Praise for *End Time Politics*

Keri Ladner's remarkable study of the theology informing Jerry Falwell's political machinations during the final decades of his life merits close attention. The significance of this important book lies in Ladner's argument that Falwell appropriated the searing cultural critique of dispensationalism—that the world is doomed and headed for judgment—and combined that critique with calls for moral reform and political activism in these "last days."

—Randall Balmer, Dartmouth College

This is an important book. By expertly tracing the theological roots of Jerry Falwell, cofounder of the Moral Majority, Keri Ladner exposes the racism, contempt for the poor, American jingoism, and blind support for untrammeled capitalism—plus a huge dose of conspiracism—that infect today's religious right. Ladner, herself an evangelical Christian, uncovers an insidious, reactionary movement "that has divorced itself entirely from the Bible" and that ultimately helped produce the January 6, 2021, attack on the US Capitol.

—Mark Potok, Senior Fellow, Centre
for Analysis of the Radical Right

Fundamentalists in America had traditionally avoided politics for the sake of spreading the gospel, but in the late twentieth century, as Keri Ladner argues in this book, the Fundamentalist Baptist preacher Jerry Falwell "created a new political religion." He blended the end-time theology of dispensationalism with the right-wing causes of the day to produce a powerful ideology sometimes labeled "Christian nationalism." Its enduring legacy is a powerful factor in the public square of the 2020s.

—David Bebbington, Emeritus Professor
of History, University of Stirling

END TIME POLITICS

END TIME POLITICS

From the Moral Majority to QAnon

KERI L. LADNER

Foreword
Randall Balmer

FORTRESS PRESS
Minneapolis

END TIME POLITICS
From the Moral Majority to QAnon

Library of Congress Control Number: 2023940355 (print)

Cover image: Digital collage with Getty Images, using Dark Flames
illustration and Capitol Building illustration by CSA printstock;
and Abstract Texture imitating oil painting on canvas by oxygen
Cover design: Kristin Miller

Print ISBN: 978-1-5064-9390-9
eBook ISBN: 978-1-5064-9391-6

For the dispossessed

But let justice roll down like waters,
And righteousness like an ever-flowing stream.

Amos 5:24 NASB

And what does the Lord require of you,
But to do justice, to love kindness,
And to walk humbly with your God.

Micah 6:8 NASB

CONTENTS

FOREWORD

Randall Balmer

Keri Ladner's remarkable study of the theology informing Jerry Falwell's political machinations during the final decades of his life merits close attention. Ladner argues that Falwell drew upon, and then markedly retrofitted, John Nelson Darby's dispensational premillennialism to advance Falwell's political ambitions. Whereas Darby's ideas, coming to America in the latter decades of the nineteenth century, gave rise to a theology of despair, an insistence that nothing could be done to make this word a better place, Falwell argued that the imminence of an event predicted by dispensationalists, the Rapture—Jesus coming to earth to collect the faithful—mandated that true (evangelical) believers must translate that urgency into political action. Falwell's political agenda included a plan for arresting the nation's moral decay, sometimes known by the shorthand "secular humanism," coupled with an insistence that the United States is and always was a Christian nation.

Falwell's message differed greatly from the dispensationalist theology of my evangelical childhood. I heard countless sermons—most of them from my father—about the imminent return of Jesus, also known as the second coming, when the faithful—my fellow evangelicals—would be taken into heaven in the Rapture.

Then, according to this theology, terrible judgment, known as the Tribulation, would be unleashed on everyone who was "left behind."

If the term "left behind" sounds vaguely familiar, it should; it was the umbrella title for a series of bestselling books written by Tim LaHaye and Jerry Jenkins. The books portray in vivid detail what life would be like during this seven-year Tribulation, when the forces of evil were unleashed following the "rapture" of the faithful into heaven. What is less well known is that these books were inspired by a low-budget motion picture called *A Thief in the Night*, which was released in 1973. The writer and director of the film, which *Time* magazine christened a church-basement classic, was my Sunday school teacher, Donald W. Thompson, and the film was inspired by my father's Sunday evening sermons at Westchester Evangelical Free Church in Des Moines, Iowa. My father, Clarence Balmer, played himself as the "good" preacher in *A Thief in the Night*.

For more than a century, this mode of biblical interpretation, dispensational premillennialism, was used as justification for evangelicals to stay away from politics. Dispensationalism taught that there was nothing believers could do to make this world a better place. The teaching directed evangelicals away from the social reforms they had advanced earlier in the nineteenth century toward an emphasis on individual regeneration—"accepting Jesus into your heart" or, in Billy Graham's words, "making a decision for Christ."

Dispensational premillennialism, the conviction that Jesus would return at any moment, had the effect of absolving evangelicals of any responsibility for social amelioration. This world, they believed, was not only transitory; it was both corrupt and corrupting, and any attempt to make the world a better place was misdirected. Better to focus on individual salvation than waste your time on politics. Premillennialism, by the way, was also responsible for some colossally bad architecture. If Jesus was returning at any moment, why waste your time on fancy or architecturally distinguished buildings; cinderblock would do just fine!

Falwell himself, earlier in his career, had affirmed this traditional understanding of dispensationalism. In his most famous sermon, "Ministers and Marches," preached from the pulpit of Thomas Road Baptist Church on March 21, 1965, the evening of the start of the march from Selma to Montgomery, Falwell declared, "Preachers are not called to be politicians, but to be soul winners." But as Ladner demonstrates, Falwell abandoned the apolitical dimensions of dispensationalism sometime in the mid-1970s in favor of a highly politicized activism.

Jim Wallis, formerly of Sojourners, tells me that Falwell responded to Richard Viguerie's promise to make the preacher a household name if he became politically active in conservative causes. Less speculatively, Falwell shed his apoliticism sometime in the 1970s in response to attempts on the part of the Internal Revenue Service to enforce anti-discrimination laws at Bob Jones University and at church-related segregation academies, including Falwell's own Lynchburg Christian Academy.

The significance of this important book lies in the author's argument that Falwell appropriated the searing cultural critique of dispensationalism—the world is doomed and headed for judgment—and combined that critique with calls for moral reform and political activism in these "last days." In so doing, Falwell created a theological hybrid, one that selected a single element of dispensational theology, the jeremiad, yet rejected its corollary of abstinence from politics.

Others can argue whether this was bad theology or ruinous politics. What is incontestable, however, is that Falwell's retrofitting of dispensational premillennialism altered the American political landscape.

Researchers are often driven by their personal experiences, and I am no exception. My descent into trying to understand some of the theological underpinnings of the Religious Right began on October 5, 1999, when I was 11 years old. My father picked me up from school early and had a packed suitcase in the backseat. Without saying where we were going, he drove out of the city of Victoria, a mid-sized urban center in South Texas, and down country roads that had more cacti than trees. He turned down a dirt road marked with a forlorn, paint-chipped sign that read, "Victory Acres Children's Home: A Place For Us." Surrounding the words were cartoonish children's faces, paled and hardened by the Texas sun. When my father pulled me out of the car and carried me inside, then drove away, my life changed in ways that I am still only beginning to understand.

Prior to that day, I had faithfully attended Southern Baptist churches with my parents, who often volunteered their time, energy, and scarce financial resources to contribute to the church's mission. I had memorized Bible verses and knew just about every story in both the Old and New Testaments. I had been given a hymnbook by the church to recognize how many hymns I had learned by heart and a Bible for being able to locate any of the sixty-six books therein within ten seconds. I had even played the leading role of defense attorney in a children's musical about a fictional court case to remove the words "In God We Trust" from US currency.

Let's stop at that fictional court case for a minute, because it represents so much of what went horribly wrong on October 5, 1999. Over the preceding two and a half decades, American evangelicalism—including the Southern Baptist Convention with which my growing-up churches were affiliated—had undergone an unexpected politicization that, at its most extreme, equated an imagined American Christian nation as the kingdom of God on earth. Evangelicals had been taught to fear secularism and liberalism, both of which allegedly wanted to strip the words "In God We Trust" from our money. In doing so, the liberals would cause God to remove his blessing from what is no longer a Christian nation. This new voting bloc of conservative Christians had to take on an offensive role by not only winning the fictional court case that my 10-year-old self helped dramatize but by pushing for government policies that would allow for a completely unregulated Christianity (at least a certain version of Christianity) in public life. And this political drama, I later learned, is how I ended up at Victory Acres.

I immediately moved not only from my family but also from the evangelicalism I had always known, into a strict fundamentalism that seemed preoccupied with an event known as the Rapture. In an instant, all true Christians would disappear from the earth to meet the Lord in the air. Was I washed in the blood of the Lamb? Of course not, because God was using my new houseparents to judge my sin and wickedness. I had to get saved immediately to ensure that I would go up in the Rapture. "Don't worry," they would tell me. "You'll never get a driver's license, graduate high school, or go to college. The Rapture will happen first. Those things are for the heathen to think about." My job was to reform my life so that I would no longer be under God's judgment and would be among those who meet him in the air.

Victory Acres was a home that received delinquent adolescent girls and turned them into long-skirt-wearing soul winners. All my roommates there had been smokers, heavy drinkers, and rebellious to the point that their parents saw no hope other than to send them off to be reformed. At least the story went that way. Many of them had been severely abused, and their parents were tempted by the promise of fundamentalist Christians "fixing" their children's behavior while blaming the kids for any abuse they had endured. Many had been victims of assault and did not even realize what had happened; only reflecting on the stories that they told me decades ago led me to understand the gravity of their experiences. My roommates there had very troubling behaviors, many of which I had never even heard of as an eleven-year-old faithful of a Southern Baptist church. But I had never smoked or even considered drinking, and part of me still wonders how any of us were able to end up in a place like Victory Acres.

At about the time I finished high school, I learned that Victory Acres was one of many residential childcare centers in the state of Texas during the 1990s and into the year 2000 that was operating without a license. George W. Bush, who served as governor of Texas before becoming US president, was part of this politically charged conservative Christianity. Many evangelical and fundamentalist churches had been operating childcare and drug-rehabilitation centers, such as church daycares and the Teen Challenge rehab homes; however, the process of acquiring a license was so burdensome that some of these faith-based centers were having to close. Governor Bush made what must have seemed like a very pragmatic move when he signed legislation that said faith-based childcare and rehab centers could operate without a state license. No minimum requirements for staff training or the level of care for those receiving services. No accountability to third parties who would ensure that children and vulnerable adults in these centers were safe. And perhaps most detrimental to me and my roommates, no investigations by children's services into allegations of abuse and domestic violence. The assumption was that the churches operating these centers would provide a level of oversight that would exceed any standards required by the state, but the opposite happened. Incidents of reported abuse and neglect at these unlicensed facilities skyrocketed, with one out of four having confirmed cases of abuse.

These faith-based initiatives of Governor Bush explain why Victory Acres was allowed to operate and led to me trying to understand the Religious Right. Yet the relationship between Victory Acres and the Religious Right went much deeper because of the doctrine of the Rapture. The Rapture comes from a biblical hermeneutic called dispensational theology, and looking back, my houseparents were strict dispensationalists. So was the man who helped bring fundamentalists—many of them dispensationalists who had been avoiding political entanglements because of their expectation of the Rapture—with non-dispensational evangelicals together in his Moral Majority. Jerry Falwell's organization, which was grounded in his dispensational beliefs, served as the flagship organization for the nascent Religious Right.

Sifting through hundreds of hours of Falwell's sermons as a doctoral student, I constantly heard what could have been my former houseparents. In the Last Days, children will be disobedient to their parents. Lawlessness will reign. Drugs will be peddled to schoolchildren. There was the constant theme of public schools not just being inadequate but being under the judgment of God. What set Falwell apart from other dispensationalists, though, was his effort to bring reform to a world that was fundamentally unreformable. He accomplished this mission not only by opening his own faith-based centers, such as homes for alcoholics and pregnant teenagers (so that their babies could be adopted by conservative Christians), but also by playing a leading role in organizing the Religious Right. Conservative Christian voters should take their nation back for God, he claimed, but at the same time, society is damned. This paradox is what my experiences at Victory Acres led me to resolve in my doctoral studies.

The critical analysis of Falwell's dispensationalism, as told in *End Time Politics*, challenges the narrative that suggests childcare facilities should be able to operate without licensure. Yet the issues at stake are so much bigger than my own experiences that center on October 5, 1999. Perpetual war in the Middle East, widespread denial of climate change, hate crimes against queer individuals, the evangelical position on so many of these concerns today is embedded in how Falwell used, even abused, dispensational theology to create the Religious Right. I say "abused" because I know many dispensationalists and am indebted to them for much of this research; the overwhelming number of dispensationalists I spoke with have profound disagreements with Falwell's use of their theology.

This entire book could have been about race and how Falwell built his movement as an antidote to the civil rights movement. That topic could be another book, and indeed, many books have been written to address the role of race in the creation of the Religious Right. While there is some content about race, including the effort to preserve oppression of Blacks in both the American South and South Africa, the experiences that led me to write this book were not those of a Black girl. I was a white girl caught up in what I thought was the absolute worst of Falwell's unholy marriage between dispensationalism and American nationalism.

Yet I must acknowledge that so many groups have suffered infinitely more than I did. Gay men who were blamed for the AIDS epidemic, supposedly God's judgment on America for tolerating their lifestyles. African Americans who saw many gains in the civil rights movement reversed seemingly overnight. Aspiring and educated women who had to begin anew the struggle to have a career outside the home. Countless children who had to remain in unsafe homes because of budget cuts to children's services. Palestinian refugees whose dispossession was legitimized through a political stance that denies them not only their homes but their right to exist. Iraqi families who watched not only their homes but entire neighborhoods be bombed into oblivion in the American invasion, before the desolations brought by ISIS. For this reason, I have dedicated this book to the dispossessed, whether the reason for dispossession be race, home country, sexual orientation, level of education, gender, poverty, abuse, or any number of other factors. The dispossessed have a shared experience of violence, and I hope to shed light on one particular cause of violence in the world today: the use of dispensationalism to promote a nationalist agenda that has no resemblance to the message of Christ.

The rhetoric from conservative Christians who have promoted policies that have increased violence around the world has essentially been the same as what my houseparents at Victory Acres told me: Society is headed for destruction, and the only solution is to become a soul-winning Christian. The denial of the problems right in front of us, be they racial disparities and even ethnic cleansing, or cases of abuse and neglect that should be investigated by children's services, coexists with a narrative centered on the Rapture and the mythical American Christian nation.

I wrote this book as an evangelical who wants to see social reform based on compassion for the poor and dispossessed, not an unflinching ideology that continually polarizes the world into "us" and "them." I hope this book helps clarify some misconceptions people may have about evangelicalism while drawing attention to how this movement has gone so profoundly wrong. I see hope for evangelicalism, perhaps even hope for fundamentalists who wish to reclaim dispensationalism from its far-right politicization, but not for the Religious Right.

Understanding how Falwell used dispensational theology can help us understand why so many evangelicals have shifted from participating in social reform to denying that reform is even necessary, even when social decay seems to be on the rise. Falwell did not invent any of these problems—they have long histories that very competent scholars have explored—but he brought them to fundamentalist and evangelical Christians in ways that wrapped the Bible in the American flag. They had to save their nation from the gays, the feminists, the environmentalists and bring it back to its Christian origins. The consequences for their failure to do so would be the wrath of God. The rewards for succeeding would be eternal. So we approach this topic not with vindictiveness and judgment, but rather with the recognition that we cannot afford to be ignorant. If we want to address what is wrong with America and what is wrong with contemporary evangelicalism, we must first understand the problem and then look for solutions. This book is a diagnosis of the problem. I hope *End Time Politics* spurs creative and innovative thinking about solutions.

INTRODUCTION

Jerry Falwell's American Christian Nation

"I Believe America to be a nation founded by our forefathers as a Christian nation and as a base for world evangelization," the Reverend Jerry Falwell declared on the steps of West Virginia's state capitol building on April 21, 1980.[1] Over the prior decade, Falwell had been traveling the country and preaching over radio and television a message of America's Christian heritage and the need to return to it. And he was effective. During the 1970s and 1980s, he built a movement that awakened evangelical Christians out of their political torpor—many evangelicals had previously considered politics too dirty to get involved in—and became the face of a resurgent conservativism. The Religious Right, as the movement became known, remained so powerful after his death in 2007 that it provided critical electoral support for Donald Trump in the elections of 2016 and 2020.

Falwell lacked formal theological training, having attended an unaccredited Bible college and deciding against going to seminary. Yet he was astute, earning the highest grade-point average in his high-school class (though he was denied the right to give the valedictorian speech at his graduation, owing to a prank that cost the high school thousands of dollars). He also had a larger-than-life personality that many in his hometown of Lynchburg,

Virginia, still remember with fondness. By 1955, at the age of twenty-two, the young college graduate had developed a reputation as a magnetic preacher and was filling in for pastors who were absent from their churches.

But in 1956, contentious politics caused a rift in the church he had attended as a teenager, and the congregation began to split. The young Falwell approached the senior pastor with the offer of starting a new church with the three dozen congregants who planned to leave. There would then be another fundamentalist Bible church in Lynchburg, Falwell reasoned, and a greater opportunity to reach those of the city who had not repented of their sins and turned to Christ. Could the two churches work together, he asked, with him and the senior pastor cooperating as they grew their sister churches side-by-side? The senior pastor disagreed with Falwell's assessment of the situation. The young preacher was barely twenty-three years old and had not even attended seminary, yet he was planning to start his own church by facilitating a church split.

Falwell took the dissenters from his home congregation and started a new church, without the senior pastor's blessing. In response, the senior pastor spoke with executives at the Baptist Bible Fellowship—the "mini denomination" to which they belonged—about the situation, and the young Falwell was expelled from the Fellowship. At twenty-three years of age and the very beginning of his career, he had helped a church split and, in the process, cut himself off from all meaningful mentorship. But he worked tirelessly to grow his new church, Thomas Road Baptist, by knocking on hundreds of doors in Lynchburg every week and by starting a radio show at a local station. That radio show became *The Old-Time Gospel Hour*, a televised broadcast of his church's services that eventually reached tens of thousands of people across the country each week. Thomas Road Baptist Church would become a megachurch with over twenty thousand members and the force behind Liberty University, which its leadership founded and would become the largest Christian university in America.

With minimal theological training, Falwell was not steeped in historical Baptist doctrines, such as the depravity of humans and separation of church and state.[2] But he had a charismatic personality and the ability to draw in a crowd that he electrified with his words. By his forties, he was regularly preaching in front of state capitol buildings to crowds that included legislators, electoral candidates, and members of the judiciary.

The message he brought to Charleston, West Virginia, on that spring day lacked theological nuance and historical clarity, yet it appealed to people who were disaffected by the liberal politics that had enabled a generation of Vietnam War protestors, civil-rights agitators, and sexual liberators. Falwell gave a voice to the concerns of those who felt that liberalism had left them behind by preaching to their elected officials about how America's moral failings of the past generation were crippling the country. "For two hundred years God has blessed this country beyond all others, simply because here, in our environment of freedom and liberty, America has, more than any nation in history, been allowed to give the Gospel out to a world for whom Jesus died." He went on, "Yet, we begin to see our country, our republic, crumbling; we see a moving away from God and away from the principles responsible for her greatness."

The claims he made were certainly dubious and by no means in agreement with those of mainstream historians of American and world history. After all, America's "environment of freedom and liberty" had not applied to Africans who had been kidnapped from their homes, brought across the Atlantic in horrifying conditions on slave ships, and forced to toil on plantations for the rest of their lives. Certainly, plenty of other countries have engaged in tremendous efforts to spread the gospel throughout the world, and there is no verifiable way to prove that America's bicentennial prosperity was the result of God's blessing. But his words resonated and helped forge a new path in how right-wing populists would think about American society and their place in it.

Historical accuracy (or lack thereof) notwithstanding, he went on. "America is certainly not for Christians only. But the Founding Fathers, though not all were dedicated Christians, were dedicated to Christian principles. It was their influence which created the contents of the Declaration of Independence, the Bill of Rights, and the Constitution." Falwell was certainly not the first person to suggest the Christian nature of the country's founding documents. Yet he was, perhaps unknowingly, disregarding the separation of church and state that has long been crucial to Baptist thought. Roger Williams, the seventeenth-century patriarch of American Baptists, insisted that the church should operate separately from civil government; otherwise, the church itself would be tainted. Yet Falwell was perilously close to—and in other places, far past—the point of suggesting that the American government should operate as an extension of the church. Four years prior, in 1976, he had preached to his church (and, via television, to the country), "We teach patriotism here at Liberty Baptist College [later Liberty University] and Thomas Road Baptist Church as being synonymous with Christianity."[3] Although Falwell was a Baptist preacher, he was out of touch with not only American history but also his own Baptist roots.

On that spring day in 1980, Falwell went on to make two declarations that perfectly summarize his message throughout his decades-long career. The first was, "[The founders] created the philosophy of the free enterprise system from the precepts of the book of Proverbs." He believed that unregulated capitalism was the economic system endorsed by the Bible and that, especially during the Cold War, America had a God-given duty to preserve capitalism against encroachments of socialism—including public schools and tax-funded nutrition and housing assistance for the poor. He had no appetite for the thought that, as Baptists and other evangelicals had historically preached, human depravity might corrupt the economic sphere; historically, evangelicals, such as the revivalist Charles Finney (who despised capitalism), had taught that the civil government must implement regulations on business to protect people from the excesses of corporate greed. Rather, Falwell had binary thinking on capitalism; any form of government regulation and government assistance was part of a diabolical agenda to cripple America into communism.

His second declaration was, "We thus feel a primary obligation, in these last days before Jesus comes, to call this nation back to God." By framing his mission within "these last days before Jesus comes," Falwell was indicating that his political activism stemmed directly from his theological beliefs. Those theological beliefs came from dispensationalism, which emphasizes the imminent fulfillment of biblical prophecy alongside radical separatism for "true Christians." Christians had to separate themselves from all things unholy while awaiting an event called the Rapture, in which dispensationalists believe they will all spontaneously leave this earth and ascend into heaven. The Rapture would precede the wrath of God on the world and the second coming of Christ, giving context to his words "these last days before Jesus comes."

Falwell's theological beliefs are not necessarily what the Baptist Bible Fellowship taught or what he learned at Baptist Bible College while studying for his undergraduate degree. To be sure, the Fellowship and Baptist Bible College taught dispensationalism, but not necessarily the same dispensationalism that he preached from state capitol buildings. By cutting himself off from the Fellowship at the beginning of his career, Falwell had the freedom to re-interpret and re-invent dispensational thought with very limited accountability. What he preached at West Virginia's state capitol in April of 1980, and in capitols and other public venues throughout the country, bore such a scarce resemblance to historical dispensationalism that his movement does not look like dispensationalism at all. His re-invented dispensationalism lacked understanding of the system's central doctrines, which actually begin with the call for "true Christians" to radically separate from the rest of the world. Instead, he relied heavily on patriotic displays, the conservative politics of the Cold War, and imagery of prophecy about the End Times. Yet despite his revisionist approach, he stood firmly in a tradition—albeit not a static tradition but rather one in constant flux—that longed for the imminent Rapture.

In organizing the Moral Majority, the flagship of the nascent Religious Right, Falwell was doing more than creating a movement. He was bringing fundamentalist Protestantism, or at least a distorted form of the dispensational faith that he had received, to the forefront of evangelicalism. To be sure, evangelicalism in America has ebbed and flowed along the lines of fundamentalism since dispensationalism first began to spread on the western side of the Atlantic in the late 1800s. By the late 1990s and in no small part because of Falwell's influence, a fundamentalism that was originally built on the doctrine of separating from all non-fundamentalist institutions, at least as much as feasible, would have absorbed much of evangelicalism. And Falwell's revision of this fundamentalist faith, a revision that included an American Christian nation that was built on faith in God and could be restored to its Christian origins, even while the rest of the world spun toward Armageddon, would turn evangelicalism into a political religion. One that, by January 2021, was so much more concerned with who occupied the halls of power in Washington,

DC than with deity, the supernatural, and the message of Christ, that many would turn a blind eye or even pardon—as morally acceptable—an attempt to violently overthrow the American government.

By grounding his movement in a retelling of America's early history and claiming that he was awakening American Christians back to the principles of the country's founding documents, Falwell was attempting to show that what he was doing was very old, as old as the nation itself. Yet by merging his reinvented dispensationalism with his own brand of patriotism, he was doing something that was actually very new: he was attempting to prepare America to face the impending wrath of God.

CHAPTER 1

American Protestantism's Civil War

"Our Founding Fathers knew that free enterprise was the best economic organization to maintain the free society they had created."[1] The sermon that Falwell preached on the steps of West Virginia's capitol building, along with numerous other state capitols, public venues, and churches throughout America in the 1970s, was called "America Back to God." It told his revision of American history, from the country's allegedly Christian origins and the biblical nature of the Declaration of Independence and Constitution to the rise of New Deal liberalism in the 1930s that had begun sinking the once-great republic. "Our Founding Fathers believed in God. They established this nation on faith in God . . . God gave to them, I believe by inspiration, not like the Bible is inspired but certainly by inspiration, a masterpiece. We call it the US Constitution."[2]

He went on to say of the nation's slide away from the faith of the founders and into immorality, "It seems impossible today, because I was born in 1933, during the days when Mr. Roosevelt was packing the Supreme Court with liberals. I have never known a Supreme Court that was capable of making a Christ-honoring decision." What had made the founders so Christ-like, he was suggesting, and the American Christian nation so great, was not merely personal repentance from sin, but an adherence to economic conservativism. Roosevelt had decisively steered the country away from those Christian principles that had ensured God's blessing on America when he implemented his New Deal. As a result, "The

United States tonight is under the wrath of God."[3] In making these bold and novel claims about the American Christian nation and God's wrath, Falwell was engaging in a form of wildcatting. The term "wildcatting" generally applies to drilling for exploratory oil wells in unproven fields; with "America Back to God," Falwell was drilling the American conscience with a new and unproven message, hoping to make a strike that would resonate with voters.

"America was founded by godly men who had in mind establishing a republic not only Christian in nature, but a republic designed to propagate the Gospel worldwide."[4] Turning the likes of George Washington and Benjamin Franklin into twentieth-century fundamentalists while ignoring their eighteenth-century Enlightenment ideals, Falwell declared that America was founded upon a faith that looked remarkably like his. He insisted that America had to return to this faith that had passed seamlessly from the founders to himself, to fulfill its destiny before the wrath of God should fall. "Dear friend," he told his audience, "the Bible is replete with stories of nations that forgot God and paid the eternal consequences." Should America continue in "unnecessary welfare spending"[5] that was wrecking the national budget while encouraging people to not work, then the country would be too weak to continue facing the End Times—what he believed the Cold War to be—and impending divine wrath.

In 1980, he expanded "America Back to God" into the 200-plus-page book *Listen, America! The Conservative Blueprint for America's Moral Rebirth.* While he waxed eloquent about the need to preserve the traditional family against the encroaching threats of homosexuality and feminism, his underlying argument throughout was that America had to return to unregulated capitalism to continue ensuring its God-given prosperity. He claimed, "The answer to every one of our nation's dilemmas is a spiritual one. When we as a country again acknowledge God as our Creator and Jesus Christ as the Savior of mankind, we will be able to turn this nation around economically as well as in every other way."[6]

In merging an apocalyptic narrative of the wrath of God with conservative economics, Falwell was following an American tradition that was, by his time, a century in the making. America's Civil War (1861–1865), between the slave-holding South and (somewhat) abolitionist North, had sparked a new civil war between the emerging forces of liberal and conservative Protestantism. This divide did not occur primarily along geographic lines but rather economic ones and was framed as liberal and conservative theology. On the liberal side emerged support for a movement known as the Social Gospel; it emphasized care for the poor by limiting the power of big business alongside the creation and expansion of social safety nets. Falwell thoroughly disparaged this approach to both economics and theology, calling it apostasy, meaning that followers of the Social Gospel had left the Christian faith.

On the conservative side emerged "biblical capitalism," which held that God has called men to work so that they can provide for themselves and their families; business leaders care for the poor by providing people with the means to earn a living and serve God's purposes by funding churches, seminaries, and missionaries. Siding with this view, Falwell claimed in *Listen, America!*,

> The free-enterprise system is clearly outlined in the Book of Proverbs in the Bible. Jesus Christ made it clear that the work ethic was a part of his plan for man. Ownership of property is biblical. Competition in business is biblical. Ambitious and successful business management is clearly outlined as a part of God's plan for his people.[7]

Biblical capitalism came from an innovative approach to the Bible that grew in America in the late 1800s. This approach merged with capitalism as a means of reacting against the Social Gospel and the new economic order it was creating.

Dispensational Node
Separatism

Falwell claimed to be a separatist, as when he said, "Anybody who knows me knows that I'm a fundamentalist. I'm a separatist . . . I believe in separatism, and I believe we should come out from the world and be separate."[8] In defining what separatism is, in a different sermon, he described it vaguely as a commitment to biblical holiness, "separatism from the world, the flesh, and the devil; separatism unto God."[9] Given his visibility on national venues ranging from CNN to the White House, many people might take issue with him professing to be a separatist. *Come out from the world and be separate?* one might ask. *Falwell, who regularly held patriotic pageants at his church and in front of state capitols? Falwell, who had a public friendship with President Reagan, spread conspiracy theories about President Clinton and First Lady Hillary, and unconditionally supported President Bush's War on Terror? On what grounds could he possibly claim to be separating from the world, when he built his empire by engaging with it?* The reason Falwell could claim to be a separatist is the same reason he agitated against civil rights, poverty-reduction programs, clean and renewable energy, and public schools: his approach to the Bible came from the tradition of dispensationalism, and he routinely distorted and abused the teachings of dispensationalism to suit his ideas about American public life. In other words, Falwell read the Bible through the lens of dispensationalism, and he read dispensationalism through the lens of American capitalism.

John Nelson Darby (1800–1882) was an Anglo-Irish evangelist who organized the theological system that came to be known as dispensationalism. This hermeneutic emerges out of his radical call for "true Christians" to separate from all worldly associations, including the established church. He said, "[God] tells me that, as His child, I am not a citizen of any country, or a member of any society; my citizenship is in heaven, and I have henceforth to do with heavenly things."[10]

In about 1863, while the Civil War was raging, Darby first traveled to the United States to spread the comprehensive approach to the Bible that he had developed.[11] Its moniker, "dispensationalism," comes from an emphasis his American protégés placed on dispensations, or different apportioned periods of time during which God dispenses grace in different ways.[12] In each dispensation, God has made a covenant with his people, and they consistently fail to live up to it. In the first dispensation, the Paradisical State,[13] God placed Adam and Eve, the primordial humans, in the garden of Eden and covenanted with them to steward his creation and obey his commands. They failed by eating the forbidden fruit and faced God's judgment in their expulsion from the garden. Every dispensation has ended (and the present one, the Church Age, will soon end) with the wrath of God falling on those who have rejected him and the terms of his covenant.

Dispensationalism fits into a form of Protestant thought known as premillennialism. Up until the Civil War, the dominant strand of Protestant thought in America was postmillennialism, meaning that Christ will return at the end of a millennium of peace. Christians help bring about this sought-after millennium through acts of love and service done in faith. Northern abolitionism that sought to end slavery, alongside churches that developed social care programs for immigrants and worked to reform factory labor, generally came from a postmillennial ethos, as Christians were striving to reform society to make it look like the kingdom of God—the millennium. Premillennialism claims that Christ will return to earth and instate the millennium—in the dispensationalist strand, when he begins his reign from the throne of David in Jerusalem. Until then, society will progressively decline, and there is nothing that Christians can do to stem this decline. Efforts to improve society will ultimately fail, as the Bible itself prophesied that society will deteriorate until Christ returns and rules the earth as King of kings and Lord of lords. Postmillennialism is inherently optimistic about the ability of Christians to improve society, while premillennialism is generally pessimistic about society being in a state of perpetual regression and decline.

The dispensational strand of premillennialism includes the events of the Rapture and Tribulation. Darby believed that the church is entirely separate from Israel—so separate, in fact, that God's purposes for the church and Israel cannot be fulfilled simultaneously. Darby taught that Jesus Christ had not originally intended to establish the church, that the church had never been part of God's primordial plan. Christ came solely for the purpose of being the King of the Jews, a literal king over an earthly kingdom. When the Jews rejected him, God's plan for a messianic kingdom on earth was delayed; during the interim, those few Jews who placed their faith in Christ became the seed of an altogether new—and unplanned—dispensation, the Church Age. During this present Church Age, God is dispensing grace through the sacrificial death of Christ. He is drawing non-Jews to himself, through faith in Christ, while Jews continue abiding by the covenant he established with them at Mount Sinai. Jews can convert and join the church if they choose, but God's plan for them as a nation has not yet been fulfilled.

This present dispensation of the Church Age will conclude with the Rapture, when all true Christians suddenly leave the earth and the church no longer exists. God's purposes will then shift from the church back to Israel, and creating the earthly kingdom over which Christ will reign. That process will include a seven-year period of God's wrath known as the Tribulation, when he will judge the world—and Israel—for rejecting Christ. Hail, fire, blood, and darkness will characterize the Tribulation, as a one-world dictator known as the antichrist—to Darby, the pope[14]—would rule over a revival of the Roman Empire.[15] Christians have no need to fear this dreaded period, as they will have been raptured and will be watching it unfold from heaven. At the end of the Tribulation, Christ will return to defeat the antichrist and begin his Millennial Reign over Israel.

Though an emphasis on dispensations formed the spine of Darby's system, especially in America, his teachings began with his call for true Christians to radically separate from apostate Christendom, both from the established church and from society as a whole. "Come out from among them and be separate, says the Lord," 2 Corinthians 6:17 (NKJV) records the apostle Paul's teaching. "Do not touch what is unclean, and I will receive you." Darby said of his own experiences, in accordance with this verse,

> It then became clear to me that the church of God, as He considers it, was composed only of those who were so united to Christ, whereas Christendom, as seen externally, was really the world, and could not be considered as "the church" . . . At the same time, I saw that the Christian, having his place in Christ in heaven, has nothing to wait for save the coming of the Saviour, in order to be set, in fact, in the glory which is already his portion in Christ.[16]

Parts of the New Testament hold "the world" in tension with the people of God, generally understood as Israel and, in the New Testament, the church. "God so loved the world," declares John 3:16, yet 1 John 2:15 says, "Do not love the world or the things in the world" (NKJV). Carefully balancing these tensions is an important task for pastors and theologians who try to help

Christians understand how they can live in the world and yet, in the words of the apostle Paul, "not be conformed to [it]" (Romans 12:2, NKJV). Darby went to an extreme by urging his followers to separate from the world as much as they possibly could, while quietly awaiting the Rapture. This separatism especially included the established church of England, the Anglican Church—with its concomitant Church of Ireland—as he saw it as a counterpart to the Roman Catholic Church. He despised Catholicism, viewing it as a worldly institution that gave worship to the pope when worship belonged solely to God, and he came to view Anglicanism in much the same way.

Darby's estimate of the church is encapsulated in a statement in his ecclesiological treatise *On the Formation of the Church*: "The Church is in ruins."[17] The poor state of the church could be found in denominationalism that perverts Christian unity, an ordained priesthood that disrupts the New Testament priesthood of all believers, and a connection to the state that denies the Lordship of Christ, in favor of the monarch. Darby's solution was not to reform the established church, as its very organization—into offices such as priest and deacon, into a hierarchy that extends to the monarch of the British state, and into denominations that divide the people of God—defiled it. He saw the Bible as foretelling the progressive deterioration and ruin of the church, beginning with the presence of antichrists within the apostolic church, and he claimed that God's will was that the church not be restored. The ruined church—Christendom—was apostate, meaning it had abandoned the true faith. True Christians, those who followed Darby's teachings, could have nothing to do with the established, and ruined, church.

"Will it surprise any one [*sic*] to hear that Satan is the god of this world, the prince of the power of the air, the manager of this stupendous system?" True Christians had to leave the

Satan-inspired system behind; Darby went on to claim of the Christian's civic duty and civic participation, in stark contradistinction to what Falwell would teach over a century later, "If, then, the true child of God refuses to vote, it is not so much that he thinks voting in itself wrong, as that he has given his vote and interest to the Man in heaven."[18] In other words, as he went on to say, "We must needs be in contact with the world-system to some degree, but this contact is never to be of fellowship."[19]

Over the decades following the Civil War and Darby's travels to America, dispensationalism would become central to conservative evangelicalism—what would become known as the fundamentalist movement—as well as the conservative economics that Falwell promoted. Because separatism formed the core of Darby's teachings, perhaps by retaining a modicum of dispensational belief, Falwell could also claim to be a separatist. While he claimed to be a dispensationalist, he would bring the church—at least the fundamentalists and conservative evangelicals that he organized into a voting bloc—into an alliance with the state. Against Darby's teachings, he would attempt to reform not only the church but the state as well, yet he never seemed to see himself at odds with classic dispensational teachings.

Dispensationalism in America would modify the system that Darby originally designed so that it applied more to an American than British and European context. Darby's system was built on the radical separatism that he taught—the separation of the church from Israel and the church from the world—which emerged from his views of the established Anglican Church and Roman Catholic Church. Yet America has no established church and is an ocean away from Rome; while American Catholics and Protestants were not famous for getting along well, the country was not party to the Protestant–Catholic tensions in Europe that still erupted into violence. Instead, America's early fundamentalists largely remained within their denominations rather than separating from them—as Darby insisted—and focused more on developing an apocalyptic narrative that would culminate in the second coming of Christ.

Less concerned about the Roman Catholic Church than Darby, American fundamentalists feasted on literature about who the antichrist would be (maybe or maybe not the pope) and what would occur in the End Times. They eagerly deciphered verses that they viewed as prophecies of the End Times and waited with anticipation for the Rapture. While Darby urged his followers to leave the world to its ruin, in America, dispensationalists became dedicated evangelists, determined to convert their loved ones so that they would go up in the Rapture and avoid the horrors of the Tribulation.

Falwell would, beginning a century after Darby first spread dispensationalism in America, bring those prophecies about the Rapture and the End Times into American public life as he strove to reform the country in accordance with his interpretation of dispensationalism. "This is a Christian nation and was so intended to be by our Founding Fathers . . . The United States tonight is under the wrath of God . . . I think our society is damned."[20] Possessing only a rudimentary education in dispensationalism—he attended an unaccredited Bible college and did not go to seminary—Falwell demonstrated little understanding of the doctrines that Darby had taught a century before. Far from separating from the Catholic church, he actively cooperated with Catholic leaders and laypeople in building his political movement. His public activism seemed to show little appetite for separatism at all, even though separatism is at the core of dispensationalism. His insistence on political engagement was the most striking innovation he made to Darby's teachings, and it helped shape a wildcatting faith that was fiercely patriotic while simultaneously declaring the damnation of America.

Much of Falwell's understanding of dispensationalism came not from the writings of Darby but rather the *Scofield Reference Bible*, which he used in crafting many of his sermons. Cyrus Ingerson Scofield (1843–1921) was a Confederate soldier who defected from the army yet went on to edit the bestselling book in the history of Oxford University Press. The *Scofield Reference Bible*, originally published in 1909 and revised in 1917 (and several times more since his death), contained commentary that explained verses from a dispensational perspective. This commentary enabled laypeople with no theological training to grasp Scofield's understanding of dispensationalism. This understanding had less to say about the Anglican and Roman Catholic Churches that Darby despised than about separating which verses apply to the church and which to the Jews. Those that apply to the church could not apply to the Jews; verses for the Jews had no application for Christians living in the Church Age.

The *Scofield Reference Bible* was nothing short of an American cultural phenomenon. It popularized dispensationalism among lay Christians and pastors who had received little to no formal theological training, and it even carried a non-dispensational audience. Shortly after the original publication of the *Scofield Reference Bible*, the outbreak of World War I (1914–1918) destroyed the cultural optimism of many evangelicals who had leaned toward postmillennialism; they became more inclined toward Scofield's (and Darby's) premillennialism. When Jews began immigrating to Palestine *en masse* following World War I, and especially with the rise of Nazism and World War II, the commentary that Scofield had put into the margins of the Bible seemed to have accurately predicted the future. Falwell's sermons about prophecy and the End Times, especially regarding Israel, frequently came directly from the 1967 edition of the *Scofield Reference Bible*. This edition had gone through significant editing to include the establishment of the state of Israel, the advent of the Cold War, and burgeoning field of young-earth creationism.

With the outbreak of World War I, Scofield's thought shifted to something that has become a hallmark of dispensationalist thought ever since. He began applying current events to specific dispensational prophecies, believing World War I itself to have been divinely prophesied. The foreword to his 1918 book *What Do the Prophets Say?* asks,

> What significance, if any, has the great war now raging over Europe and the East in the light of prophecy? May it be confidently affirmed that this particular war is mentioned in the prophetic Word? If it be true that "prophecy is history written beforehand," it might well seem a strange thing if a war wholly without parallel in human history should be passed without notice in the Scriptures.[21]

According to Scofield and the millions he influenced, postmillennial Christians who sought to bring the kingdom of God to earth were sorely mistaken in working for a world of peace and righteousness. God himself had decreed that war was to be the fate of humanity until the Prince of Peace comes to instate his kingdom from the throne of David in Jerusalem. Falwell would claim half a century after the original publication of the *Scofield Reference Bible*, "We have the foolish idea today that we are going to create a utopia. We are going to give people better education, and by giving better education, we'll outlaw sin; we'll outlaw crime. We'll have no more rebellion."[22] America may be a Christian nation, but ultimately, all of society is damned.

The Social Gospel and Liberal Protestantism

"What a terrible thing when we, preachers of the gospel, no longer preach the gospel, but preach some other gospel," Falwell lamented in an early sermon, undated but likely preached in the 1960s. "Ecumenicalism, and all the other 'isms,' are preaching that kind of thing. It's called the social gospel."[23] Here, he drew a line to another trans-Atlantic movement that, in some ways, paralleled and in other ways completely diverged from the rise of dispensationalism in America. The Social Gospel, as this movement became known, served as the antithesis of dispensational fundamentalism in America and the foil against which he built his movement.

At about the same time that dispensationalism was beginning to spread in America—during and immediately after the Civil War—another approach to the Bible was also gaining traction. This approach has been variously termed biblical criticism, higher criticism, and historical-critical exegesis and sought to unpin the Bible from its sacred moorings so that it could be studied as an ancient text. Previously, biblical studies had tended to start with the assumption that the Bible was a divine book, inspired by God and penned by men under his direct guidance. While Christians did not always take everything that the Bible says literally—Did Jonah really survive inside a fish for three days before being spit back onto dry ground?—they did not question the book's divine origins. Biblical criticism challenged that assumption by examining the Bible as an ancient text penned by human authors who were not working under divine inspiration. Not only was the garden of Eden no longer seen as a real place; the virgin birth of Christ and his resurrection from the dead also came into question, thereby leaving doubt as to the supernatural roots of Christianity.

Biblical criticism originated primarily in German academic circles during the 1700s and was making inroads in America by the 1830s. During the first half of the nineteenth century, this approach to the Bible shaped the emergent Unitarianism—which denies the Trinity—and Transcendental Meditation movements.

By the post–Civil War years and especially the 1880s, biblical criticism had gained respectability in centers such as Yale, Harvard, and Union Theological Seminary. Pastors trained in these schools carried biblical criticism with them to the pulpits of their churches, in the process transforming the thought and praxis of mainline American Protestantism. These churches gave rise to a new expression of Christianity, liberal Protestantism—in sharp contradistinction to their dispensationalist brethren. To be sure, many Protestants considered themselves to be moderates, not desiring to take a position in the growing tensions between liberal Protestantism and what would become fundamentalism. But the battle lines were being drawn, whether the moderates planned to join the fray or not.

Liberal Protestants had little room for doctrine, such as historical teachings on sin, heaven, and hell, and preferred to focus more on life experience. They were less interested in reforming theology than they were in reforming society, and they became deeply connected with the movement known as the Social Gospel or Social Christianity. This movement had already been spearheaded by evangelical clergy, both in Britain and in America, who had become distressed at the rapidly deteriorating conditions of the inner-city slums and rural farming communities. These evangelicals adopted principles of civic liberalism—such as freedom, equality, and self-determination—and married them with Christocentric theologies. Eager to bring reform to the inner-city poor and struggling rural farmers, evangelical clergy of the Social Gospel developed schools, advocated for labor laws (at a time when many children under twelve were working twelve-hour days, seven days a week in factories), and promoted women's rights. Some of these evangelical Social Gospelers considered themselves to be incarnating themselves among the poor, just as Christ had left heaven and incarnated himself among humans. Some saw their work as one of atonement that reconciled the poor with God, parallel to how Christ's sacrificial death on the cross provided atonement by making sinful humans one with God. In this way, these progressive evangelicals merged secular thought with sacred principles, though they never left the sacred behind in their quest to bring the kingdom of God to earth. They did not dispense with the concept of individual salvation—that one's soul must be regenerated through the atonement of Christ—and they also applied the concept to social salvation. In the postmillennial ethos of the Social Gospel, society could be redeemed in such a way that would usher in the millennium.

To the emergent liberal Protestantism, people, rather than texts or doctrines, were inspired, and liberal theology was incomplete without the Social Gospel. Sometimes dispensing with evangelical language of the sinful individual and sinful human heart, liberal Protestants of the Social Gospel came to see sin as applying more to social institutions than to individuals. Additionally, some strands of the Social Gospel that were more inspired by liberal theology than evangelicalism taught socialism over capitalism. This socialism did not refer to *collectivism*, as would be found in communist thought and practice (though some Social Gospelers were influenced by Marxist ideas), but rather the application of Christian principles to social relationships. At the time, *laissez-faire* capitalism—capitalism with no regulations—had led to a steady upward flow of material wealth, leaving the poor increasingly destitute and the wealthy with unparalleled riches. To bring atonement and redemption to the poor—or to more liberal Protestants who did not use such evangelical language, to bring justice to the poor—Social Gospelers sought to reform the economic sphere by reigning in corporate corruption and bringing accountability to those in power. Doing so would require regulations be placed on a capitalism that was, at that point, not regulated.

Nowhere was their work more pressing than in the redistribution of resources, away from the immensely wealthy and toward the poor that they championed. Among the Social Gospelers who advocated socialism, "socialism" lacked a coherent definition but was broadly understood as an alternative to capitalism that could (but not necessarily would) promote human welfare above moneyed interests. Walter Rauschenbusch, whose pastorate in the Manhattan neighborhood of Hell's Kitchen led to his leadership in the movement, saw socialism as a means that could help alleviate urban poverty. However, the philosophy was ultimately material and could not promote character and moral development. He saw Christianity as capable of providing a corrective to the material focus of socialism so that people's character could also be lifted out of poverty. As such, to the more theologically liberal leaders of the Social Gospel, "Christian Socialism" existed along a continuum that went from what they saw as the true religion of Jesus and the early church to an economic system that supported human flourishing over moneyed interests by employing the New Testament mandate to love neighbor as self.

America's early dispensationalists—proto-fundamentalists—believed that this preoccupation with temporal affairs distracted Social Gospelers from the realm of the spiritual. Further, the growing role of liberal Protestantism in the Social Gospel led many dispensationalists to view the movement as making the church itself a secular institution rather than bringing the kingdom of God to earth (something that, Darby taught, could not happen in the present dispensation). Still, the evangelicals and liberal Protestants of the Social Gospel strove to reform a society that they believed could be reformed.

By the time Falwell began his career as pastor of Thomas Road Baptist Church in 1956, dispensational fundamentalists had come to see the idea of socialism—socialism as a first cousin to the collectivism of communism, rather than the Christian Socialism intended by early leaders of the Social Gospel—as piecemeal to liberal theology. Just as Darby had declared the established Anglican church of his day as apostate, Falwell and other dispensationalists saw liberal Protestantism, along with what he viewed as its communist-inspired socialism, as apostate. He declared, "We're in the day of the apostasy that the Bible predicted; we're in the day of the falling away. We're in a day when we're hearing all this business about building the kingdom, social reform . . . It's called the Social Gospel."[24] Disparaging all forms of socialism as part of the apostasy, he urged not only churches but America as a whole to return to the true faith of the Bible, one that necessarily included unregulated capitalism against any kind of "Christian Socialism." This true faith, dispensationalism, was inherently separatist, and Falwell was more than ready to exploit separatism to promote his anti-communist, anti-liberal agenda.

The Economics of Modern Biblical Interpretation

Both of these developing expressions of Protestantism were very modern. Though premillennialism as a broader category does have a much longer history in Christian thought, dispensationalism uses nineteenth- and twentieth-century methods of classifying and cross-referencing within the text; the result is a highly complex system of prophecy and interpretation that resembles a feat of engineering more than the "plain-text" interpretation that American evangelicals had long favored. According to B. M. Pietsch, "Far from simple literalism, proof-texting, or conservative retrenchments, dispensationalist understandings of interpretation reveal thoroughly modernist assumptions."[25] Meanwhile, liberal theology required biblical criticism, which was based on Enlightenment philosophies of religion alongside scientific developments, such as evolution and archaeology.[26]

The milieu that gave rise to both liberal Protestantism and dispensational fundamentalism was one of change in how people thought about economics, and much of that thought centered around a commodity powering the era: oil. These competing Protestantisms would lay unique claims to the world of oil, giving followers a stake in how the industry would (or would not) be regulated and in how its economics would shape the future of American society. The civil war in American Protestantism was not merely the competing theologies of liberal Protestantism and dispensationalism; it was also how their followers laid stake to the economics of oil.

In the early oil years of the late 1850s and 1860s, drilling for oil was the industrial equivalent of gambling, with vast fortunes or crushing bankruptcies to be made overnight (and sometimes both in the same night). Many independent oilmen, who were fiercely evangelical and often leaned toward dispensationalism, saw their successes or failures in a highly volatile market not as the product of hard work but as the result of divine favor. Wildcatting, the highly risky venture of drilling exploratory wells, fit in with this notion that wealth was from on high, as God blessed those whom he would with an oil strike and left others empty.

These wildcatting oilers were entrepreneurs who sometimes bet everything on the bit of earth that they drilled into. Their faith in the ground often mirrored their faith in the God who would bring forth divine riches in the form of oil. In the words of Darren Dochuk, "Countless numbers of [wildcatters] chased the black stuff as if it was *their* divine calling and drew on their biblical studies . . . to engineer better methods of tapping the earth's bounty . . . in hopes of achieving a prosperity that could signal their blessedness and allow them to save society in anticipation of the end times."[27] This wildcatting ethos imbued capitalism with a holiness that saw prosperity in terms of supernatural blessing rather than hard work. When Falwell traveled the country preaching "America Back to God," he presented that same wildcatting view to his audiences, claiming that capitalism made America righteous before God and that her prosperity came directly from his hand.

Lyman Stewart (1840–1923) was a postmillennial Christian whose vision of a peaceful world during the millennium helped fuel his desire to become a missionary. His childhood home was near Titusville, Pennsylvania, the birthplace of the oil industry. Oozing petroleum frequently caught his young eye, and in 1859, two years before the Civil War broke out, Edwin Drake created a makeshift derrick in Titusville that could pull oil out of the ground. Stewart decided to follow in Drake's footsteps, believing that the riches he could gain from the oil under his feet could finance his missionary dreams. Yet before the war, his first two ventures at drilling failed.

Growing up in Pennsylvania, a state where escaped slaves were able to cross into freedom, Stewart was gripped by preaching from abolitionist conductors on the Underground Railroad. When the Civil War began, he joined the Union Army and, in 1863, was part of a unit headed toward Gettysburg. He missed the landmark battle, due to a bout with typhoid fever that left him incapacitated for months. Yet he did not escape the horrors of the war, as his time in medical care made him a constant witness to the war's brutality. Men with body parts blown off, men with gangrene, men whose stories and injuries must have rattled his soul. After the war, Stewart went back to drilling, this time with more success. By 1870, he was earning $1,000 per week and believed that God was guiding him toward prosperity in the incipient oil industry. Around 1880, he began reading dispensationalist works, and by the 1890s, he had become a firm dispensational premillennialist.

No longer believing that Christian service could improve the world, he committed his life to evangelism that he believed would save people from the coming Tribulation.

At that time, the Social Gospel was taking hold in the Northeast, shifting the focus of churches from doctrine to "Christian Socialism." Perhaps the most contentious figure in the Social Gospel movement was John D. Rockefeller (1839–1937), the titan of oil. Rockefeller was born into a family with modest financial means and devout Baptist faith. His shrewd mother taught him the value of hard work and discipline, while his father was a con artist. In 1870, shortly after the Civil War ended and while both dispensational fundamentalism and the Social Gospel were beginning to develop, he incorporated the Standard Oil Company.

When Rockefeller and Stewart were first building up America's oil industry, there were no regulations around it, and the "rule of capture" dominated the field. The rule of capture essentially said that the wildcatter who claimed the land and built the derrick owned whatever oil came from it. As a result, oilers scrambled to build derricks practically on top of each other, often covering entire hillsides with derricks, while crude oil oozed down the slopes and into rivers. Further, without regulations, prices were highly unstable, so much so that one could strike oil and it be nearly worthless because the market was so saturated. There were no efficient means of transporting or storing oil, other than in barrels to be carried on trains, so whatever the oil was worth when it was struck was what the oiler got. Sometimes, he made millions; sometimes, he struck black gold and still lost his shirt.

Rockefeller entered the oil industry and changed it from a free-for-all to a monopoly with his Standard Oil Company. With no stability at the time, he knew that he would go bankrupt if he went by the rule of capture like the wildcatters did. Instead, he made back-room deals with railroad companies to transport his oil more cheaply than his competitors, thereby enabling him to lower his prices so much that others would go out of business. By 1872, just two years after founding Standard Oil, he owned nearly all the refineries in Cleveland, Ohio, and by the next decade, he controlled 90 percent of the country's oil market.

This dominance over the oil industry led to a series of state and federal investigations into the Standard Oil Company. Several legal challenges attempted to break it up but only led to Rockefeller separating it into multiple companies, of which he maintained control. Standard Oil ultimately became a trust that held all his companies, which came to include Standard Oil of New Jersey (Exxon), Standard Oil of California (Chevron), and Standard Oil of New York (Mobil). He also went into overseas markets, especially China—where he marketed kerosene lamps to peasants who had previously relied on vegetable oil—and the Middle East. There, his ARAMCO became Saudi Aramco, the state-run oil company.

Rockefeller used his massive oil wealth to engage in philanthropic causes, many of which were connected to the Social Gospel. He funded some fundamentalist causes, such as the fire-and-brimstone revivalist Billy Sunday and foreign missionaries (including the parents of the media mogul Henry Luce), but his two longest-lasting causes were the University of Chicago and the Rockefeller Foundation. The Rockefeller Foundation aimed to promote the public good in keeping with the Social Gospel, but not all Social Gospelers were keen on using Rockefeller dollars. In 1902, a muckraking journalist named Ida Tarbell published a series of articles exposing Standard Oil as a ruthless monopoly that had been making deals with railroad operators to transport its oil more cheaply than other oil companies while also systematically buying out the competition. In 1904, she compiled the articles into *A History of the Standard Oil Company*. The next year, the Social

Gospel leader Washington Gladden led a campaign for $100,000 (the equivalent of $2.7 million in 2019) of "tainted" Rockefeller money to be returned to the tycoon. Yet despite the money being "tainted," Social Gospelers relied on the philanthropy of millionaires (and in Rockefeller's case, billionaires) to fund their causes, allowing them to put faith into action for social redemption.

Rockefeller's University of Chicago taught the liberal theology of the Social Gospel at the divinity school, while other university departments ultimately secularized the movement by applying its principles outside of explicitly Protestant contexts. The world's first sociology department was at the University of Chicago, and the department built on the successes of the Social Gospel. In part, the university itself functioned as part of the Social Gospel from which it developed, with local outreaches such as Professor John Dewey's University Elementary School that promoted community uplift in Chicago. This local outreach reflected the broader model of Rockefeller philanthropy in that the goal was not to promote individual achievement but rather to create new standards and conditions within which communities can thrive. Both Rockefeller philanthropy and the Social Gospel focused on the collective uplift of communities rather than individuals, setting the ideologies at odds with both wildcatters and fundamentalists. Falwell called this approach, spawned by the Social Gospel and advanced by Rockefeller, "secular humanism," the belief that man is his own god.[28] He claimed in *Listen, America!* that "Humanism in some form has taken the place of the Bible. Secular humanism has become the religion of America."[29]

With Standard Oil in solid control of the oil industry and the Social Gospel transforming churches, there was little wildcat ethos left in the eastern and midwestern parts of America. Stewart and his partner, Wallace Hardison, sold their business interests to Rockefeller and, in 1883, moved to California.

In the Wild West, they were unencumbered not only by Rockefeller but also by the Social Gospel. Stewart could develop his wildcatting profession into a new kind of Protestantism that blended capitalism with dispensationalism. The West was more anti-establishment than the Northeast, and Protestants who had settled on the frontier had developed a home-grown faith that celebrated their hard work. By this point, Stewart was engaging with dispensational thought and applying it to his business ventures—and by now, overwhelming success—in the oil industry. Dispensationalism taught that the Bible was full of prophecies that had remained mysteries until God revealed them to his chosen ones, and there seemed to be a parallel to how oil was hidden inside the earth until he revealed its secret location. Stewart had to rely on God to uncover both the secrets of the Bible and the secrets of the earth.

According to B. M. Pietsch, "Twisting the clear causal connections between labor and success, oil wildcatting re-enchanted the Protestant ethic, and replaced it with a new, holier spirit of capitalism."[30] This holier spirit of capitalism was the product of wildcatting and saw wealth as the result of supernatural blessing rather than human investment. Pietsch went on to say,

> Contrary to classical theories, [Lyman] Stewart believed that religion and capitalism were not dichotomous forces. Max Weber's Protestant work ethic did not entirely disappear, but it was reconfigured by wildcat capitalism in which speculative risk-taking and superstitious beliefs led to either great riches or quick bankruptcy, or often both. Riches were no longer a natural reward for work, but a consequence of divining supernatural signs.[31]

Stewart went on to use his oil wealth to finance the infrastructure of what would become Protestant fundamentalism. Whereas Rockefeller had endowed the University of Chicago as a place that built on the successes of the Social Gospel, in 1908, Stewart endowed the Bible Institute of Los Angeles, now known as Biola University. He wanted to train ministers in the literal truth of the Bible, from a dispensational perspective, empowering them to convert people so that more would go up in the Rapture and be spared the Tribulation.

Thus began a uniquely American version of dispensational separatism. While Darby had urged his followers to separate from apostate Christendom and leave the world (including the established church) to its ruin, Stewart and other American dispensationalists taught separatism from liberal churches and liberal doctrine. Though Stewart himself did not diametrically oppose the Social Gospel, he did oppose its growing association with liberal theology, the concept of Christian Socialism, and especially the financier of much of the movement, J. D. Rockefeller. Stewart's growing crusade, centered in Los Angeles and somewhat partnered with Chicago's Moody Bible Institute, emphasized separatism from these liberal teachings and institutions—such as University of Chicago, Yale, and Harvard—that spread them. In other words, dispensational separatism in America was heavily predicated on economic interests.

In time, these dispensationalists would build their own subculture, with not only their own schools and churches but even their own beauty parlors and clothing stores. Against the bobbed hairstyles, short dresses, and androgynous form of the 1920s flapper, fundamentalist women could showcase styles that emphasized modesty; with their own bookstores, fundamentalists could altogether avoid sexually candid novels, such as F. Scott Fitzgerald's *The Great Gatsby* and Zora Hurston's *Their Eyes Were Watching God*. As such, they could come out from the world and be separate, all while remaining part of mainstream America. After all, dispensational fundamentalism was becoming a distinctly American movement, and though anti-liberal, it emphasized longstanding American Protestant ideals of hard work and evangelism.

To Falwell, whose ministry began nearly half a century after the founding of Biola, the American Christian nation functioned almost as a church, and he applied dispensational separatism to it. In other words, his approach to nationalism was grounded in ecclesiology, or a doctrine of the church. He told his church, "This is a Christian nation . . . And if we lose our liberties as Americans, the cause of world evangelization, as I see it, will be down the drain."[32] The obligation to pay taxes was as significant as the obligation to tithe to the church; he said in the same sermon, "It's just as wrong to cheat Uncle Sam as it is to cheat the Lord."[33] While he may have been referring to the need for Christians to deal honestly, the broader context of his nationalism indicates that he meant more than mere honesty. He also claimed that the president of the United States should have the same qualifications as a pastor; those qualifications did not include seminary training—Falwell himself did not attend seminary—but referred to what he saw as moral qualities, particularly regarding the traditional, male-headed family.[34]

Nowhere did Falwell's national separatism apply more than on his stance regarding the United Nations. The liberal UN was for Falwell what the ruined church was for Darby: apostate. Similar to how Darby urged his followers to leave the apostate church, Falwell wanted Christian America to leave the apostate UN. In a series on biblical prophecy that he likely taught in 1974, he said that the United Nations is an instrument that Satan will use during the coming Tribulation to bring together all the nations of the world under the antichrist.[35]

Darby wrote, "Nationalism was associated with the world; in its bosom some believers were merged in the very world from which Jesus had separated them."[36] Doubtless "nationalism" meant something different in Darby's day than in Falwell's, but Falwell's brand of political engagement is nothing if not an innovation within dispensational thought. He taught that as a Christian nation, America had to pursue its own agenda, regardless of what the UN determined. Yet America was more than a Christian nation; it was a church, and its president was not merely a political leader but a pastor of sorts, steering the church away from worldly entanglements and the apostasy of the End Times.

Biblical Capitalism versus the Social Gospel

Stewart saw evangelism and business as counterparts to each other, with a daily devotional from the first edition of Biola's journal, *The King's Business*, saying,

> "Do Business till I come." It is enough that the disciple shall be as his Lord. Our Lord was a business man [*sic*]. "My Father worketh hitherto and I work," are his words. What ceaseless energy was manifested by Him "who went about doing good and healing all that were oppressed of the devil." While He lived here He labored hard. When He left the world He laid the burden of service upon his followers.
>
> In the parable of the pounds, the Lord represents Himself as the nobleman going into a far country. To his servants He commanded, occupy (do business) till I come.[37]

The article goes on to affirm—against the ethos of the Social Gospel's more theologically liberal strands—the individual, rather than the societal, imperative to conduct the Lord's business. In the aforementioned parable of the pounds, the nobleman gave some pounds to each of his servants; they had to individually—not collectively or socially—give an account for what they did with what they had been entrusted. A collection of daily devotionals affirmed the need of the individual to work and not expect social safety nets; under a section entitled "Private Revenge, 'An eye for an eye,'" is written, "'Give to him that asketh,' but not what he asketh. A child might ask a razor, or a tramp a drink of liquor. Against this text put its opposite, 'If a man will not work, neither shall he eat' (2 Thess. 3:10)."[38] The text seems to carry an undertone that those who expect social safety nets want things that are not beneficial, such as the tramp who wants more liquor. Falwell echoed this sentiment, albeit more derogatorily than Stewart, in how he talked about people who received welfare benefits. They were bums "who wouldn't work in a pie shop eating the holes out of donuts,"[39] but even worse, they squandered the public money that was meant to provide for them and their children. Hard work and capitalism, not socialism and labor unions, would save them.

Despite having moved across the country, Stewart was not finished with his archnemesis, Rockefeller. Following Tarbell's muckraking expose on Standard Oil, Stewart envisioned a similar treatise that would expose the side of Rockefeller that she had missed, that of liberal theology. He brought together the most brilliant evangelical scholars of his time, both conservative and progressive, to publish a collection of essays that would defend a divinely inspired Bible against the poison of liberal theology: *The Fundamentals*.

A theological rationale for capitalism over socialism and for a rejection of liberal theology's biblical criticism featured prominently in *The Fundamentals*. Though not strictly dispensationalist—many of the writers, including B. B. Warfield of Princeton Seminary, were postmillennialists—the essays thoroughly denounced the conclusions produced by the biblical criticism that underpinned the more theologically liberal strands of the Social Gospel. While *The Fundamentals* may have symbolized the high view of Scripture promoted by those who rejected liberal theology, some of the essays take direct aim at the idea that socialism and Christianity can have anything to do with each other. One such essay is entitled "The Church and Socialism," by Professor Charles Erdman. Erdman claimed,

> "Christian Socialism," however, is not only a [*sic*] imperfect name; it is in most of its forms an unfortunate thing. In some cases, it is true, it is only the expression of a benevolent desire that a spirit of justice and brotherhood should be shown by men in their social and industrial relations. This is innocent enough; but as presented by the great masses of its advocates, "Christian Socialism" is neither Christian nor Socialism. It is disappointing to Christians and irritating to Socialists. It minimizes or denies such Christian truths as the incarnation, the virgin birth, the atonement, the resurrection, justification by faith, the work of the Holy Spirit, the second coming of Christ, and insofar it ceases to be true Christianity.[40]

Erdman went on to suggest that properly understanding the social teachings of Jesus requires that Christians voluntarily tithe and help those who are in need. Another essay, entitled "Our Lord's Teachings About Money," uses texts from the gospels, particularly Matthew, to illustrate that the capitalist system embodies the ethos of stewardship taught by Jesus. Christian giving kept one from being a slave of personal wealth and allowed one to receive more abundant blessings from God.

Falwell claimed in *Listen, America!*, in a manner consistent with Erdman, "The way to defeat welfarism in America is for those who wish to see God's law restored to our country to tithe fully to organizations that will remove from government those tasks that are more properly addressed by religious and private organizations."[41] The key to ending welfare programs and restoring the capitalism promoted by *The Fundamentals* was for Christians to tithe to churches; churches could then assume full responsibility for social programs that, by Falwell's time, were being run by the government.

Stewart was not the only oiler who used his wealth to finance fundamentalist institutions. In January 1901, the company that Patillo Higgins and his partner, George Carroll, had formed struck oil at Spindletop; Higgins used the riches that he believed God had blessed him with to finance many Baptist causes. Charles Fuller, a graduate of Biola, used his oil wealth to fund his radio broadcast *The Old-Fashioned Revival Hour*—Falwell credited the show for his own conversion to Protestant fundamentalism and modeled the name of his show, *The Old-Time Gospel Hour*, after it—and later to endow the opening of Fuller Seminary in 1947. Oral Roberts, another dispensationalist-leaning evangelical whose ministry was inextricably connected with Oklahoma's oil industry, was motivated by his beliefs in the impending End Times and particularly regarding the restoration of the Jewish people to the land of Palestine. He founded Oral Roberts University in 1963 to train young scholars in similar beliefs, as well as to endow them with the gift of faith healing. I refer to this network of fundamentalist institutions that were funded with oil money and promoted "biblical capitalism" as the fundamentalist-oil empire.

Perhaps as important as Stewart, in the world of dispensationalism and oil, was the Pew family. Around the time that Stewart was building Union Oil and advancing the idea of biblical capitalism, Joseph Newton Pew (1848–1912) was organizing the Sun Oil Company. Pew was born into a devout Presbyterian family and never left the Presbyterian faith, but the Pews may have been influenced by dispensationalism. Joseph's nephew, J. Edgar Pew (1870–1946), helped manage Sun Oil's holdings in Texas and seems to have tied prophecies into the oil industry, as seen in a 1923 publication for the American Association of Petroleum

Geologists: "Never yet has the oil producer failed to bring forth the hidden deposits of this invaluable commodity when needed, and a fair prophecy is that they will not fail."[42] Indeed, Joseph's son, J. Howard Pew (1882–1971) (who would help create the Pew Charitable Trusts), would serve as the principle investor in *Christianity Today*, the magazine of the committed dispensationalist Billy Graham.

With the rise of communism in Russia and post-war unrest, a Red Scare was brewing in the 1910s and 1920s. The Red Scare of the post–World War I era was driven in part by radical labor unions that promoted socialism, communism, and anarchy. In 1917, members of the anarchist Industrial Workers of the World (IWW) chapter in Tulsa, Oklahoma, planted a bomb in the Pew home that, surprisingly, did not kill anyone but destroyed the house. To the Pews, socialism was not only a threat to Christianity and their oil company; socialism was a threat to their family, as they experienced the teaching as inciting workers against managers and even calling for violence. Addressing the socialist menace, J. Howard Pew would, during the later Red Scare of the Cold War, preach a sermon entitled "The Oil Industry: A Living Monument to the American System of Free Enterprise." He became a major financial donor to Fuller Seminary, as well as to many other fundamentalist causes.

To the Pews, oil promoted the values of industry and stewardship, against the idleness that would surely follow the implementation of socialism. Whereas in the 1920s the government was attempting to increase oil taxes to pay off its debt from World War I, the politically active Pews advocated for the reduction of oil taxes so that this industry, so central to American life, could thrive. They claimed that lower taxes would result in less regulation from the government and a freer hand for wildcatting oilers to stake their claim on this piece of americana. The biblical capitalism promoted by Lyman Stewart and later the Pews was the key to a well-ordered Christian life as well as abundance in the world of oil.

The Economics of the Fundamentalist-Modernist Controversy

Dispensationalists were not the only evangelicals who maintained a high view of the Bible as the divinely inspired word of God. Many Christians have held to that view since long before Darby; it was never limited to dispensationalism. Princeton Seminary, founded in 1812, developed and taught the Princeton Theology, a postmillennial approach to the Bible that upheld its divine origins. A Presbyterian school, Princeton Seminary would later attract some dispensationalist thinkers, and several of its professors contributed to *The Fundamentals*. However, the administration dismissed ideas such as the Rapture and favored the more evangelical aspects of the Social Gospel.

Despite not being dispensationalist, Princeton Seminary was embroiled in a dispute in the 1920s that came to be known as the Fundamentalist-Modernist Controversy. With a loose and informal alliance between Princeton Seminary and dispensationalist thinkers, both the Princeton Theology and American dispensationalism came to be known as "fundamentalism"; Curtis Lee Laws, an editor for the *Watchman-Examiner*, coined the term when he said that a fundamentalist is one who is ready to do "battle royal" for the fundamentals of the faith—fundamentals that relied heavily on the high view of scripture contained in the Princeton Theology.[43] The Fundamentalist-Modernist Controversy, a series of clashes between liberal Protestants and fundamentalists, led to a schism in the Presbyterian church and the reorganization of Princeton Seminary. A Princeton professor named J. Gresham Machen left and formed Westminster Theological Seminary to continue teaching the Princeton Theology, while Princeton Seminary began leaning more and more toward biblical criticism and liberal theology.

Dispensationalism did not feature too heavily in the Presbyterian schism (though there were several Presbyterian churches that taught dispensationalism, the center of the split was Princeton Seminary, which was avowedly non-dispensationalist), but American-style dispensationalism's emphasis on biblical capitalism versus the Social Gospel set the stage for an even more significant struggle. The tensions between Stewart and Rockefeller would continue, with many independent oilers (especially the Pew family) taking up the mantle of biblical capitalism, at the time when the liberal economics of the Social Gospel were becoming mainstream.

While studying at Brown University and especially under the mentorship of Professor Elisha Benjamin Andrews, John Rockefeller Jr. (1874–1960) began considering how he could apply the principles of the Social Gospel to the world of business. He and Lyman Stewart both saw business as a Christian enterprise, though for different reasons. Stewart saw business as a means of generating wealth that could be used to fund pastors and missionaries; in the process, businessmen provided jobs so that people, rather than being idle and lazy, could occupy themselves diligently while earning an income. John Jr. rejected all forms of sectarianism, including dispensationalism; against the separatist and premillennialist ethos, he actively engaged with the challenges facing contemporary society and believed he could solve them. As a civil millennial (someone with a postmillennial ethos who does not believe in a literal millennium) and liberal Christian, Junior saw business as a means toward philanthropy, which he could use to improve human society. In his view, the world was not destined for the judgment of God but rather could—and should—be improved by those who have the ability.

In 1901, Junior played a significant role in the opening of the Rockefeller Institute for Medical Research, the first biomedical institute in America. Later known as Rockefeller University, the institute significantly elevated the status of science and health in American public life. In 1909, he began the Rockefeller Sanitary Commission, which had the goal of eradicating hookworm in the Southern United States, at a time when the parasite affected two out of every five southerners. Though the commission failed to accomplish its goal, in the process, Junior set an important precedent in philanthropy's vision of disease eradication. Concerned with prostitution and venereal disease, he created the Bureau of Social Hygiene and effectively catalyzed a movement of education and medicine around sexual health. Rather than urging prostitutes to repent of their sinful ways, he strove to ameliorate the social conditions that drove women to prostitution while developing treatments for the illnesses that plagued them. When he helped open the Rockefeller Foundation in 1913, he saw his work as capable of curing evil.

There was a deeply religious component to Junior's philanthropic career. His pastor was Henry Emerson Fosdick, a liberal Protestant and staunch Social Gospeler in Manhattan who would become a central figure in the Fundamentalist-Modernist Controversy; Fosdick's brother, Raymond, would become the president of the Rockefeller Foundation in 1936. After Fosdick's preaching stoked fires in the Fundamentalist-Modernist Controversy and led to him leaving his pastorate, Junior commissioned the construction of Manhattan Riverside Church with the intention of Fosdick serving as the senior minister. The church's sculptures reflect a liberal, almost secular

Christianity that is less preoccupied with the supernatural than humanitarianism: carvings of Pythagoras, Hippocrates, Charles Darwin, and Albert Einstein are among the intellectual lights featured. Junior's was a faith that, lacking a supernatural focus, had nothing in common with dispensationalism and the growing fundamentalist movement.

Meanwhile, President Warren Harding (in office 1921–1923) was promoting an approach to economics that bore a striking resemblance to President Ronald Reagan's (in office 1981–1989) trickle-down economics decades later. Believing that lower taxes and fewer business regulations would naturally create a balanced market and economic prosperity, he slashed tax rates and took a hands-off approach to business. Following Harding's death, President Calvin Coolidge (in office 1923–1929) and his successor, President Herbert Hoover (in office 1929–1933), promoted not the Social Gospel but rather the *laissez-faire* economics that underpinned "biblical" capitalism. J. Howard Pew, the scion who took over as president of his family's Sun Oil Company in 1912, championed the deregulation of Hoover in particular; later in life, he kept a framed picture of the former president in his office, claiming that Hoover was one of the Americans he most admired. Coolidge and Hoover's *laissez-faire* economy boomed during the Roaring Twenties, as did the Pew family's Sun Oil Company. Yet trouble was on the horizon.

In 1929, the year that Princeton Seminary was reorganized along the lines of liberal Protestantism, came the climax of "biblical capitalism's" war with the Social Gospel when the stock market crashed. The country soon found itself in the throes of the Great Depression, and no amount of biblical capitalism could stop the foreclosures of farms, the lines of hungry people waiting for bread and soup, and the growth of shanty towns. Unemployed and starving masses helped elect Franklin Roosevelt, a Democrat who had been deeply influenced by the Social Gospel, to the presidency in 1932.

President Roosevelt established a series of government initiatives known collectively as the New Deal. These initiatives included social security, government-funded jobs in areas such as construction and forest conservation, and agriculture assistance, all intended to help lift people out of crushing poverty. In addition, he began the Federal Deposit Insurance Corporation (FDIC) and Securities and Exchange Commission (SEC) to help prevent another stock-market crash. These programs built on the Social Gospel, especially how Roosevelt saw its principles as applicable to government. In other words, the New Deal was a government-wide appropriation of the Social Gospel. No longer confined to progressive evangelical and mainline churches and schools such as the University of Chicago, the Social Gospel was now government policy.

Roosevelt led America through most of World War II, passing away soon before it ended. As the Cold War set in, liberalism seemed to be the dominant strain of intellectual thought and public life, holding sway in both the Democratic and Republican parties. Rockefeller Junior's son, Nelson (1908–1979), was a liberal Republican who held public office for decades. When Barry Goldwater (1909–1998), a conservative Republican, lost the 1964 presidential election in a landslide, scholars and journalists generally agreed that his conservativism had been lost on the Republican party, which still had a strong liberal streak. Yet the revived communist threat of the Cold War helped stoke the tensions between capitalism and socialism that underpinned American Protestantism's civil war. Following the success of the New Deal, liberals may have declared victory too soon.

The Rise of Communist Magog

As the New Deal's systemic implementation of the Social Gospel was providing social safety nets for Americans and regulations (as well as taxes) on businesses, the network of fundamentalist institutions funded by oil money was expanding its influence, almost without public notice. J. Howard Pew was funding far-right, libertarian institutions, including the Christian Freedom Foundation, Christian Economics Foundation, John Birch Society, and the *Christian Economics* magazine. *Christian Economics* was based on Friedrich Hayek's Austrian school of economics, which teaches that any form of government intervention prevents markets from self-correcting. According to this thought, deregulation of private property and private business allows the market to dictate the economic sphere and provides the greatest possible freedom for people. With the help of Pew's funds, the Christian Freedom Foundation sent biweekly copies of *Christian Economics* to 180,000 ministers across the country; similar to Stewart's mass distribution of *The Fundamentals*, Pew also paid to distribute Hayek's *The Road to Serfdom* to Christian ministers. Through these enterprises, the fundamentalist-oil empire was quietly growing and turning public opinion away from liberalism.

Less extreme than his promotion of Hayek, though certainly consequential, was Pew's partnership with a Christian evangelist whose star was rapidly rising, Billy Graham. Graham and his father-in-law, L. Nelson Bell, envisioned starting a Christian periodical that would provide for the spiritual edification of evangelicals and a Christian worldview on current events. With Pew's influence and especially his dollars, *Christianity Today* would emerge during the Cold War as a vehicle for promoting conservative economics—what had since Lyman Stewart become enmeshed with fundamentalism. Pew and his siblings also established the

Pew Memorial Trust in 1948. Though the later Pew Charitable Trust would promote humanitarianism not unlike the Rockefeller Foundation, the Pew Memorial Trust supported conservative causes. As late as the 1980s, the Pew Memorial Trust was financing the conservative thinktank American Enterprise Institution, which advocated the hyper-conservative, libertarian economics of Hayek.

Despite the political convictions of Pew's philanthropy and public face of Graham's crusades, dispensationalists after the Fundamentalist-Modernist Controversy were generally unconcerned with social reform. Carl McIntire had put tremendous energy into political organizing among fundamentalists in the mid-twentieth century, but he was unable to create a large-scale movement. Falwell said as late as 1965, in a manner consistent with Darbyite separatism rather than the nationalist ecclesiology, that he would soon come to embrace, that God has not called upon Christians to reform the externals of the world—the liquor stores, bootleggers, and other social ills—but to preach the gospel so that souls might be saved. Much of dispensationalists' intellectual activity and engagement with public life centered on the interpretation of biblical prophecy, especially as the Cold War went into full swing.

Dispensationalists during this time merged the idea of biblical capitalism with some of the most sensationalist imagery in the Bible, especially with what they saw as End Times prophecies regarding Magog. Ezekiel 38:2-3 says, "Son of man, set your face against Gog, of the land of Magog, the prince of Rosh, Meshech, and Tubal, and prophesy against him, and say, 'Thus says the Lord God: Behold, I am against you, O Gog, the prince of Rosh, Meshech, and Tubal'" (NKJV). The rest of the chapter describes an invasion by Gog, the leader of the people of Magog, into the land of Israel, followed by God's supernatural judgment on the invaders. The identity of Magog had long been debated by theologians, with Medieval apocalypticists believing Magog referred to either tribes beyond the Caucasus Mountains or the Ottoman Turks. The Turkish identification of Magog persisted through the 1800s, when another Magog contender arose: Russia. Darby himself identified Magog as Russia, as did many other non-liberal biblical scholars of the 1800s. The 1917 Bolshevik Revolution in Russia, followed by the collapse of Turkey's Ottoman Empire in 1922, led prophecy interpreters to a near-unanimous identification of Magog as Russia.

The wildly popular *Scofield Reference Bible* unambiguously asserted that Magog was, in fact, Russia. Commentary on Ezekiel 38:2 identifies "Meshech" as Moscow and "Tubal" as Tobolsk, both major cities in Russia; further, the passage speaks of a "northern people," and no country is farther north than Russia. It was actively persecuting the Jewish people within its borders and, according to prophecy, would eventually launch an invasion into Israel.

With the rise of communism following World War I, Magog as Russia increasingly allowed dispensationalists to merge prophecy with economics. Communism was irreconcilably opposed to the God-ordained system of capitalism, making America's enmity with the Soviet Union during the Cold War not merely a political struggle but also a theological one. To America's dispensationalists, prophecy was unfolding in real time. According to Paul Boyer,

> A 1919 prophecy writer saw "THE BOLSHEVIST GERM" as an unequivocal sign of the last days. Articles with titles such as "The Red Menace" and "When Russia's Bear Meets Judah's Lion," which combined apocalyptic foreboding about Russia's Mideast invasion and communism's spread to the United States, filled prophecy journals of the interwar years. And Soviet

atheism provided a more compelling motive for the assault: a nation that denied God would naturally seek to destroy God's chosen people.[44]

The conclusion of World War II and beginning of the Cold War brought another reason for dispensationalists to read Russia into biblical prophecy: the rise of nuclear weapons. Second Peter 3:10 says, "But the day of the Lord will come as a thief in the night, in which the heavens will pass away with a great noise, and the elements will melt with fervent heat; both the earth and the works that are in it will be burned up" (NKJV). In this view, the Bible had predicted the atomic bomb that destroyed the Japanese cities of Hiroshima and Nagasaki, and the bomb surely meant that the End Times were at hand. Thousands of years earlier, the Hebrew prophet Zechariah had asked, "For who has despised the day of small things?" (Zechariah 4:10 NKJV). The prophet was ahead of science, as he had unknowingly foretold that the atom, the smallest of all things, would be used in the devastation of the End Times.

As America descended into an arms race with the Soviet Union, especially with the 1957 deployment of Sputnik and then the 1962 Soviet Missile Crisis, dispensationalists looked more and more toward what the Bible says about Russia. In his 1967 book *The Nations in Prophecy*, leading dispensationalist thinker John Walvoord (1910–2002) pointed believers to the Ezekiel 38–39 passages about Magog's End Times invasion of Israel. With an almost fatalistic approach, Walvoord assured his readers that this invasion would happen, that world events are aligning in this way; there was no reason to believe Christians could, or should, try to affect world events as prophecy was unfolding. This fatalism generally followed the Americanized form of Darbyite separatism, in which fundamentalists retreated from mainstream, liberal society to create their own cultural enclaves. While the world was careening toward the Tribulation, Walvoord taught that true Christians were to concern themselves with heavenly things, especially evangelism and the study of prophecy.

In 1970, Walvoord's protégé, Hal Lindsey (who studied under Walvoord at Dallas Theological Seminary), published the bestselling nonfiction book of the decade, *The Late Great Planet Earth*. The book is about prophecy and its fulfillment in current events; other than the 1948 creation of the state of Israel, which signaled God's purposes returning to the Jews, the surest sign of biblical prophecy's fulfillment was the role of Russia in current events. With over 15 million copies of the book sold, dispensationalism was moving out from the shadows and becoming a national force, one that would soon rival the liberal establishment that had prevailed since the New Deal.

In 1973, Walvoord made public the dispensationalist thinking regarding conservative economics and dispensationalism in the fundamentalist-oil empire. In the wake of an economic crisis caused by an oil embargo, he published *Armageddon, Oil, and the Middle East Crisis*; he claimed that God was using the complex oil politics of the Middle East, alongside the restoration of Palestine to the Jewish people, to drive biblical prophecy and ultimately lead the world toward the climactic battle of Armageddon. The real question for dispensationalists was if America would succumb to communism—the socialism of liberal theology and the Social Gospel could only have been precursors to the rise of the communist Soviet Union—or might somehow remain free until the Rapture. Walvoord insisted that God's wrath on America was long overdue, but the country's support of Israel and role in evangelizing the world may be why this wrath has not yet fallen. Still, there was no escaping the Tribulation; it would strike America with equal ferocity as the rest of the world.

"What has gone wrong?" Falwell lamented in "America Back to God." "What has happened to this great republic? Why are we under the wrath of God?" He pointed to the 1973 oil embargo as symptomatic of America's economic problems, saying of the energy shortage, "This is all, I believe, the wrath of God upon a nation who has inside her borders a sleeping church." He went on to compare America to the biblical Jonah, who tried to run from God by boarding a ship; God sent a storm that nearly overtook the ship, until Jonah confessed his misdeed and had the crew throw him overboard. "It wasn't because of those godless mariners aboard [that the ship began to sink]," Falwell declared. "It isn't because of a bunch of godless Democrats and Republicans that God is judging this country." He then laid the blame for God's wrath squarely at the feet of the church, for allowing America to slide into the apostasy of liberalism. He urged national repentance of this sin and a turning back to God and unregulated capitalism. This call for repentance emerged from the separatism that underpinned Darbyite dispensationalism, albeit with the nation, rather than the true church, chosen by God to "come out from among them and be separate" (2 Cor 6:17 NKJV). The nation was under the wrath of God, but the nation—not merely individuals or even the church, but the nation itself—could repent and be saved.

This climate of the 1970s, in which Cold War fears of Russia and a communist takeover—alongside an economic collapse caused by an international oil embargo—were inducing a public surge of prophecy belief, is the one that Jerry Falwell stepped into. He had been preaching since the 1950s, but until the early 1970s, his sole concerns were evangelism and upholding segregation. Massive social upheaval of the 1970s, upheaval that reflected the longstanding economic tensions of American Protestantism's civil war, caused him to move away from a separatist approach, in which the only public issue he concerned himself with was segregation, to a hyper-nationalist approach that read American patriotism into the Bible. His new form of nationalism married the myth of the American Christian nation with the dispensationalism of the fundamentalist-oil empire—biblical capitalism merged with prophecy fulfillment—and used this narrative to bring the conservative economics of Stewart, Pew, and other soldiers in this civil war into the public eye. Though liberalism took a hit with the presidency of the more conservative Richard Nixon (president 1969–1974), it would begin losing its public credibility with the rise of Falwell's friend and fellow believer in Armageddon, Ronald Reagan.

Falwell's movement was, first and foremost, an economic one, grounded in longstanding fundamentalist beliefs about biblical capitalism. He was convinced that liberal theology, the Social Gospel, and the New Deal were the apostasy of the End Times that the Bible prophesied. Just as Darby's apostasy was the established church, Falwell's was established liberalism, and America had to repent of this national sin. The country had to reject its liberal ways in favor of biblical capitalism—no business taxes or regulations, no social safety nets, not even public schools—and reclaim its Christian heritage. Otherwise, the country would be unequipped to face the impending Tribulation; rather than one nation under God, America would be one nation under God's wrath.

Abortion and the Economics of Civil Rights

ON FEBRUARY 26, 1978, Jerry Falwell cautiously preached a sermon that would reshape America's conservative movement. The sermon had little fanfare, lacking not only the patriotic flamboyance and pageantry that had come to define his preaching style but also the airwaves that would transmit the message across the country and to the corners of the earth. He preached the landmark sermon "Abortion on Demand: Is It Murder?" during his church's evening service, when the cameras were not rolling and only the most committed of his church, along with a curious few who visited, attended. The sermon was his first one about abortion, and it did not come until a full five years after the Supreme Court's 1973 *Roe v Wade* decision legalized abortion in all fifty states.

Despite the lack of pomp and circumstance, Falwell made clear in his 1978 sermon the gravity of the topic that he was bringing to his congregation. "Tonight, we are talking about a very, very important issue," he began. "As a matter of fact, I feel that on the American scene today, there is no issue more important to the spiritual health and welfare of our nation than the one on which I am speaking tonight." He then affirmed the sanctity of human life, based on the biblical view that God created humankind in his own image, saying, "Man is God's highest creation on earth. And for that reason, we approach the subject of abortion . . . As a gospel minister, I am against every law that has been passed in our nation legalizing abortion on demand. Whether on the federal or the state level, it brings upon our land divine retribution." In his view, legalized abortion was threatening the future of America, not only because the practice was ripping apart the country's social fabric but also because it would bring about divine judgment on the land. The wrath of God, language that he generally used to speak about the coming Tribulation, would descend on America because of the national sin known as abortion.

Up until then, conservative American Protestants had not exactly ignored abortion. While Billy Graham was urging support of programs that would help women facing crisis pregnancies, the Southern Baptist Convention was advocating for policies that would improve access to abortion; the impetus was primarily concern for women experiencing significant challenges that would impede their ability to raise children, as well as for children who would be born with life-limiting conditions. In 1971, two years before *Roe v Wade*, the Southern Baptist Convention issued a statement encouraging "Southern Baptists to work for legislation that will allow the possibility of abortion under such conditions as rape, incest, clear evidence of severe fetal deformity, and carefully ascertained evidence of the likelihood of damage to the emotional, mental, and physical health of the mother."[1] Succeeding statements throughout the 1970s issued stronger calls for protection of the "sanctity of human life," speaking against "the practice of abortion for selfish non-therapeutic reasons" and an "indiscriminate attitude toward abortion."[2] Despite the convention adopting an increasingly uncompromising stance, Southern Baptists of the 1970s, and evangelicals more broadly, remained largely ambivalent about engaging with abortion as a political issue.

Nothing about the context of Falwell's 1978 sermon suggested that the topic of abortion would soon become a galvanizing issue of American conservativism, as well as the most public feature of the new Religious Right, well into the twenty-first century. Abortion came to feature so prominently that the origin myth of the Religious Right is that the voting bloc formed in response to *Roe v Wade*. Falwell claimed as much in his 1997 autobiography, saying,

> In growing horror and disbelief, I read and re-read the short article describing the historical case titled *Roe v. Wade*. The Supreme Court had just made a decision by a seven-to-two margin that would legalize the killing of millions of unborn children. In one terrible act they struck down all the state laws against abortion and legalized infanticide across the land. I could not believe that seven justices on the nation's highest court could have so little regard for the value of human life . . . It wouldn't be easy for this Baptist preacher to become politically active.[3]

The year following his first anti-abortion sermon, in 1979, Falwell partnered with associates, including Tim LaHaye and Paul Weyrich, to form the Moral Majority. The goal of the Moral Majority was to promote conservative politics that aligned with Falwell's understanding of biblical morality, as part of a larger conservative coalition that Weyrich was building. In the newsletter that Falwell sent out in August of 1979 to explain what the Moral Majority is, he wrote in the introduction, "For six long years we have stood by helplessly while 3 to 6 million babies were legally murdered through abortion-on-demand—each baby a precious living soul in the eyes of the Lord. Can you imagine what this means to Almighty God?" Other topics that he touched on in the newsletter included the stains of feminism, homosexuality, and "social welfare bills that would further erode our precious freedoms." Subsequent publications from the Moral Majority highlighted the anti-abortion movement that Falwell began building in 1978 alongside calls for delegitimizing queer lifestyles, dismantling social welfare policies, and increasing military spending. Throughout these publications, he consistently placed abortion as the single most important issue in America.

Yet the abortion story, that *Roe v Wade* provided the motivation for Falwell to organize the Religious Right, is a myth. His own telling of how he got into political activism simply does not fit the record, beginning with the fact that he did not preach his first sermon about abortion until five years after *Roe v Wade*. The second problem with the abortion story is that he had been engaged in political activism long before *Roe v Wade*, not by advocating against abortion but by preaching against racial integration. Something other than abortion was going to bring the wrath of God upon America: the economics of civil rights.

Dispensational Node
The Apostasy

Falwell's conservative advocacy began with a reaction to a different Supreme Court decision, one that came nearly two decades before *Roe v Wade*. In 1954, the Supreme Court ruled in *Brown v Board of Education* that segregated schools were inherently unequal and therefore violated the Fourteenth Amendment's Equal Protection Clause. Thus began a decades-long process of integrating America's public schools, a process that met fierce resistance in the American South, including Falwell's hometown of Lynchburg, Virginia. In 1958, he was part of a resistance strategy that aimed to close Virginia's public schools altogether to prevent integration. He even served as the chaplain to a local chapter of Defenders of State Sovereignty and Individual Liberty, an organization dedicated to upholding segregationist norms.

When efforts to prevent desegregation showed sure signs of failure, he employed a more creative strategy that was growing throughout the South, the opening of so-called "segregation academies." Segregation academies were private schools that either only enrolled white children or set their tuition fees so high that Black families could not afford them. Falwell opened a segregation academy, Lynchburg Christian Academy, as a parachurch ministry of Thomas Road Baptist in 1967; LCA had an all-white student body upon opening. In 1968, when George Wallace ran as a third-party candidate for president on an openly segregationist platform, Falwell invited him to speak at Thomas Road Baptist.

During this time, he was teaching a form of dispensationalism that maintained some level of separatism, unlike his sermons and public forays after about 1973. Yet what featured more prominently than separatism, in both his preaching and political activism of the 1950s and 1960s (and well beyond) was the dispensational concept of the apostasy. "Apostasy" refers to a departure from the faith, indicating that there was, at least primordially, an adherence to what might be considered the "true" faith. Someone who grew up in a Christian home yet, as an adult, abandoned the faith, or perhaps even converted to a different faith, would be considered an apostate. In dispensationalism, "apostasy" is perhaps better understood as "heresy." "Heresy" refers to a teaching (or even an institution) that is at odds with the Bible, church teachings, or tradition, and a "heretic" is a person (or again, an institution) following a teaching that is considered "heresy." While an apostate has left the faith, a heretic may have never held to the true faith at all, or at least never been a dispensationalist. Despite this difference, because dispensationalism uses the language of "apostasy," I will, as well.

In the nineteenth century, John Nelson Darby taught that the established church was unequivocally apostate. Shortly after he began a brief tenure as a clergyman for the Church of Ireland, the archbishop of Dublin (allegedly, as the facts are disputed) issued a circular declaring that all Catholic converts to Protestantism had to swear an oath of loyalty to the British monarch. Darby saw this measure as making the church of God subservient to the state, something that accounted to a reformulation of Catholicism, with allegiance to the pope transmuted into allegiance to the king. In a tract published shortly thereafter, in 1828, he said,

> In the first place, it is not a formal union of the outward professing bodies that is desirable; indeed it is surprising that reflecting Protestants should desire it: far from doing good, I conceive it would be impossible that such a body could be at all recognized as the church of God. It would be a counterpart to Romish [Catholic] unity; we should have the life of the church and the power of the Word lost, and the unity of spiritual life utterly excluded.[4]

Compounding Darby's disillusionment with the established church was the contemporaneous Oxford Movement, what he referred to as "Puseyism" and saw as the church betraying its heavenly nature through an alliance with the state.[5] The Oxford Movement sought "to revive a conception of the Church of England as a branch of the ancient catholic and apostolic Church"[6] through emphases on high-church components, including the venerated priesthood and the sacraments as vessels through which communicants receive divine grace. With the Anglican church now, in Darby's view, drawing perilously close to Roman Catholicism, there was no hope for the church to be restored; it was utterly apostate, and he taught his followers to have no association with it.

Darby later expanded on his reasons for leaving the established Anglican church. He said,

> I find no such thing as a National Church in Scripture. Is the Church of England—was it ever—God's assembly in England? I say, then, that her constitution is worldly, because she

contemplates by her constitution—it is her boast—the population, not the saints. The man who would say that the Church of England is a gathering of saints must be a very odd man, or a very bold one. All the parishioners are bound to attend, by her principles. It was not the details of the sacramental and priestly system which drove me from the Establishment, deadly as they are in their nature. It was that I was looking for the body of Christ (which was not there, but perhaps in all the parish not one converted person); and collaterally, *because I believe in a divinely appointed ministry.* If Paul had come, he could not have preached (he had never been ordained); if a wicked ordained man, he had his title and must be recognized as a minister; the truest minister of Christ unordained could not. *It was a system contrary to what I found in Scripture.*[7]

Darby recognized that there have been numerous apostasies in the church, going back to the apostolic church of Christianity's first century. Yet there was something different about the present apostasy in which he lived; he believed it had been prophesied in the opening of Revelation. As Darby pointed out in his "Commentary on the Book of Revelation," the apostle John wrote in his vision of the resurrected Christ that he would spew the church out of his mouth (Rev 3:16). While the passage refers specifically to a church in Laodicea that is "lukewarm," neither cold nor hot, Darby seems to have interpreted the passage as a prophecy for the apostate church of his day. This great apostasy, rather than the different apostasies throughout church history, heralded the imminent End Times.

When dispensationalism traveled to America, the lack of an established church (along with geographical distance from the Vatican) led to different understandings of what the apostasy of the End Times is. James Hall Brookes (1830–1897), one of the first Americans to convert from postmillennialism to Darby's dispensational premillennialism, recognized an apostasy—the emergent liberal Protestantism—without holding denominations in the same contempt that Darby did. Brookes mentored Cyrus Ingerson Scofield, and the original *Scofield Reference Bible* contains almost no commentary on the lukewarm Laodicean church which Christ said he would spew out of his mouth. Yet Scofield saw the seven churches featured in the opening chapters of Revelation as different periods of time within church history. The first church, the one at Ephesus, was the apostolic church; the second church, at Smyrna, was the persecuted church under emperors such as Nero, until finally, the seventh church at Laodicea was the apostate church at the end of the present dispensation. American dispensationalists were able to see the present church as apostate—especially with the rise of liberal theology that was leading Christians to reject the supernatural—without a Darbyite disdain for the Catholic church overwhelming their ecclesiology.

Many American dispensationalists came to live out their separatism by rejecting the ecumenical movement that sought to bring harmony and Christian unity to different denominations. The 1910 Edinburgh World Missionary Conference helped create a spirit of ecumenism among attendees, for the sake of evangelizing the world, and the ecumenical movement began in earnest in the conference's aftermath. America's Federal Council of Churches had formed in 1908 (associated with the Social Gospel and initially endowed, in part, with Rockefeller dollars), and in 1950, it became part of the National Council of Churches, America's branch of the World Council of Churches (which formed in 1948). American dispensationalists largely remained within their own denominations but rejected these ecumenical bodies, seeing them as the apostate church of the End Times.

Charles Ryrie (1925–2016) was a contemporary of Falwell who took a more scholarly approach to dispensationalism, having studied at the University of Edinburgh (not a dispensationalist school, but one where he could attain scholarly credentials) before serving as a professor and dean at Dallas Theological Seminary. In his 1986 book *Basic Theology*, which built on decades of dispensational exegesis, Ryrie suggested that apostasy refers to unbelief, especially a defection from those who did believe. This defection will increase in the build-up to the End Times, as people will deny the Trinity, the Incarnation of Christ (including both his deity and humanity), and the imminent return of Christ. As a result, there will be widespread decline in morality, as prophesied in 2 Timothy 3:1-5. During this time of apostasy, a foundation will be laid for a one-world church; this church is fundamentally apostate, as it is not only unfaithful doctrinally but also persecutes true Christians. This one-world church, whose being could already be seen in the ecumenical movement and especially the World Council of Churches, would ultimately give rise to the antichrist.

Still, up through the 1950s, American dispensationalists tended to see the apostasy more in terms of liberal theology than any church establishment. Liberal theology was, in dispensational teaching, subverting the economic order while denying the fundamental truths of Christianity, all through the Social Gospel. There was a both/and to the apostasy: liberalism had spawned both the ecumenical movement that was already leading to the one-world church of the antichrist and the Christian Socialism that had upended Protestant orthodoxy. Dispensationalists separated from this great apostasy, the sign of the imminent End Times, and strove to live lives of personal holiness and doctrinal purity, rejecting liberalism in all its guises.

Then an obscure woman named Rosa Parks refused to give up her bus seat to a white man, and Martin Luther King Jr. became the de facto leader of the civil rights movement.

In 1965, eight years before *Roe v Wade*, Falwell preached a sermon called "Ministers and Marchers" as a response to the Selma

March that King was leading in Alabama. Falwell preached many sermons against the civil rights movement during the 1950s and 1960s—so many that he began to alienate his own congregation in Lynchburg—but recalled them in the early 1970s, when he publicly claimed to have changed his views on race. "Ministers and Marchers" had been distributed so far and wide that it could not be recalled, and it provides possibly the best glimpse into the theological underpinnings of his early conservative activism.

Falwell began "Ministers and Marchers" by asking the question, "Does the church have any command from God to involve itself in marches, demonstrations, or any other actions, such as many ministers and church leaders are doing so today in the name of civil rights reforms?"[8] Before answering that question with an emphatic no, he made clear his view that many civil rights leaders, including King, were communists and intent on taking advantage of racial tensions to advance the communist cause. To Falwell, any association with socialism or communism was a product of the apostasy—liberal theology and the Social Gospel—and he viewed the civil rights movement through that lens.

Though not a communist, King advocated socialism, and a week before he died, he claimed after meeting with disaffected youth in New Jersey,

> The trouble is that we live in a failed system. Capitalism does not permit an even flow of economic resources. With this system, a small privileged few are rich beyond conscience, and almost all others are doomed to be poor at some level. That's the way the system works. And since we know that the system will not change the rules, we are going to have to change the system.[9]

King recognized what is now referred to as *racial capitalism*, a collection of systemic inequalities that prevents African American communities from rising out of deep poverty. As an alternative,

King and his associates pressed for a redirection of economic and material resources so that the angry and frustrated poor could have what they need to thrive. Socialism, as part of a liberation movement to uplift communities that have been intentionally marginalized not only by individuals but also by government policies, is what I refer to as the economics of civil rights. Not socialism writ large, especially since "socialism" is such a slippery term that it defies clear definition, but rather socialism as advocated by liberationists such as Walter Rauschenbusch, Martin Luther King Jr., and later the South Africans Desmond Tutu and Nelson Mandela.

"We are asked quite often why we don't belong to the National or World Council of Churches," Falwell said in a 1973–1974 series on how prophecy was unfolding.[10] "The reason is, very frankly, that I don't want to get caught up in [Revelation] 17, because there is coming a day when God himself is going to deal with the one-world church." King was part of the ecumenical movement that had been spawned at Edinburgh 1910, and Archbishop Tutu would become leader of South Africa's branch of the World Council of Churches; both leaders promoted socialistic policies that would allow for the downward flow of material wealth. Falwell continued in what was a thinly veiled indictment of the economics they promoted as part of their liberationism by saying, "We are caught up in socialism, even promoting communism. We are talking about togetherliness, with no regard for principle or doctrine." Then, to show just how evil the ecumenical movement was, that it came straight from hell, he said, "The ecumenical movement is the attempt of Satan to bring together Babylon . . . Their idea was that they would build a tower into heaven, that they would go to heaven by the works of their own hands." The economics of civil rights—socialism and ecumenism as part of liberation movements—was apostate and would soon face the wrath of God.

From the Social Gospel to the Cold War

The civil rights movement, along with a renewed emphasis on a downward flow of material wealth in order to advance the uplift of minority communities, came during the Cold War. On the far right, leaders such as Robert Welch, the founder of the John Birch Society, had been banging the drum against communism since at least President Franklin Roosevelt began enacting his New Deal policies in the 1930s. In Welch's view, socialism, including the socialism that King advocated, was part of a communist infiltration of America. He claimed, in his 1958 address that became *The Blue Book of the John Birch Society*, that the racial agitation of the civil rights movement was being generated by communists.

"I must personally say that I do question the sincerity and nonviolent intentions of some civil rights leaders, such as Dr. Martin Luther King Jr., Mr. James Farmer, and others, who are known to have left-wing associations," Falwell declared to his congregation on the day that King was leading thousands of marchers over Alabama's Edmund Pettus Bridge, from Selma to Montgomery. "It is very obvious that the communists, as they do in all parts of the world, are taking advantage of a tense situation in our land and are exploiting every incident to bring about violence and bloodshed." The words that Falwell preached on March 21, 1965, could have come straight from *The Blue Book of the John Birch Society*. After all, Falwell and Welch were both reacting against the same New Deal, but for Falwell, the struggle was a religious one. The New Deal was, in a sense, the government appropriation of the Social Gospel, and therefore, it represented the apostasy of liberal theology.

This struggle was compounded by the onset of the Cold War. Dispensationalists since Darby had been interpreting prophecies about Magog as referring to Russia in the End Times; for

Falwell in particular, the Cold War put beliefs about Magog into overdrive. According to his interpretation of Ezekiel 38–39, the Soviets would launch an invasion into Israel halfway through the Tribulation period, as part of their campaign to achieve total world domination. The Russians had long been persecuting Jews, since at least the days of the Romanovs, and their hatred of the modern state of Israel—coupled with their anti-God communism—set them at complete enmity with God. Yet this enmity was not merely the product of Russian actions; it was biblically prophesied and therefore immutable: God himself was against Russia and especially against communism. The Cold War struggle between Christian America and communist Russia was essentially between God and anti-God, and the American Christian nation could not let anything that remotely resembled communism into its borders.

In other words, the apostasy of the Social Gospel and Christian Socialism was threatening to put the American Christian nation at enmity with God. The threat of the apostasy increased when the Social Gospel became government policy via the New Deal, at a time when Russia, God's own enemy, was experimenting with communism. To Falwell, the socialism of the New Deal was merely a cousin to communism, and America was on track to becoming communist, as well. Now with the civil rights movement, the likes of King were making demands that were not only communist in nature but were part of a communist conspiracy to create violence and upheaval in America. Should America succumb, the civil rights movement would be the end of the Christian nation and bring about the wrath of God.

"Ministers and Marchers" reveals that, long before Falwell claimed to get involved in politics, he was deeply invested in the far right. Rather than opposing abortion, he, like Welch, expressed his political commitments by preaching against communism and the civil rights movement. The point of "Ministers and Marchers" was that Christians had no business engaging in the movement. In fact, contrary to his later activism that included the anti-abortion movement, he claimed, "Nowhere are we commissioned to reform the externals." The church of God had no business in enacting political reform, not only through the civil rights movement but also by addressing "bootleggers, liquor stores, gamblers, murderers, prostitutes, racketeers, prejudiced persons or institutions, or any other existing evil as such." The sermon did not explicitly promote segregation, as did many of Falwell's actions during the time period and other sermons he preached that are no longer extant. Yet the message was clear: preserve the status quo, including the status quo of segregation, and do not attempt to reform society. By disavowing reform, he came close to representing the separatism that underpinned Darby's development of dispensationalism.

Much of the racial element found in "Ministers and Marchers" had an antecedent in Welch's John Birch Society that Welch founded in 1958. In *The Blue Book of the John Birch Society*, he claimed,

> The whole slogan of "civil rights," as used to make trouble in the South today, is an exact parallel to the slogan of "agrarian reform" which they used in China. And the Communists, who are pulling innocent and idealistic Americans into promoting this agitation for them, have no more real interest in the welfare of the Negroes and no more concern about the damage they actually do to our colored population, than the Chinese Communists had with regard to the welfare of the Chinese peasants.[11]

Though there is no extant evidence that Falwell's early days of conservative activism included involvement in the John Birch Society, his resistance to the civil rights movement came from the same mold. He was very much operating within the far-right political tradition of the 1950s and 1960s by baptizing his antagonism toward the civil rights movement in communist terms. His innovation was to bring that approach to the civil rights movement into a dispensational view of history and then broadcast it through his growing televangelical empire. The critical element in bringing the civil rights movement under the dispensational umbrella was the apostasy, and what he was keenly aware of is that the civil rights movement was itself a product of the Social Gospel. As such, the preaching of King and his associates was part of the End Times apostasy.

Two of the greatest influences in King's life were his father, Martin Luther King Sr. (1899–1984), and the African American theologian Howard Thurman (1899–1981), whose works include the 1949 classic *Jesus and the Disinherited. Jesus and the Disinherited* reflects Thurman's—and King Sr.'s, whom Thurman knew well—merging of the Social Gospel with personal transformation through spiritual salvation, as a means of addressing racial injustice. King Jr. studied liberal theology at Crozer Theological Seminary, the same place where Thurman studied, and he encountered the thought of Social Gospel leaders, such as Walter Rauschenbusch and Washington Gladden. While King was pursuing his doctorate at Boston University, Thurman was serving as the Chapel Dean and personally mentored him.

As leader of the civil rights movement in the 1950s and 1960s, King, like his Social Gospel forebears, advocated socialism as a means of advancing a "beloved community" in which all people had the same rights and economic opportunities. Yet King went further and, like Thurman, applied the framework of the Social Gospel to his own Black Baptist roots to create a radical social gospel for oppressed Blacks. Personal transformation through a salvation experience allowed, in Thurman's language of "the disinherited," "the awareness of being a child of God, [which] results in a new courage, fearlessness, and power."[12] From this new core of the disinherited's relationship with God, the oppressed could challenge the social powers that act against them by engaging with human dignity and nonviolence.

The significance of Falwell connecting the civil rights movement to the Social Gospel is not his own historical accuracy but in what he meant by this belief. To him, the civil rights movement was part of the End Times apostasy. Whether or not the civil rights movement advocated individual salvation, in keeping with Thurman's and King's Baptist roots in the South, its teachings built on the Social Gospel and its concomitant advocacy of socialism. To Falwell, socialism was the apostasy, and anyone who could advocate socialism while professing a transformative salvation experience was incomparably deceived. Given his belief that socialism was merely the brother of communism, the only conclusion he could see was that the civil rights movement stemmed from the same godless communism as that of the Soviet Union. The aspect of personal transformation through salvation was not merely irrelevant; it was deceptive, as those who had truly been transformed by Christ—dispensational fundamentalists—would surely be ardent capitalists.

Just how were Christians to respond to the civil rights movement, seeing as it was not only sponsored by communists but also a product of the End Times apostasy? In a word, they were to pray. Falwell claimed in 1965, in "Ministers and Marchers,"

> If as much effort could be put into winning people to Jesus Christ across the land as is being exerted in the present Civil Rights Movement, America would be turned upside-down for God. Hate and prejudice would certainly be in a great measure overcome . . . Good relations between the races would soon be evidenced . . . May we pray toward this goal.

The way that Falwell tied this far-right, communist-infused worldview into a dispensational understanding of history laid the foundation for his preaching and conservative activism throughout his entire life. Like Welch and other leaders in the far-right political tradition of the twentieth century, anything that did not correspond with Falwell's understanding of how the world should be was communist. All who opposed fundamentalist Christianity, especially the progressives of the Social Gospel (including the civil rights movement), were part of the End Times apostasy and ultimately would lead America down the path of communism. Like other fundamentalists of his day, he believed that the only cure for social ills was the Bible and conversion to fundamentalist Christianity. The natural outcome of this conversion would be an unwavering support of unregulated capitalism.

By the early 1970s, Falwell was no longer using overtly racist language in his sermons and public engagements. In 1980, he apologized for his history of racism and claimed that the message of "Ministers and Marchers" constituted "false prophecy." He opened his church and school to non-whites in 1968, in an effort to distance himself from his past segregationist rhetoric; in the 1980s, he began working with Black pastors to recruit more actively for his Moral Majority. Yet a closer look shows that while he may have no longer been using the pulpit to promote segregation, he merely changed the language that he used about race, especially in his "I Love America" rallies in which he preached his stump sermon of the 1970s, "America Back to God."

Even though his "I Love America" rallies did not directly challenge the new status quo of integration, he brought into the "America Back to God" sermon a trope that had begun to be used to vilify African Americans, that of the welfare queen. The mythological welfare queen is a Black single mother who keeps having babies so that she can collect more welfare payments. Rather than using the publicly provided resources to care for her children, she squanders her checks at beauty parlors and department stores while her children sit alone in a filthy home with inadequate food and clothing. Though a fair amount of white people have historically received welfare assistance, and before the civil rights movement welfare was largely unavailable to non-whites, the welfare queen is always Black. Anti-welfarism in the 1970s and 1980s was code for racism.

During that decade, the trope of the welfare queen came to dominate American public discourse about the burgeoning welfare state. Hard-working taxpayers complained to their government representatives that their money was being stolen to pay people to not work; the media often portrayed welfare recipients as using their public funds irresponsibly and adding more children to the welfare roster. Falwell said in "America Back to God," "There are many, many people in America who would not work in a pie shop eating the holes out of donuts. We feed them and encourage their laziness and worthlessness. You can't give them a job because they can make more money on unemployment than they can working." He went on to tell a story about his dogs, saying that a friend from church gave them to him. At first, the dogs were accustomed to eating meat, but Falwell gave them dog food instead. They refused to eat until four days later, when they were hungry enough to eat the dog food. He then said, "If we get these bums hungry enough, they'll work." In this statement, he may not have directly referred to African Americans as dogs, but given the anti-welfare rhetoric of the 1970s, conservatives listening to him would have gotten the message.

When Falwell began substituting overt racism for condemnation of people on welfare, he was—as with his association of the civil rights movement to communism—operating firmly within the far-right political tradition of his era. Yet Falwell also went beyond the politics of his day to continue submerging his views about race into his interpretation of dispensationalism, which featured heavily the apostasy and the economics of civil rights. To him, unregulated capitalism was the only economic system endorsed by the Bible, yet the civil rights movement had created fresh demands for African Americans to receive public assistance. If the success of the civil rights movement could be measured by the expansion of welfare rosters, then America was dangerously sliding away from godly capitalism and toward the communism of King and other civil-rights leaders. The End Times apostasy—liberal theology that had led to government-sponsored welfare programs and now the expansion of a welfare state to support Black people who refused to work—was devouring America. American Christians could stem the tide of this End Times corruption by dismantling welfare programs and forcing Black people to work.

In his view, not only was welfare feeding a communist mentality in America, but it was also wrecking the national budget. Touring the country preaching "America Back to God," he claimed that the only thing needed to balance the national budget is to "drastically cut, if not totally eliminate, this blooming welfare program at home and abroad, and use those monies to intensify our defense development." Public funds that were being diverted to welfare programs could be much better appropriated for national defense, especially strengthening the nuclear arsenal. America's military machine was necessary to protect the country's borders from an attack by the Soviet Union, which would end the godly economic system of capitalism once and for all. In other words, the only antithesis to communism was a return to unregulated capitalism—ironically, the kind of capitalism that led to the Great Depression, against which President Roosevelt began institutionalizing welfare programs.

The Rise and Fall of Segregation Academies

Despite this change of rhetoric, the issue of school integration remained prominent in Falwell's political engagement during the late 1970s and into the 1980s. As segregation academies proliferated during the 1960s—in Mississippi alone, the number of children enrolled in segregation academies skyrocketed from 2,290 in 1963 to 30,939 in 1970—the government began questioning their function as charitable institutions because they were not promoting the public good of integration. In the 1970 *Green v Kennedy* case, the Supreme Court ruled that the IRS could revoke the tax-exempt status of segregation academies, as a kind of economic sanction that would threaten their financial viability. By then, Falwell's Lynchburg Christian Academy was formally open to non-white students, but only about 0.0043 percent of the student body was Black, in a community that was one-quarter Black. Though Falwell was no longer actively promoting segregation, he had a clear stake in the future of what he called the "Christian school movement," the rise of segregation academies.

The premier segregation academy of the 1970s was Bob Jones University, a dispensationalist school opened in 1927. Its founder, Bob Jones, insisted that segregation was biblical; therefore, the school had a holy mandate to refuse integration. Until 1975, no African Americans were permitted admission to Bob Jones University (other than one part-time student admitted in 1971), and after 1975 only married African Americans were allowed admission, in order to ensure no miscegenation would occur; the penalty for interracial dating was expulsion. Racial discrimination at the school was so severe that by 1982, only a dozen out of about six thousand students were African American. In 1981, the Supreme Court agreed to hear the case of *Bob Jones University v United States* to challenge the effort of the IRS to revoke the school's tax-exempt status. Though Falwell was actively trying to distance himself from his past segregationist stance, he supported BJU throughout the case.[13]

"First of all, what about that basic system called the public school?" he asked his audience in "America Back to God." "There is no question about the fact that the American public school system is damned." He laid the blame for the state of the country's public schools at the feet of a Supreme Court which, in the 1960s, ruled that teacher-led prayer and Bible reading in the classroom violate students' freedom of religion. These liberal rulings, in *Engel v Vitale* and *Abington v Schempp*, came from the same liberalism that had led FDR to implement the New Deal. Falwell went on to lament, "It is not safe for a Christ-loving teenager to attend school in that public school system."

To Falwell, the issue went beyond the understanding of religious freedom held by the Supreme Court during the 1960s. The public schools were themselves part of the apostasy, having emerged alongside the same Social Gospel that had spawned the civil rights movement. When the Supreme Court ruled in *Brown v Board of Education* in 1954, it effectively sided with the apostasy that was sending America careening toward the wrath of God. Yet by the 1970s, Falwell was savvy enough to realize that he could not continue building his movement by opposing integration. Instead of framing the BJU case within the apostasy of the civil rights movement, he framed it in terms of the apostate one-world church that was emerging as part of the End Times.

To many dispensationalists, the liberal church that had become part of the ecumenical movement following Edinburgh 1910 was on track to become a one-world church that denied all fundamental doctrines of the faith: the virgin birth, the deity of Christ, and his imminent return within history, to name a few.

This one-world church had been prophesied and would ultimately, during the Tribulation, become the throne from which the antichrist would declare himself to be God. Especially during the Tribulation but likely also in the days leading up to it, the one-world church would persecute true Christians who, like Falwell, clung to these timeless truths. Further, this one-world church was the conduit of socialism, as it had been emerging from the apostasy, and was therefore the enemy of unregulated biblical capitalism.

With this dispensational framework in mind, the issue at stake for Falwell was religious liberty, although not as the Supreme Court had interpreted religious liberty in *Engel v Vitale* and *Abington v Schempp*. Should America continue on this track of the apostasy and toward the wrath of God, Christians would soon begin facing persecution in what had once been a Christian nation; they will have lost their religious freedom to the one-world church. He framed the case as one of the government overstepping its boundaries by violating the First Amendment's separation of church and state. In a revised version of "America Back to God" that Falwell preached in 1980, while BJU was engaged in litigation, he said,

> America is locked in a moral battle for her very life. It started back in, well, I guess 30, 35 years ago in a very significant way. Symptoms began to crop out all along the way—abortion on demand legalized, prayer and Bible-reading kicked out of the public schools. And then as the Christian school movement began to accelerate, opposition from bureaucratic agencies. But oh, thank God, he has raised up his people everywhere.[14]

This moral battle began with the movement to desegregate public schools that led up to *Brown v Board of Education* in 1954. *Brown* was followed by Supreme Court decisions such as

Engel v Vitale in 1962, which ended school-sponsored prayer in public schools, and *Abington v Schempp* in 1963, which ended Bible-reading. Concerned Christian citizens had opened their own schools—segregation academies—to teach children the fundamental truths of the Bible, and now the government was attempting to shut those schools down. To Falwell, fundamentalist Christians were losing their religious freedom.

What Falwell called the "Christian school movement" stood against not only removing school-sponsored prayer and Bible reading but also the integration of public schools. In other words, the Christian school movement of the 1960s and 1970s which he spoke of was the rise of segregation academies, including Lynchburg Christian Academy, Liberty Baptist College, and Bob Jones University. The "bureaucratic agencies" was a reference to the IRS, which was attempting to sanction BJU by removing its tax-exempt status. Ultimately, the Supreme court ruled against BJU, a move that Falwell also labeled a blow to religious liberty.

In the 1970s, Falwell built his movement by challenging the successes of the civil rights movement, and though his language changed, those challenges never ended. Randall Balmer, a premier historian of the Religious Right, recalled attending a 1990 meeting hosted by leaders of the Religious Right—including Paul Weyrich, who co-founded the Moral Majority with Falwell—and said of the meeting,

> In the course of one of the sessions, Weyrich tried to make a point to his Religious Right brethren (no women attended the conference, as I recall). Let's remember, he said animatedly, that the Religious Right did not come together in response to the *Roe* decision. No, Weyrich insisted, what got us going as a political movement was the attempt on the part of the Internal Revenue Service to rescind the tax-exempt status of Bob Jones University because of its racially discriminatory policies.[15]

Taken into the broader context of the civil rights movement and stretching back to the 1950s, the real issue at stake was the changing economics that would be required to guarantee civil rights for non-whites. Falwell's organizing principle, for both how he understood dispensationalism, especially within contemporary American politics, and the Cold War, was the need to re-instate *laissez-faire* "biblical capitalism" against the economics of civil rights.

The Economics of Civil Rights in South Africa

For Falwell, resisting the economics of civil rights was much more far-reaching than the American South's opposition to integration and national efforts to dismantle welfare programs. The 1980s saw increasing violence in South Africa, which had been operating under a governmental system known as apartheid. Critics compared apartheid to segregation, as Blacks in South Africa could not be present in white spaces and had severely limited economic opportunities, resulting in dire poverty. A growing international movement, determined to confront the human-rights violations occurring under apartheid, began imposing economic sanctions on South Africa. President Ronald Reagan, alongside Falwell, resisted the anti-apartheid movement by promoting a policy called "constructive engagement." Constructive engagement intended to increase trade with South Africa and invest in the country's currency, the Krugerrand. The intent was to promote capitalism against the rising tide of communism and ultimately prevent a communist takeover of South Africa. Instead of apartheid and granting civil rights to Blacks, for Falwell, the issue at stake was, yet again, the communist threat.

In August 1985, escalating tensions in South Africa between Blacks and the apartheid government, and the effort of the

US Congress to impose economic sanctions on South Africa, inspired Falwell to lead a cohort of associates to visit the beleaguered country. The South African president, P. W. Botha, had declared a state of emergency in July amid increasing violence by the apartheid regime and Blacks seeking liberation; additionally, the African National Congress, which represented many oppressed Blacks, had just held its second national conference, and the anti-apartheid movement was gaining international support. Soon after the declaration of the state of emergency, government-backed squads killed the anti-apartheid lawyer Victoria Mxenge. On August 15, shortly after Falwell returned from his visit, Botha gave his "Rubicon speech," in which he doubled down on enforcing apartheid.

Of the trip Falwell wrote in a fact sheet, "In recent years, I have watched the entire continent of Africa threatened by Communist takeover. It has broken my heart to watch the Soviets and the Cubans steal nation after nation across Africa. This must not happen to South Africa!"[16] He went on to list several points about South Africa, which included,

1. South Africa does, indeed, operate a racially unfair social and political system called apartheid. *I AM against apartheid!* [emphasis in original]
2. South Africa is torn by civil unrest. This is being instigated primarily by Communist-sponsored persons who are capitalizing on many legitimate grievances that are created by apartheid, unemployment, and police confrontations.
3. The Marxist-leaning organizations—African National Congress (ANC), United Democratic Front (UDF), and AZAPO are constantly creating violence and bloodshed among the blacks of the country who are the true victims.[17]

Shortly after returning, Falwell was interviewed on C-SPAN to give his opinion of the situation in South Africa. The reason he gave for engaging in the political issues facing the country was not about race; he began the interview by insisting that he is not racist and has hundreds of non-whites in his congregation. Rather, his stated reason was, "I have watched this blood-red river of communism flow over Eastern Europe, Asia, Africa. South Africa is the only one of the 53, 54 African states now that has any hope of ever becoming a democracy . . . Regardless of what you think of the Soviets, they do a pretty good job of keeping what they steal."[18] To him and his associates, racism may be an evil, but communism was far worse; while denying the vote to a large part of the population may deprive people of dignity, a communist takeover would deny millions of people the right to live. In Falwell's words, "The number one problem in South Africa is the Soviet takeover of a country that, number one, if they take it over, 30 million of all colors will suffer."[19] He did not dispute that presently, the Blacks of South Africa were suffering, and he did call for apartheid to end. Yet should the United States impose economic sanctions against the apartheid government, the communists would certainly conquer South Africa.

To Falwell, central to the growing communist threat was the imprisoned Black liberationist and leader of the African National Congress, Nelson Mandela. An international movement sought his release from prison, but Falwell insisted that he was a "self-confessed terrorist" who should remain in prison. Even more, Falwell claimed Mandela was supported by communists, and allegedly his African National Congress aired radio broadcasts on how to build homemade bombs. Similar to King, Mandela did hold socialist beliefs and insisted that the government had to actively promote the uplift of marginalized Black communities. To Falwell, Mandela's release from prison would be a victory for communism and ultimately lead to a Soviet takeover of South Africa.

Second only to Mandela in terms of the communist threat to South Africa was Desmond Tutu, the archbishop of the South African Council of Churches (SACC) and anti-apartheid activist. The SACC is the South African branch of the World Council of Churches (WCC), which is a product of the ecumenical movement and the Social Gospel. Falwell connected the WCC with the End Times apostasy alongside communism, and he similarly saw Tutu in those terms.

In the C-SPAN interview, as Falwell was deriding the communist sympathies of Black liberation organizations in South Africa, he positioned the SACC as the enemy of true liberation for Blacks. Referring to conversations he had with elected Black leaders of Soweto, he said, "With tears running down their faces, [they] told us of the atrocities they go through. Sometimes they're brutally treated by the Marxist radicals who drive around in those big cars, they said, funded by the South African Council of Churches to do their mean-ness and so on."[20] To further tighten the association between Tutu and communism, Falwell's *Moral Majority Report* wrote, "Bishop Desmond Tutu of Johannesburg said last November that 'if the Russians were to come to South Africa today, then most Blacks who reject Communism as atheistic and materialistic would welcome them as saviors.' Anything would be better than apartheid."[21] Yet to Falwell, communism was infinitely worse than apartheid, as communism reflected the apostasy of the End Times and was central to the anti-apartheid movement.

Despite claiming repeatedly that apartheid must end, Falwell and his associates did not believe that Blacks should be part of the national government. In the C-SPAN interview, he derided Tutu's statement that one day, Mandela would be the president of South

Africa. While this derision was in the context of explaining that Mandela is a communist terrorist, race was certainly a component. Falwell's associate, Ed Hindson (who worked at Thomas Road Baptist Church), wrote in Falwell's publication *The Fundamentalist Journal*,

> The South African government fears that by moving too fast the country will fall into the hands of the nation's black majority—a majority that is uneducated, unskilled, hostile toward whites, and influenced by Marxist-Communist organizations. Such a move, the government maintains, would destroy the nation's political, social, and economic stability.[22]

The Blacks of South Africa, particularly those in the African National Congress and who supported Mandela, were not only unfit to govern whites (Hindson noted that Blacks were allowed to govern their own homelands while chafing at the thought that they would govern whites) but, more importantly, were supported by communists.

To Falwell, the solution to the racial inequity and violence in South Africa was not economic sanctions that would force the government to cater to the anti-apartheid movement. Not only was the anti-apartheid movement inherently communist, but restricting trade with South Africa would give the Soviets increased influence over the government. Sanctions would lead to a communist takeover, not civil rights for Blacks (which were admittedly not his primary concern). Reagan's constructive engagement, which he supported, would eliminate the communist threat by promoting unregulated capitalism. He claimed in his fact sheet,

> Sanctions against South Africans by the United States and disinvestment by American business will, in my judgment, eliminate all leverage we might have toward pressuring the Pretoria government to abolish apartheid as rapidly as possible. Worse

than that, the non-whites in unison, advised us that sanctions and disinvestment cause unemployment among poor blacks—which then causes starvation, violence and bloodshed—while doing little or nothing toward effecting governmental policy changes . . .

We should, if possible, accelerate investments in South Africa, including the purchase of Krugerrands, because this inevitably improves the standard of living for non-whites in South Africa.[23]

In these views, Falwell continued operating within the far-right political and theological traditions of his day. As with the civil rights movement, he baptized his political view—extreme anti-communism that rejects all government programs to benefit the poor—into his understanding of dispensationalism by framing the anti-apartheid movement in terms of the End Times apostasy. As such, he could claim that the issue was communism rather than race, showing again that the core of his political and theological ideas was the economics of civil rights.

The Illuminati

While Falwell's political views were firmly aligned with the far-right movement that included Robert Welch, his associate, Tim LaHaye, was a card-carrying member of Welch's John Birch Society. A dispensationalist like Falwell who was constantly innovating, LaHaye followed Welch's conspiratorial thinking that included belief in the Illuminati as a group of global elites controlling world events. In his book *Rapture Under Attack*, LaHaye called the Illuminati "the Master Conspirators"[24] and went on to claim,

I myself have been a forty-five-year student of the satanically-inspired, centuries-old conspiracy to use government, education, and media to destroy every vestige of Christianity within our society and establish a new world order. Having read at least 50 books on the *Illuminati*, I am convinced that it exists and can be blamed for many of man's inhumane actions against his fellow man during the past two hundred years.[25]

In his 1980 manifesto *Battle for the Mind*, he insisted that a global elite—presumably the Illuminati—are on a mission to replace Christianity, and its concomitant system of capitalism, with the religion of secular humanism and its economy of socialism. To LaHaye, there was no difference between socialism and communism, and the people agitating for socialism ultimately wanted to turn America into the dystopia of the Soviet Union.

The "Master Conspirators" of secular humanism and socialism were supposedly behind the liberation movements of the 1960s and 1970s. LaHaye claimed, "The 1960s saw the battle for racial rights. In the 1970s, it was sexual rights. But the 1980s have been designated for the battle against religious rights."[26] In his view, these liberation movements that advocated socialism as a means of advancing the uplift of marginalized communities were being masterminded by the Illuminati. The ultimate goal of the Illuminati was to abolish Christianity, thereby explaining why the next front in this war by the global elite was against the church. Falwell did not share the depth of LaHaye's conspiratorial thinking (at least not publicly, though Falwell was also a conspiracist), but both agreed that the struggle of their day was to preserve Christian freedoms against the rising tide of socialism, humanism, and civil rights. For Falwell, the struggle was exemplified by the need to maintain the rights of segregation academies to operate without government intervention. For LaHaye, the visible aspect of the struggle was squarely on liberation movements.

The civil rights movement preoccupied Falwell well into the 1980s, but there were other liberation movements in the 1960s and 1970s that had threatened the status quo, as well. LaHaye collaborated with Falwell on mobilizing against the gains of the gay rights movement of the 1960s and 1970s. In 1978, LaHaye published *The Unhappy Gays* to promote his belief that homosexuality was a pathology that could be cured; the high suicide rate of queer people served as evidence that queerness was a disease. He claimed, "As a minority movement in America, [the gay rights movement] demands that we give official sanction and acknowledge its 'rights.'. . . What was once a secret sin, rarely mentioned, has become an epidemic sweeping the land."[27] Efforts to legitimize queer lifestyles were sponsored by the same global elite seeking to destroy Christianity and impose secular humanism and a socialist economy on the world. When the AIDS epidemic began in 1980 and publications associated it with the gay community, Falwell and LaHaye were quick to point to the new disease as God's wrath on America for advancing gay rights.

In addition to agitating against civil rights for African Americans and queer people, LaHaye and his wife, Beverly, became leading spokespeople among American fundamentalists for pushing back against the women's liberation movement. Horrified by the rhetoric of Betty Friedan, Gloria Steinem, and the National Organization for Women (NOW), the LaHayes organized Concerned Women for America (CWA) to provide conservative men (the organization targeted men to advance its cause) and women a platform to voice their concerns. Along with the well-known antifeminist Anita Bryant, CWA organized against the ratification of the Equal Rights Amendment (ERA), which would have prohibited discrimination based on gender. *The Unhappy Gays* claimed that lesbians had taken over the effort to ratify the ERA, so opposing it was necessary to push back against the gay rights movement. The LaHayes helped the men and women of CWA envision an America in which all children were raised in two-parent families, with the father as the breadwinner and the mother as a housewife. Women did not need the equal rights that the ERA would guarantee because they did not need to be in the workplace; their husbands would provide for them while they raised the children.

This picture of the two-parent family, with a working father and a stay-at-home mother, was the essence of how LaHaye and Falwell imagined capitalist, Christian America should operate. Any policies that pushed back against this ideal, such as free daycare that would support working mothers or welfare programs that would presumably encourage African American women to become welfare queens, were part of the humanist conspiracy to replace capitalism and Christianity with socialism. The ultimate success of the women's liberation movement, and by extension the cause of socialism, was the legalization of abortion through *Roe v Wade*. The nation-wide legalization of abortion devastated the future of this capitalist utopia that was upheld by a two-parent family. Rather than women getting married early and serving their husbands as housewives, they could murder their unborn children without their husbands (or even their various sexual partners) knowing that they were pregnant. Even more, their increasing presence in the workforce, due in no small part to the availability of birth control (LaHaye saw abortion as a kind of birth control), meant that the humanists were succeeding in dismantling the Christian foundations of America.

The Pro-Life Movement

Alongside the liberation movements that took on increased social capital in the 1960s was the pro-life movement. Here, I will be cautious about the use of the terms "pro-life" and "anti-abortion," as the anti-abortion movement is concerned solely about abortion, while the pro-life movement opposes abortion as part of valuing all human life. Abortion was largely illegal in America through the nineteenth and early twentieth centuries, but in the first decades of the twentieth century, some doctors began calling for abortion to be legalized. Women had been obtaining abortions since time immemorial, and without proper medical care, thousands were dying every year following the procedure. Campaigns for birth control that began in the 1920s also signaled shifting public opinion regarding human sexuality and reproduction. In response, Catholic clergy throughout America began organizing against efforts to legalize birth control and abortion, as they saw both practices as attacks on human life. The genocidal horrors of World War II gave them new reasons to resist abortion, especially in cases of suspected fetal abnormality or concerns about the mother's emotional or financial well-being; if people could legally kill off humans in utero on thin claims that they did not deserve to live, then America was a small step away from sending entire classes of people to a new Auschwitz. Yet their primary arguments stemmed from the natural law theory of the medieval theologian Thomas Aquinas, and their rationale for opposing abortion was overwhelmingly theological. Few non-Catholics supported their anti-abortion crusade, as they did not share the language and theology of natural law.

By the 1960s, public opinion had moved so firmly to favor the widespread legalization of abortion—roughly three-quarters of the American public supported allowing abortion in situations where, if the pregnancy should be carried to term, the mother or child would be deprived of quality of life—that even state legislators who had previously been influenced by the Catholic clergy on matters of abortion voted for legalization. But in the 1960s, a dramatic shift happened that brought the anti-abortion movement into the progressivism of the era's liberation movements. Vatican II (which met from 1962 until 1965) led to *aggiornamento*, or updating the church's doctrines and opening Catholicism to the new social norms and mores of the modern era. Consequently, many anti-abortion Catholics in America realized that if they continued campaigning on theological grounds, they would continue losing the struggle against the increased legalization of abortion.

Following Vatican II and all the changes that went with it, leaders of the Catholic pro-life movement began using the language of universal human rights instead of natural law. Rather than church doctrine, they began appealing to secular documents, such as the United Nations Declaration on the Rights of the Child (1959), which included unborn children as needing protection. Post–Vatican II leaders also shifted their position from merely speaking out against the looming liberalization of abortion to advocating a more holistic valuing of all human life, not just fetal life. On December 8, 1966, the Catholic Cardinal James McIntyre held the first meeting of the Right to Life League. According to Daniel Williams, "'Right to Life' was an appropriate phrase because, from the very beginning, Catholics had defined their cause as protecting the 'sanctity of human life'. . . By calling themselves 'right-to-life' or 'pro-life' rather than 'anti-abortion,' they signaled that their cause was about more than merely stopping an objectionable medical procedure."[28]

By making their cause a human rights one, the leaders of the new pro-life movement were able to begin drawing in non-Catholic supporters who embraced liberal social values. To be sure, many of the liberal Protestants who were concerned about abortion joined the movement to expand abortion rights; by the late 1960s, however, there were also quite a few liberal Protestants who came to see fetal rights along the lines of human rights. Liberal Protestants who became part of the pro-life movement were also active in the civil rights movement and opposed the Vietnam War.

Additionally, they called for a nuclear freeze and alleviating the degrading poverty in which so many African Americans were raising their children.

Meanwhile, Falwell and LaHaye expressed disgust for Vietnam War protestors and saw the civil rights movement as part of the End Times apostasy. If African Americans were poor, the problem was simply that they did not want to work and preferred to collect welfare payments. Had these dispensationalist leaders been aware of the incipient pro-life movement of the 1960s, they would have had nothing in common with it. In what may be one of the greatest ironies of twentieth-century politics, prior to *Roe v Wade* in 1973, the far-left senator Ted Kennedy supported the pro-life movement while Ronald Reagan, the favored politician of Jerry Falwell, was expanding abortion access in California. Between Vatican II and *Roe v Wade*, the pro-life movement—though it did not encompass feminist calls for abortion as a woman's right, in keeping with the contemporaneous women's liberation movement—was thoroughly liberal.

Just how did a liberal social cause, one that drew in supporters of a nuclear freeze, ending the war in Vietnam, and extending civil rights to beleaguered African Americans, become central to a movement whose political origins are so far to the right that it denounced the civil rights movement as a communist conspiracy?

From Pro-Life to Anti-Abortion

There were whispers of conservative evangelical support for the pro-life cause in the 1960s. Billy Graham's periodical, *Christianity Today*, which became the flagship magazine of conservative evangelicalism, published some articles on abortion in the 1960s that largely reflected Graham's own view: abortion should not be used as a form of birth control, but the practice could be considered in cases of rape and medical emergencies. Falwell would claim in his 1978 sermon on abortion that a study of 3,000 rape victims showed that not a single one of the women became pregnant, indicating that when he first tested the anti-abortion waters, he did not share Graham's view that rape might be a legitimate reason for abortion. Nothing about the evangelical pro-life movement of the 1960s suggested that the forthcoming *Roe v Wade* decision would spark a political firestorm—and, as the record shows, the decision had very little effect among conservative evangelicals for several years.

C. Everett Koop was a pediatric surgeon with an evangelical faith, and unlike many other evangelicals, he was advocating against abortion long before *Roe v Wade*. Though Koop would later serve as Surgeon General under President Ronald Reagan and was lauded by anti-abortion evangelicals, including Falwell and LaHaye, abortion was not necessarily a political issue to him. In fact, while under interrogation by the US Senate before his post as Surgeon General was approved, he claimed that he would not use the appointment to advance his personal beliefs. As Surgeon General, Koop turned his focus to fighting the AIDS epidemic, despite Falwell's claim that AIDS was God's wrath on America for toleration of queer lifestyles. He also worked to curtail smoking and brought attention to domestic violence; when Reagan asked Koop to compile a report on the effects that abortion has on the mother, he could not comply because of a lack of evidence.

Yet Koop was a firm pro-lifer, and he had pioneered procedures that would enhance the lives of children with complex medical needs. He began working as a pediatric surgeon in 1945, when pediatric surgery was not yet even recognized as a medical specialty and doctors largely ignored children with complex needs. Decades before *Roe*, Koop recognized that many of the children he serviced might have been candidates for therapeutic abortion, and he spent thirty-five years in pediatric surgery before becoming Surgeon General. When the *Roe* decision came, he began speaking publicly about abortion; in 1975, he partnered with Ruth Bell Graham (Billy Graham's wife) and the evangelical professor Harold O. J. Brown to form the Christian Action Council to advance the pro-life cause. Soon, he partnered with the Christian apologist Francis Schaeffer to create the film and book *Whatever Happened to the Human Race?*

Schaeffer was a Presbyterian missionary from America who moved to Switzerland in 1948 and opened a community called L'Abri in 1955. He wrote so prolifically on theology and the role of Christianity in Western culture that by 1970, he had become a household name among evangelicals and is still quoted today. He preached several times at Falwell's church, and LaHaye quoted him extensively in his writings about the encroaching influence of humanism. In the 1970s, Schaeffer's son, Frank, approached him about taking up the cause of abortion, and initially, Schaeffer balked on the grounds that abortion was a Catholic issue. But Frank helped his father and Koop produce the movie *Whatever Happened to the Human Race?*, which came out in 1979, followed by an accompanying book the next year. The movie, along with Schaeffer's other pro-life works, utilized the liberal Catholic thought that had underpinned the pro-life movement since the New Deal of the 1930s.

Yet while Catholic thought placed a high emphasis on liberal values that were also associated with the philosophy known as Christian humanism, Schaeffer, serving as the inspiration for LaHaye, saw all forms of humanism as an anti-God movement that sought to eradicate the influence of Christianity on Western culture. Ironically, Thomas Aquinas is credited with the development of the natural law theology that Catholics used in the incipient pro-life movement, prior to Vatican II; LaHaye said of Aquinas that he was "responsible for reviving an almost dead philosophy, which has become the most dangerous religion in the world today—humanism."[29] In other words, the man whose thought had laid the foundation for the pro-life movement was deeply reviled by LaHaye as being responsible for the apostate religion of humanism, which was the religion of the emerging one-world church. Additionally, while Catholics had begun the pro-life movement in the 1930s and women had been performing do-it-yourself abortions for millennia, Schaeffer pointed specifically to *Roe v Wade* and the court's secular values, as if the 1973 decision was the sole cause of abortion.

Schaeffer brought his newfound concern about abortion to the attention of Falwell, who was by then growing a conservative movement of evangelicals fighting for the rights of Christians to operate segregation academies. A few months later, Falwell preached the sermon "Abortion on Demand" and made a national crusade out of efforts to overturn *Roe v Wade*. Within a few years, Falwell and LaHaye had co-opted the pro-life movement of liberal Catholic thought to create today's anti-abortion movement.

If the cause to overturn *Roe v Wade* had any meaningful purpose in the development of the Religious Right, the reason was only because the new anti-abortion movement was embedded in a larger movement that was mobilizing against the advances of marginalized communities. Martin Luther King Jr. was one of many African American liberationists who had advocated for socialism that would elevate those living in absolute poverty. To Robert Welch and the far-right movement that he began organizing in the 1950s, the civil rights movement was part of a communist conspiracy, and Falwell echoed that view using dispensational rhetoric. Socialism and communism, as the products of American liberal theology, were the End Times apostasy that he believed the Bible prophesied would come before the Rapture. He viewed Desmond Tutu and Nelson Mandela through the same lens, as communist conspirators who would rather see South Africa "liberated" by the Soviets than continue living under apartheid.

The gay rights movement and women's liberation movement likewise fell under this umbrella of socialist and communist conspiracy because of how they also advocated the uplift of marginalized peoples. By pinning the *Roe v Wade* decision on feminism, LaHaye was able to tie abortion into this broader conspiracy of humanist attempts to make America socialist rather than Christian and capitalist.

By the 1980s, Falwell was using the anti-abortion movement— which was overwhelmingly composed of white conservatives—in a way that allowed him to compensate for his past advocacy of preserving segregation. In about 1980—the date of the sermon was not preserved—Falwell preached a sermon entitled "One Nation Under God on the Rebound," in which he claimed,

> Suddenly, in 1973, by a 7–2 vote, the Supreme Court decides that little unborn babies are not human beings and therefore have no human rights. Strange that in 1857 by the same 7–2 vote, the same Supreme Court ruled that black people were not human beings, that they had no human or civil rights, and that they could be bought and sold as cattle.[30]

He had compared the *Roe v Wade* decision of 1973 to the *Dred Scott v Sandford* decision of 1857, in which an enslaved man unsuccessfully sued for his freedom. Abortion had become the new civil rights issue, and this time, Falwell would not be found advocating for the continued oppression of those being denied their constitutional rights. No longer a segregationist, Falwell had become an abolitionist.

The anti-abortion movement was the new liberation movement, and it was led by men who had labeled the liberation movements of the past three decades as part of a communist conspiracy. Soon, ending abortion became more urgent than guaranteeing civil rights for African Americans, women, queers, and other marginalized peoples, in no small part because, in this conspiracy-laden mindset, overturning *Roe v Wade* meant the defeat of socialism and the victory of capitalism. The movement quickly became a cover for ongoing efforts to reverse the gains of these earlier liberation movements, beginning with the BJU case against the IRS for revoking the tax-exempt status of segregation academies. Falwell could not have helped organize the anti-abortion movement with the goal of saving the lives of the unborn. Rather, this movement was part of a broader economic agenda that promoted "biblical capitalism" against liberationist movements; in this manner, the anti-abortion movement served as a smokescreen for racism.

Nuclear Family Values

Moral Majority Inc. is made up of millions of Americans, including 72,000 ministers, priests, and rabbis, who are deeply concerned about the moral decline of our nation, and who are sick and tired of the way many amoral and secular humanists and other liberals are destroying the traditional family and moral values on which our nation was built.[1]

So BEGAN A 1979 pamphlet that Falwell distributed far and wide in his effort to gain support for the conservative movement he was building. Showing that this movement went far beyond dispensational fundamentalists like himself, the pamphlet declared, "We are Catholics, Jews, Protestants, Mormons, Fundamentalists— blacks and whites—farmers, housewives, businessmen . . . united by one central concern . . . providing a voice for a return to moral sanity in these United States of America." He claimed that they wanted a return to "family and moral values," the foundation on which Falwell claimed America had been built. People from all the aforementioned demographics—and then some—could not argue with a political agenda that highlighted "family values." But what were these family values, and what did Falwell mean by them?

"We believe that the only acceptable family form begins with the legal marriage of a man to a woman," the pamphlet reads. "We feel that homosexual marriages and common-law marriages should not be accepted as traditional families. We oppose legislation that favors these kinds of diverse family forms, thereby penalizing the traditional family unit." While the pamphlet claimed that Falwell's Moral Majority does not intend to agitate against civil rights for queer people, his 1980 manifesto *Listen, America!* was much less ambiguous. "[Homosexuals] are an indictment against America and are contributing to her downfall,"[2] he wrote before connecting this national sin to the impending Tribulation. "We cannot allow homosexuality to be presented to our nation as an alternative life style [*sic*]. It will not only have a corrupting influence upon our next generation, but it will also bring down the wrath of God upon America."[3] He showed that dismantling the gains of the gay rights movement was central to his "family values" of Christian America by saying, "I am against the flaunting of the homosexual life style [*sic*] before impressionable children. This is detrimental to the basic tenet of Christian society, the home. The home must be protected, and America must turn around before she suffers the wrath of God."[4]

"Family values" went beyond attacking the gay rights movement by also taking aim at women's liberation. The women's liberation movement had led not only to the *Roe v Wade* decision but also to a growing number of women who were leaving the home to join the workforce. He said in *Listen, America!*, "In a drastic departure from the home, more than half of the women in our country are currently employed. Our nation is in serious danger."[5] Meanwhile, the civil rights movement had coincided with an expansion of the social safety net, at the expense of Godly unregulated capitalism. These liberation movements were part of the apostasy of the End Times, and Falwell had to act to save America before all Christians departed the earth in the Rapture. "Family values" became the means by which he communicated an agenda that pushed back against the economics of civil rights and brought America back to biblical capitalism.

The Moynihan Report

Falwell was far from the only politically motivated leader of his era who was concerned about America's family values. In 1965, the year that he preached "Ministers and Marchers" and one hundred years after the Thirteenth Amendment attempted to end slavery, President Lyndon Johnson's liberal administration released a report entitled *The Negro Family: The Case for National Action*; it was colloquially known as the Moynihan Report, after its author, Daniel Patrick Moynihan. As the civil rights movement was leading to increased economic opportunities and civil gains for African Americans,[6] the Moynihan Report sought to address an emerging paradox: At the same time that unemployment levels among African Americans were decreasing, welfare rosters were growing. Theoretically, increased employment should mean fewer people receiving welfare assistance, but among African Americans during the 1960s, the opposite was happening. The report claimed,

> Indices of dollars of income, standards of living, and years of education deceive. The gap between the Negro and most other groups in American society is widening. The fundamental problem, in which this is most clearly the case, is that of family structure. The evidence—not final but powerfully persuasive—is that the Negro family in the urban ghettos is crumbling.[7]

Moynihan suggested that based on traditional measures, such as level of education achieved and unemployment levels, African Americans were experiencing higher standards of living; however, while some were rising into the middle class, widespread positive results were not being seen. The real problem lay in something that could not be measured through more traditional means: family breakdown.

Outward markers of poverty, such as income, unemployment, welfare, and education, were only symptoms, suggested the Moynihan Report. The cause of poverty among African Americans was weak family structures, and the cause of weak family structures was centuries of oppression and domination through slavery and Jim Crow. While the families of white suburbia were largely stable, consisting of a breadwinning father and caring mother, African American families in the inner cities were pathological. Moynihan referred to a "tangle of pathology" that afflicted African American families, in both rural and urban settings, that created a culture in which they could not rise out of debilitating poverty.

The report cited statistics claiming that, among African American women who had been married, over a quarter were divorced or separated or had absent husbands. Similarly, nearly a quarter of African American children were now born out of wedlock, compared to a mere 3 percent among whites. As a result, there were far too many female-headed households among African Americans, and more and more children were growing up without fathers. This phenomenon was causing African American single mothers to increasingly depend on welfare—helping give rise to the trope of the "welfare queen." Moynihan went on to say of these matriarchal African American families, "Ours is a society which presumes male leadership in private and public affairs . . . A subculture, such as that of the Negro American, in which this is not the pattern, is placed at a distinct disadvantage."

He called on the national government to implement programs that would support families, especially African American families, as a means of addressing the root causes of poverty in America. "In a word, a national effort towards the problems of Negro Americans must be directed towards the question of family structure. The object should be to strengthen the Negro family so as to enable it to raise and support its members as do other families." The report implied that the desired outcome of family-support programs would be less dependence on welfare assistance as more patriarchal families among African Americans created more stability and economic prosperity for children.

About the time that the report was released, in August of 1965, allegations of police brutality in Los Angeles led the predominantly African American neighborhood of Watts to erupt in a week of rioting. The governor called in nearly 14,000 members of the California National Guard to establish order; thirty-four people died, over 1,000 were injured, and nearly 3,500 were arrested. The contemporaneous Moynihan Report led pundits to conclude with ease that the cause of the riots was not the police brutality that was endemic in the inner-city neighborhoods where many African Americans lived; rather, the riots were the result of African American children growing up without fathers.

The Moynihan Report sparked controversy among both liberals and conservatives. While liberals applauded efforts to strengthen domestic life among African Americans as part of creating economic equality, they derided notions that the patriarchal family was superior. Indeed, the women's liberation and gay rights movements were upending long-held assumptions about gender roles, while creating greater opportunities for women. Pursuing greater equality for women, alongside ensuring civil rights and economic opportunities for African Americans, would strengthen families and free them from the "pathologies" that were keeping children mired in poverty. At the same time, liberals criticized the report for victim-blaming, because of how it focused on family structures rather than systemic oppression that, even with the passage of civil rights legislation, persisted. Still, Martin Luther King Jr. praised the report, as he saw the uplift of African American families as essential to the uplift of African

American communities; national policy was key to undoing systemic oppression that had caused deterioration of African American families.

Conservatives saw the report as highlighting the need for racial self-help. Instead of relying on welfare programs that could never help children escape poverty, African Americans needed to examine their own cultures and family relationships. African American leaders needed to focus more on instilling family values rather than demanding national legislation that would redistribute resources from the wealthy and toward poor African American communities. However, the calls for racial self-help did not include a national policy to continue dismantling centuries of oppression that had caused the dire poverty of so many African Americans. Indeed, many of the conservatives who saw the Moynihan report as a "self-help" document were the same ones who derided civil rights legislation as part of a communist conspiracy. As Falwell insisted in his "America Back to God" sermon, those "bums" needed to stop relying on welfare programs and instead get jobs. They were not caring for their families, as welfare queens were frittering away their checks while neglecting their children. His solution was a family-values agenda that did not include national action to support African American families, as this action was inherently socialist and part of the End Times apostasy. Rather, his family values agenda was one aspect of a larger economic agenda of biblical capitalism.

Dispensational Node
The Wrath of God

"The wrath of God is revealed from heaven," declared the apostle Paul in the opening chapter of Romans, "against all ungodliness and unrighteousness of men, who suppress the truth in unrighteousness"

(Rom 1:18 NKJV). The 1909 *Scofield Reference Bible* says of this verse that the "Gospel [is] a revelation of wrath also." Scofield's notes go on to explain the apostasy, in accordance with the rest of the chapter; there are "seven stages of Gentile world apostasy" within this present dispensation of the Church Age, and the consequence for this apostasy is the judgment—wrath—of God.

The wrath to come at the end of this dispensation will be the Tribulation, but dispensationalism teaches other forms of wrath, as well. All people are under God's wrath until they receive his mercy through the substitutionary death of Christ; those who do not make this decision and remain under his wrath are doomed to an eternity in hell. In his commentary on Romans, Darby wrote of God's wrath that "all men are under sin and judgment."[8] For this reason, as Paul declared, "the wrath of God is revealed from heaven." This wrath was not merely the natural consequences one might face on this earth for sin, as in when lying causes a relationship to be severed or stealing leads to imprisonment. Rather, this wrath is revealed from God "in connection with the grace which delivers from this very wrath." God is a God of both love and wrath; "God is now fully revealed in Christ: and all sin, whatever and wherever it is, being set in the light of heaven, is unsupportable." Dispensational teachings on the wrath of God are complex and nuanced, and this wrath is not limited to the worldwide desolation that will come at the end of this dispensation.

For Falwell, however, the wrath of God always referred to the Tribulation. There were times when he attempted more complex exegesis, but he simply was not able to teach doctrine. What he could teach was how current events were in alignment with prophecy, and in this area, he had a lot to say about the wrath of God. Especially with government officials and members of the public pressing for programs that would benefit African American families.

When Falwell toured the country preaching "America Back to God," he claimed that to balance the national budget, the government needed to "drastically cut, if not totally eliminate, this blooming welfare program at home and abroad, and use those monies to intensify our defense development." In this bold statement, he was urging the government to step back from all programs meant to support families, especially African American families. The conservative attitude at the time was that hard-earned tax dollars were paying welfare queens to not work, and Falwell was baptizing this grievance into his use of dispensationalism. Liberals who had responded to the Moynihan Report wanted to see more government programs that would help minority families rise out of debilitating poverty and become self-sufficient, and Falwell rejected this notion entirely. In other words, the battle line that he was drawing was both *economic* and *racial*, and by siding with the economic calls for racial justice, America was giving in to the apostasy and making itself a target of God's wrath. "God is judging America," he declared in the sermon, "because America's religious leaders have joined up with the Philistines and have begun to worship false gods and to create golden idols and calves." Biblical capitalism, not more welfare programs, was the solution.

Instead of using tax dollars to fund poverty-reduction programs to help African American families, he urged investment in "defense development." By "defense development," he was referring to increasing America's stockpile of nuclear weapons that served as a deterrent to the Soviet Union; the two countries were locked in an arms race of nuclear development and spending significant portions of their national budgets toward that end. In his view, welfare programs that encouraged African Americans to not work and rewarded the laziness of welfare queens were part of the apostasy that was leading up to the Tribulation, but nuclear build-up would help avert God's wrath.

One warning of God's impending wrath on America was the country's floundering nuclear arsenal. "For the first time since we have been a nation, we are second militarily," he declared in "America Back to God." To him, America's military might seems to have always been tied to its standing before God, as when God blessed the colonial revolutionaries, who fought on God's own side to establish a Christian nation and ultimately prevailed against the British. Now in the nuclear age and especially with the rise of Soviet Magog, America's standing before God as a Christian nation was tied into its nuclear arsenal, and the facts were grim: "The Soviet Union not only has more conventional military might but almost twice the nuclear might." The Tribulation was surely at hand, and America was not prepared. In other words, Falwell's understanding of the wrath of God is tied into his fascination and even obsession with nuclear war; his relentless advocacy of nuclear build-up, against poverty-reduction programs for marginalized communities, is inseparable from his understanding of the Tribulation.

Second Peter 3:10 says, "But the day of the Lord will come as a thief in the night; in the which the heavens shall pass away with a great noise, and the elements shall melt with fervent heat, the earth also and the works that are therein shall be burned up" (KJV). Dispensationalists have long used the term "as a thief in the night" to describe the rapidity and spontaneity with which the Rapture will occur. In the blink of an eye and with no warning, before people realize what has happened, their loved ones will disappear; they will have gone to be with the Lord in the Rapture. Following the explosion of the atomic bomb on Hiroshima and Nagasaki in August 1945, dispensationalists began claiming that the second part of the verse—"the heavens shall pass away with a great noise, and the elements shall melt with fervent heat"—was a prophecy about the nuclear age. Falwell said of the verse, in a 1983 sermon entitled "Nuclear War and the Second Coming of Christ,"

> In 2 Peter chapter 3, there's no question that we do have a clear indication that after the thousand-year reign of Christ and prior to the ushering in of the new heavens and the new earth, that there will be a melting of the elements. The very elements of the universe shall melt with a severe heat caused by an indescribable explosion. I personally feel that is nuclear in nature.[9]

Second Peter 3:10 places bookends on the events of the End Times, as many dispensationalists understand the End Times. This period will begin with the Rapture and end with a nuclear explosion that will destroy the entire universe.

During the Cold War, which could be said to have begun with the end of World War II and the advent of the nuclear age, the threat of nuclear war took on particular significance in dispensational thought. Perhaps God had used nuclear fission in the destruction of Sodom and Gomorrah in the book of Genesis, and he would use it again when his judgment would fall to earth during the Tribulation. The sheer terror that people felt at the new reality of a potential nuclear war fulfilled Luke 21:26, which says, "men's hearts failing them for fear, and for looking after those things which are coming on the earth: for the powers of heaven shall be shaken" (NKJV). The advent of the nuclear age was a sure sign that biblical prophecies were speeding toward their ultimate fulfillment in the Rapture, Tribulation, and Millennial Reign.

Not all Christians shared the dispensational view that the atomic bomb was part of biblical prophecy. With the end of World War II, the Catholic *Pax Christi* movement emerged as an effort to forge reconciliation between the peoples of France and Germany. As the Cold War progressed, *Pax Christi* promoted pacifism with regard to the nuclear threat, in accordance with Catholic social teachings. Pope John XXIII, in his *Pacem in Terris* letter in 1962, called for nuclear disarmament and the banning of nuclear weapons in all countries of the world. The early 1980s saw a growing nuclear-freeze movement, with a 1982 march in New York City drawing over a million people in favor of a nuclear freeze. In 1983, the National Conference of Catholic Bishops published a letter entitled *The Challenge of Peace*, which said, "Today, the possibilities of placing moral and political limits on nuclear war are so minimal that the moral task is prevention: as a people, we must refuse to legitimate the idea of nuclear war."[10] In a 1985 declaration, the United Church of Christ said that, because just war is impossible in a nuclear age, the church had to begin "to move beyond Just War thinking to the Theology of a Just Peace."[11] Among Catholics and more liberal Protestants, there developed a strong movement for disarmament in favor of programs to support social uplift.

Falwell fiercely rejected this view in favor of nuclear build-up. In 1979, a revision of the Strategic Arms Limitations Talks/Treaty (SALT II), which would limit the nuclear build-up of the United States and Soviet Union, came up to a vote in Congress. He declared that God had caused the Iranian hostage crisis—in which revolutionary forces in Tehran took fifty-two Americans hostage from the US embassy and held them for 444 days—to show the US government the dangers of SALT II and prevent ratification. As the movement for nuclear disarmament was building up, he claimed in 1982 that his ministry was providing one-way airfare to the Soviet Union for "peaceniks" and "freezeniks." He believed that those opposed to nuclear build-up were "putting this country down, and saying that the Soviet Union is utopia, and America is a slave labor camp."[12] In a booklet that accompanied his 1983 prime-time special "Nuclear War and the Second Coming of Christ," he opened by claiming, "Nuclear War and the Second Coming of

Jesus Christ—the one brings thoughts of fear, destruction, and death while the other brings thoughts of joy, hope, and life. They almost seem inconsistent with one another. Yet, they are indelibly intertwined."[13] Operating out of a dispensational approach to the Bible, Falwell saw nuclear build-up as consistent with Christian values.

Yet ironically, he believed that there would not be any nuclear war during the present Church Age, which would end at the Rapture. He even claimed in the 1983 sermon "Nuclear War and the Second Coming of Christ," "And so question one, will nuclear holocaust destroy this earth? The answer clearly, if you believe the Bible, is no." The world still had seven years of Tribulation ahead, following which would commence the thousand-year reign of Christ over the world. Simple mathematics meant that the world could not be destroyed for 1,007 years—following which the entire universe would melt in a nuclear explosion. For now, Americans had no need to worry about nuclear war because God would supernaturally preserve the planet for the next 1,007 years. Even those who would be left behind at the Rapture and have to face the horrors of the Tribulation had no need to fear nuclear war. In fact, in Tim LaHaye's original *Left Behind* novels (not the movies or later novels based on the original series), as the Tribulation began, the antichrist introduced a policy of nuclear disarmament; while he engaged in a bombing campaign that was destroying cities all over the world, there was no trace of nuclear fallout (except in London). Though nuclear weapons had been prophesied in the Bible, Falwell and LaHaye saw no reason to believe that they would actually be used.

So why should the United States expend billions of dollars on a nuclear arsenal while eliminating the country's public schools, job-development programs, and social safety net? For Falwell, the goal of nuclear build-up was to preserve American Christianity and its consequent economic system of capitalism. Having a superior nuclear arsenal served as deterrence, to prevent the Soviet Union from attempting a nuclear strike on US soil. Should the Soviets succeed in such a strike and then take over the United States, "if America should lose her freedom, if that flag, Old Glory, should come down, I don't know how any other part of the world could remain free from the hammer and the sickle."[14] Nuclear build-up was the only way to ensure that capitalist, Christian America did not fall under communism.

Yet there was also an internal threat, as liberals were agitating for socialist, even—as Falwell believed—communist, policies, in the name of "family values." These social programs—Aid to Families with Dependent Children, food stamps, and now movements toward universal health care and children's daycare—threatened to turn America into a communist state without the Soviets having to fire a single missile. *All* resources had to be diverted to fighting the communist threat. Monies that had been used to support social—socialist—programs in America had to stop flowing in that direction, as they were building up to a communist government. Instead, they had to flow toward nuclear build-up to deter a Soviet strike.

Because Falwell saw capitalism and Christianity as inextricably intertwined, should America's capitalist economy become communist (or even socialist), the repercussions would extend beyond economics. Christianity itself would collapse, not only in America but throughout the world. He followed the statement, "I don't know how any other part of the world could remain free from the hammer and the sickle," by saying, "and I don't know how we could get the gospel out to the world in our generation, and I personally feel that this is the last generation before Jesus comes." The purpose of nuclear build-up was to preserve American capitalism; capitalism was not only the safeguard of Christianity but the very essence of it. By adding the phrase, "I personally feel that this is the last generation before Jesus comes," he indicated that his perspective on nuclear build-up, in conjunction with capitalism and Christianity, emerged from his understanding of dispensationalism, not studies in economic theory or the science behind nuclear weapons. This dispensational understanding of capitalism, Christianity, and nuclear weapons is what informed his stance on "family values."

Capitalist Family Values

The liberal response to the Moynihan Report showed that supporting families was critical to the liberal agenda. Yet when Falwell spoke about family values, he was not referring to the Moynihan Report and its implied assent to the civil rights movement, or government efforts to enhance life for working mothers, disabled fathers, and disadvantaged children. These efforts were part of the apostasy—the socialistic New Deal, as it was reinforced in President Lyndon Johnson's War on Poverty. Rather, Falwell rejected the need for women to work outside the home and called on them to become housewives so that they could dedicate all their time to caring for their children and husbands. While feminists allegedly supported pornography—he insisted in *Listen, America!* that they wanted to have their own "dirty magazines"[15]—the most holy thing a woman could do was marry, bear children, and allow her husband to support her financially while she raised their children and cared for his needs.

Falwell defined a family strictly as "one man and one woman together for a lifetime with their biological or adopted children."[16] Here he was appealing to an idea that certainly does have a long history and received reification in the early twentieth century, when the term "nuclear family" began to be used. Nuclear families are, generally speaking, heterosexual families that consist of two parents and their own biological and/or adopted children. Combined with his belief that women must be housewives, Falwell's idea of nuclear families left no room for matriarchal families, single parents, divorcees, foster families, or any other approach to family life. Indeed, he decried the idea of family diversity, referring specifically to queer families but inevitably including all non-patriarchal families.

Falwell's "family values" included rejecting all gains of Women's Lib as well as attacking the queer community, as he claimed homosexuals were corrupting children and steering them away from the ideal family. He also invoked Tim LaHaye's language of humanism, claiming in the inaugural flyer for the Moral Majority,

> For too long now we have witnessed the concerted attack waged by ultraliberals and so called "feminists" against the family structure in America. . . For too long we have watched pornography, homosexuality, and godless humanism corrupt America's families.

The end result of this corruption was "socialism, which is a first cousin to communism."[17] In his 2015 book *Family Values and the Rise of the Christian Right*, Seth Dowling noted that to conservatives of the Cold War era, "The American way of life emphasized the triumph of capitalism but was best epitomized by the nuclear family."[18] To Falwell, the patriarchal nuclear family, in which children attended private Christian schools or were homeschooled by their mothers, was America's first line of defense against a communist takeover.[19]

These family values were incompatible with federal programs, such as what the Moynihan Report called for, to enhance the domestic life of American families. In 1980, the US House and Senate both passed the Domestic Violence Prevention and

Treatment Act to provide federal, state, and local governments with support in addressing domestic violence; the bill did not become law because it passed in two different forms, and the differences between the House and Senate versions were not resolved. In *Listen, America!* Falwell castigated the bill, saying that if it passes, "the federal government could become directly involved in the area of husband-wife relationships . . . Women could sue their husbands for rape."[20] Though America admittedly had a problem with domestic violence, "it is an inappropriate response to legislate a federal bureaucracy to take care of this problem."[21] Government attempts to implement programs that would strengthen the family were part of the encroachment of humanism that was threatening to devastate Christian America.

In fact, Falwell wanted the repeal of all government programs that he saw as threatening to the male-headed "nuclear family." He supported the Family Protection Act, the first title of which "Abolishes the Department of Education and nullifies all regulations, contracts, licenses, or privileges issued by such Department prior to the effective date of this Act."[22] The country's public schools were teaching godless humanism rather than Christianity and leading children down the dangerous path of socialism and communism, not capitalism. In fact, the public schools were part of the socialist agenda that emerged from the Social Gospel of the post–Civil War years, thereby making them antithetical to America's Christian and capitalist standing before God. Therefore, he called on the government to shut down the public schools in favor of Christian schools—the segregation academies that arose throughout the South in the 1960s and 1970s—and homeschooling.

The nuclear family served another purpose, in addition to supporting Christian America's capitalism against the socialism of the liberation movements that made notable gains in the 1960s and 1970s. The God-ordained nuclear family itself was America's front line of defense against nuclear war. Because the American government was spending so much on socialist programs that were meant to support families but were actually destroying the nuclear family, there were less funds available for nuclear development. In the *Listen, America!* chapter about families, Falwell claimed that in the event of a nuclear strike, America would lose ten people for every Soviet life lost because of how much the Soviet Union had been investing in nuclear development. More Americans than Soviets would die in the event of nuclear war, he believed, because America's liberal government had been diverting too much money from nuclear development to welfare programs. The only solution was emphasizing nuclear families.

Further, he claimed that the government of communist Russia, having no use for families, took children away from their parents to put them in state-sponsored education facilities; Falwell likened this approach to American feminists who wanted the government to provide universal daycare so that women could work. Yet these programs would place the country—and its families—at greater risk of a nuclear attack. No, fathers needed to work, and mothers needed to stay home with their children. God might then bless this Christian America enough to supernaturally prevent a Soviet takeover.

Therefore, the socialist policies that began with the Social Gospel and that the government assumed under the New Deal had to end. The gains of the civil rights movement had forced the government to expand its welfare programs, as Martin Luther King Jr. had called for a more equitable distribution of resources than what capitalism permitted; the clock needed to be turned back on these gains, and African American leaders needed to focus more on the moral development of their people than clamoring for government handouts. Politicians had to stop listening to queer-rights activists calling for the repeal of sodomy laws and civil rights for the queer community. Feminists advocating for government-supported daycare programs so that women could go to work instead of staying at home with their children had to get out of the way. America was capitalist, not socialist, and the country had something of much greater importance on the horizon: the threat of nuclear war.

The Anti-Family Apostasy of the United Nations

At the center of this nuclear confluence lay the United Nations and the impending Tribulation period. The UN declared 1979 to be the International Year of the Child (IYC), as part of efforts to address problems facing children throughout the world and reinforce the 1959 Declaration of the Rights of the Child (DRC). Falwell saw the IYC and DRC as part of a world socialist agenda to steer children away from Christian families, values, and lifestyles. He claimed that widespread family planning would require parents to become licensed before they could bear and raise children. In a manner consistent with the dystopia of Soviet Magog, governments would begin taking children away from their parents, and all responsibility for child-rearing would shift from parents and families to governments. Children would be forced to reject patriotism, capitalism, and Christianity as a means of liberating them from traditional values. Most alarmingly to Falwell, leaders of the IYC called for nuclear disarmament and urged that children have the opportunity to grow up away from militarism. The only possible outcome of these goals, should they be fulfilled, would be the creation of a one-world socialist government.

In fact, that one-world socialist government already existed in its incipient form, the United Nations. "There is in America today an effort towards internationalism that would eliminate, actually eliminate the sovereignty of the United States of America,"[23] Falwell proclaimed in 1980, with reference to the UN. "And when there are those who advocate the surrender of our sovereignty and the joining of a one-world community with a great one-world supreme court and one-world government, we need to say in a big, loud, sophisticated tone, baloney!"

When dispensationalism first emerged in Britain in the mid-1800s, followers pointed to the Roman Catholic Church as a one-world government and one-world church from which the antichrist—the pope—would emerge during the Tribulation. An ocean away, America did not experience the depth of Protestant-Catholic tensions that had historically erupted in war throughout Europe; following World War I, American dispensationalists pointed to the League of Nations, not the Vatican, as the one-world government and to the ecumenical Federal Council of Churches as the one-world church. Following World War II, the one-world government of the End Times became the UN, and the one-world church became the World Council of Churches (WCC). As the prophetic calendar continued to count down toward the End Times, dispensationalists generally believed the UN and WCC would gain greater levels of power. During the Tribulation, the antichrist, as a one-world dictator, would use the WCC to create a one-world religion and turn the UN into his seat of power to rule over the planet. To many (though not all) American dispensationalists, the UN was Satan's instrument for moving people away from capitalism, Christianity, and national self-defense (nuclear build-up) to socialism, humanism, and religious toleration.

This dispensational view of the UN is what informed Falwell's approach to the IYC, DRC, and all other UN initiatives. If the Satanic UN was calling for nuclear disarmament, the American Christian nation had to spend larger and larger sums of money enhancing its nuclear arsenal. When the UN called for children's rights, Falwell called for parents' rights. When the UN called for national governments to invest more in social programs—such as public schools and public health—Falwell labeled these programs as "socialist" and doubled down on his support of unregulated capitalism. Because history was nearing its end and the UN would soon give rise to the reign of the antichrist, the American Christian nation had to oppose all UN efforts and stand for Christianity, capitalism, and nuclear weapons. Most importantly, it had to support the nuclear family against government efforts to "liberate" children from the influences of religion.

Nuclear Family Values

Note: This section and the next, in particular, will use objectionable language to describe Falwell's views on the queer community. As painful as this language is, the author believes that repeating it is necessary for readers to understand the vitriol and harassment that queer people in America have been facing.

Despite the world careening toward the wrath of God, there was a divine plan for America and for America's families. According to Falwell, capitalism and the work ethic handed down by the Puritans had enabled the American Christian nation to become the wealthiest and most blessed country in world history. Consequently, Americans supported half of all Protestant missionaries in the world and had a divine mandate to carry out the task of global evangelization. Falwell claimed in "America Back to God," "Our Founding Fathers came to this country for the advancement of the Christian faith. They came here to develop a worldwide missionary enterprise." The problem today was that liberal churches were more concerned with socialist policies—the Social Gospel—than with helping others convert to Christianity.

Coupled with the country's wealth, America's military strength enabled the Christian nation to support the state of Israel against Arabs who, Falwell claimed, were hostile to Jews and bent on their destruction. Falwell's understanding of the End Times centered on Israel, and the ultimate goal of history was the establishment of Christ's Millennial Kingdom from the throne of David in Jerusalem. As such, one of the most sacred tasks America could perform was providing military support to arm the Jewish people living in Israel. By reinforcing Christian America's capitalism, against calls for social programs to benefit marginalized families, the country could continue its efforts at world evangelization and support of Israel. As history was drawing to a close, world evangelization and support of Israel were the two imperatives of God's plan, and America was the only country in the world with the resources to carry out those sacred tasks.

But modern efforts to support non-patriarchal families took America away from its divine mission. Falwell believed socialism would soon cripple America's economy so severely that the country would no longer be able to send out missionaries; it would also spiritually weaken the country so that it could no longer provide Israel with the military support needed. And unless Christian America could complete the twin tasks of world evangelization and military support of Israel, the country would soon fall under the wrath of God, just like the rest of the world. In "America Back to God," Falwell said,

> It isn't because of a bunch of godless Democrats and Republicans that God is judging this country. It's because we have a country full of Jonahs who are not carrying out God's commission, who are no longer preaching repentance, who no longer know what sin is . . . If America falls, it will be because of people like you and me. Judgment begins at the house of God. God is judging

America because America's religious leaders have joined up with the Philistines and have begun to worship false gods.

He listed a litany of sins that were causing God's judgment to come on America: public schools, pornography, drugs, and socialism (notably, abortion was not on the list until after 1978). One of the greatest sins was homosexuality, not merely that some people practiced a queer lifestyle but that liberal churches were endorsing it as a legitimate lifestyle.

> Add to that the fact that just recently, three mainline denominations accepted into membership the gay church, the church for homosexuals. They have accepted the fact that homosexuality is normal, and that these people ought to have a Christian church of their own, and they have been so accepted. Regardless what the World Council of Churches endorses, or the Methodists or the Baptists or the Episcopalians or the Presbyterians or the Catholics endorse, God still says it is reprobate.

In *Listen, America!* he claimed that God's wrath would soon fall on America for how Christians were not only tolerating but endorsing, even embracing queer lifestyles. He did not have to wait long before he could declare that the wrath of God had fallen.

The Centers for Disease Control and Prevention reported its findings on the first cases of the disease that came to be known as AIDS on June 5, 1981. This first report centered on a cluster of five gay men in Los Angeles, and the association with male-to-male sexuality led to the disease being initially known as GRID, or gay-related immune deficiency. Notwithstanding the fact that most people with AIDS were not gay men and that lesbians had an extremely low chance of contracting the HIV virus, Falwell began claiming that AIDS was God's punishment for the advances of the gay rights movement. In his 1986 sermon "Is America a

Christian Nation?" he said, "Someone asked me, do you think AIDS is God's judgment against homosexuals? No, it is God's judgment against America . . . You mark it down, God is angry with America because we have violated and ignored his moral rules of decency."[24] God was not punishing gay people with AIDS; he was punishing America with AIDS for tolerating the gay lifestyle.

"The traditional, monogamous family may cease to exist during this decade,"[25] Falwell declared at the start of the 1980s. At stake was primarily the Christian home, the patriarchal nuclear family. Falwell believed that gay men were not manly and able to lead families as could heterosexual men, and lesbian women were not feminine and submissive as God required. As such, queer individuals were breaking down the fabric of society, not only by exploiting children—"Why must they prey upon our young?"[26]— but primarily by existing in a way that defies gender roles and disregards God's order for the family. The way that queer individuals were ripping apart America's society was a prelude to how society around the world would collapse when all true Christians departed in the Rapture. Similarly, the AIDS epidemic that God had brought to America was a prelude to the utter destruction that would soon come during the Tribulation. Should America not heed this warning, should Christians continue tolerating queer lifestyles and the government allow this behavior to continue, the wrath of God that came in the form of the AIDS epidemic would pale in comparison to the wrath of God during the Tribulation.

America had to scale back the gains of the gay rights movement in favor of the nuclear family, nuclear build-up, and unregulated capitalism. Only in this way could the country recover its Christian role, including its divine tasks of evangelizing the world and supporting the state of Israel. Otherwise, the wrath of God via the AIDS epidemic would only get worse.

The Anti-Family Conference

"Now government that permits, allows, or encourages immorality is an enemy of the family,"[27] Falwell said of President Jimmy Carter's White House Conference on Families. The pledge to support American families was a part of Carter's 1976 presidential campaign, and both social conservatives and social liberals supported the intent. In 1980, Carter brought together a panel of experts who would help determine the strengths of families and how public policies could support them. Social conservatives, including many evangelicals, who voted for him in 1976 largely expected that the conference would focus on the nuclear family, with a bread-winning father and stay-at-home mother. Yet the experts he convened wanted to examine the challenges facing gay families and single-parent families—an echo of how the Moynihan Report fifteen years earlier had sought to gain federal support for African American families.

The backlash was fierce. Falwell, horrified that the president of the United States was on a trajectory to recognize same-sex couples and their children as constituting a family, called the conference the Anti-Family Conference. "The Russians have been delighted with the course we Americans have taken," he said in *Listen, America!* "Our improper priorities are leading us down the road to weakness."[28] America needed God's blessing to ensure its survival, and possibly even victory, in its struggle against the Soviet Union. Yet instead of enacting policies that would ensure this blessing—policies that moved resources away from social services and toward nuclear build-up, policies that privileged nuclear families over queer and single-parent families—America was incurring God's wrath by supporting the rights of queer people. As an alternative to Carter's White House Conference on Families, Falwell partnered with Phyllis Schlafly (who organized anti-feminists across the country to defeat the Equal Rights Amendment), Bill Bright (founder of Campus Crusade for Christ), and Tim LaHaye to promote a Pro-Family Conference. The Pro-Family Conference was held to promote support for the nuclear family as the only true family.

A newsletter for this conference grouped foster families alongside the diverse family forms against which Falwell railed by sarcastically quoting Richard John Neuhaus, an advisor for the White House Conference on Families. "Foster parents, lesbians and gays, liberated families, or whatever—all can do the job as long as they provide children the loving and the permanent structure that traditional families have typically provided."[29] The Pro-Family Conference made no caveat for foster families, who received government support to care for abused and neglected children; foster families, the newsletter seemed to imply, were not real families because they did not follow the nuclear model.

Present at the Pro-Family Conference was the politician who embodied the conservative movement that Falwell was building: Ronald Reagan. While New Deal liberalism had led to "Uncle Sam [replacing] dad as provider of food and clothing,"[30] Reagan promised to cut social programs that rewarded people for not working. While feminists had been clamoring for the government to support daycares so that women, including single mothers, could work to provide for their children, Reagan saw no reason for the government to be involved in such a measure. Reaganomics, as his economic theory came to be known, dramatically cut government funding to social services, especially services that were intended to support families, in favor of lower taxes, especially for the wealthy and for businesses. The "trickle-down" reasoning behind Reaganomics was that money that the wealthy saved in tax cuts would "trickle down" to the poor, thereby helping everybody rise out of poverty. In other words, "trickle-down economics" was a re-packaging of nineteenth-century *laissez-faire* economics—what became the biblical capitalism that rejected liberal theology and the Social Gospel—and had long been the goal of this strand of American dispensationalism.

Perhaps most importantly, alongside policies that favored Falwell's ideal of the nuclear family, Reagan supported nuclear build-up. "We should build for our military defenses in this country," Falwell said, referring to the country's nuclear arsenal against the Soviet Union's. "I support what the president's trying to do."[31] Ending all socialist policies and inclinations toward communism within the United States, from welfare programs to public schools to efforts at universal daycare, was certainly significant in protecting America's nuclear families. Ultimately, however, the only way to preserve them was through a strong military machine, which included a nuclear arsenal that rivaled that of the Soviet Union, to prevent a communist invasion.

Falwell's Pro-Family Conference spawned a surge of national organizations that supported the nuclear family. Focus on the Family, which has advocated prolifically against the queer community, was founded by Dr. James Dobson in 1977 and rose to prominence in the years after the Pro-Family Conference. Similarly, the American Family Association, which Donald Wildmon had founded in 1977, had a strong presence at the Pro-Family Conference and soon increased its following. The year 1978 saw the founding of the anti-feminist group Concerned Women for America by Tim LaHaye and his wife, Beverly, as well as Christian Voice by Robert Grant and Richard Zone; Christian Voice was located at the conservative thinktank The Heritage Foundation in Washington, DC. The next year, in 1979, Falwell formed his Moral Majority to help churches organize their communities in voting for pro-family, pro-military values. In 1981, Dobson founded the Family Research Council as a thinktank in Washington that would promote his anti-queer agenda in the halls of government. Dozens of similar organizations sprang up in the late 1970s and early 1980s.

Reaganomics and the 1980 Child Welfare Act

Family values meant something entirely different to populations that liberal policies supporting families had intended to serve. Carter convened the White House Conference on Families on June 6, 1980. Less than two weeks later, on June 17, he signed into law the 1980 Adoption Assistance and Child Welfare Act, which had the intent of strengthening the country's foster-care system. Throughout the 1970s, "foster-care drift" had become so severe that many state governments had no records of where many of their foster children were. The 1980 Child Welfare Act aimed to improve outcomes for foster children by preventing family separation in the first place; a judge had to determine that "reasonable efforts" had been made to keep the family intact before a child could be removed and placed into state custody. When removal did occur, children's services had to focus on "permanency planning," meaning that within a certain amount of time, children had to either return to their families of origin or become eligible for adoption into a stable and nurturing home.

"Economic and social trends are fueling a collapse in children's services,"[32] read the foreword to a 1989 government report on the implementation of the 1980 Child Welfare Act. "Federal oversight and funding are weak to nonexistent. There are too few resources in these service systems to meet the increasingly complex needs of children." The report did not mention Reaganomics specifically, but all 229 pages might as well have served as an indictment of the new economic policies that had crippled America's social services and marked the end of New Deal liberalism. Even though preventive services that aimed to keep children with their families were remarkably successful and cost-effective—family preservation efforts in Virginia during the 1980s prevented 93 percent of participating families from experiencing foster care, at a cost of $1,214 per child versus foster-care expenses of $11,173 per child—they were curtailed by a lack of funding for the most basic services, such as housing and nutrition assistance. The report summarized, "Our findings are alarming."

Earlier in the decade, there were signs that the Child Welfare Act was helping children and families. The number of children in foster care dropped, from approximately 302,000 in 1980 to 262,000 in 1982. Yet during that time, increases in poverty, homelessness, and teenage pregnancies, alongside an exploding drug epidemic and AIDS crisis, were leading to increased reports of child abuse and neglect. During 1981, while the number of children in foster care was declining, there were 1.2 million reports of child abuse and neglect; that number increased to 2.2 million in 1988. Further, more children were dying of abuse and neglect by the end of the decade, with over 1,100 reported fatalities between 1986 and 1988.

There had never been a legal definition of what "reasonable efforts" constituted, even though the 1980 Act required that they be implemented before a child could be removed and placed into foster care. Ostensibly, the framers of the Act intended services such as subsidized housing and crisis counseling, under the guidance of a social worker, to be available to families at risk of having their children removed. Yet with Reagan's cuts to social spending, those services were not available. According to the 1989 report, "Recent research has shown that services are being offered unevenly at best. There is some indication that they still may be triggered more by placement [of children into foster care] than offered in preventing placement."[33] Families in crisis were receiving little to no support, and any services that they received were only available *after* their children were removed; there were too few services to help prevent children from going into foster care, even though family-preservation programs saved states as much as $10,000 *per child*.

Further, a growing drug epidemic, which the White House responded to with Nancy Reagan's "Just Say No" campaign, helped fuel the explosion in child abuse and neglect. The 1989 report showed that rehabilitative services for those suffering from addiction were inadequate for the rapidly growing number of drug users, and services for addicted pregnant women were almost nonexistent. As a result, babies born with addictions to hard drugs were being abandoned in hospitals, and social workers were scrambling to find foster homes for them.

Instead of supporting poor families to help them stay together, in 1984, President Reagan signed legislation that would financially cripple parents whose children had been removed and placed into foster care. Those parents would have to begin paying child support to the state, sometimes thousands of dollars a year—per child— when they were already suffering from homelessness and drug addiction. Many had already lost their children because of growing poverty that had kept them from finding safe housing, sufficient food, and childcare while they tried to work. Now, they were also receiving bills from the government, bills that were putting them tens of thousands of dollars into debt. Children began spending longer and longer amounts of time in foster care because, instead of their parents receiving the support that they needed to put their families back together, they had to pay a monthly bill to the state.

After a few years of decline, by 1985, the number of children removed from their families and placed into foster care was rising steeply. Many of these children had been in foster care previously and reunified with their families when the Act was first implemented; however, reunification ultimately failed, in no small part because of the lack of support services. Because of the increasingly harsh conditions in which these children had lived before experiencing family breakdown, they entered foster care with greater trauma and psychological challenges. Foster parents received only about $10 per day to care for severely emotionally disturbed children. That small stipend could not begin to pay for property damage caused by their erratic behavior; waiting lists for these foster children to receive mental-health services sometimes were years long. As a result, there was a severe shortage of foster homes for the rapidly growing number of children entering foster care. "Calling the shortage of foster parents 'critical,' the GAO [Government Accountability Office] . . . found that 'increasing numbers of foster parents are ceasing to provide care because they do not receive support and positive recognition in dealing with difficulties they face in caring for today's foster children.'"[34]

Instead of "reasonable efforts" to prevent family breakdown in the first place, many children who had been removed from their families were diverted to the juvenile justice system and incarcerated; others experienced prolonged stays in residential facilities. When foster children ran away or aged out of care, whichever came first, a lack of resources often meant that they had to fend for themselves on the streets. Like their parents before them, far too many had no way of obtaining safe housing, nutritious food, mental-health counseling, or addiction rehabilitation. The nuclear family values of capitalist, Christian America had failed them.

"The Spirit of the Lord is upon me," Luke 4:18 records Christ as saying, "because he anointed me to bring good news to the poor" (NASB). But Falwell's innovative approach to Christianity, his family-values gospel of unregulated capitalism and nuclear build-up, at the expense of programs such as housing and nutrition assistance, was news of family breakdown for hundreds of thousands of children. It was news of separation from brothers and sisters because there were not enough foster homes to keep siblings together, news of homelessness and incarceration for children aging out of foster care.

In Texas, then-governor George W. Bush's "solution" was to allow religious organizations to form their own accrediting bodies that would license residential childcare centers, without the government or tax dollars getting involved at all. According to a report from the Texas Freedom Network, "Loosening regulations over faith-based providers has not served the faith community at large, but has instead provided a refuge for facilities with a history of regulatory violations, a theological objection to state oversight and a higher rate of abuse and neglect."[35] People of faith who responded to Bush's provision that faith-based organizations could accredit their own homes for children in need overwhelmingly believed that the government did not have a duty to aid these children. These people, like Falwell, had "a theological objection to state oversight," and this objection helped fuel the "higher rate of abuse and neglect" that the children in their care experienced. Few social services, including waitlists for housing assistance that can be five to ten years long, continue to cause tens of thousands of children to be removed from their families and placed into foster care each year.

I wrote this chapter for kids like me. We have to do better for them. And for Christians who want to assist kids and families in crisis, the gospel has to be good news.

CHAPTER 4

The Politics of Armageddon

"Do you ever get the feeling sometimes that if we don't do it now, if we let this be another Sodom and Gomorrah, that maybe we might be the generation that sees Armageddon?"

AT THOMAS ROAD Baptist Church, Fourth of July services rival the spectacle of Christmas and Easter, and the one held on July 3, 1983, was no exception. Falwell had purchased a scarlet flag and asked two of his associates to hold it up, in juxtaposition against the red, white, and blue. Even though America is nowhere in the Bible, Falwell had prepared his Fourth of July sermon around Old Glory and its cosmic nemesis. "That flag stands for bondage, for slavery,"[1] he said of the hammer and sickle. "It's properly colored, bloody . . . That flag stands for death." Speaking of the Soviet Union engaging in "nuclear blackmail" against America, he asked his audience, "Is the president right in being against an immediate [nuclear] freeze that would lock us into inferiority? Of course the president's right."

Falwell's audience must have known that the sermon, entitled "The Two Flags in Today's World," was really about the End Times. He had preached so regularly on the events of the End Times through the 1970s—the oppression of Israel and soon-to-come persecution of Christians, wars in the Middle East, the Magog invasion into the Holy Land—that prophecy was piece-meal to how his followers viewed current events. Videos of church services in which he preached about nuclear war and the Soviet

Union show members of the congregation nodding eagerly, leaning their heads forward so as to not miss a word of how current events were leading society toward the Tribulation. The Soviet Union, better known as Magog, was the enemy of God, as foretold in prophecy and manifested in the country's communist structure and oppression of its Jews. The threat of nuclear war meant that the Tribulation was imminent, as Falwell predicted a nuclear strike within the next five years or less; America was doing God's work by building up its nuclear arsenal.

A few months later, in the fall of 1983, Cold War tensions would reach a fever pitch when the Able Archer 83 NATO military drills led Soviet leaders to believe that a nuclear attack from the West was imminent. At about that time, Falwell bought a prime-time television slot to enthrall a national audience that was living on edge regarding nuclear war. He began "Nuclear War and the Second Coming of Christ" by asking, "Are we going to be roasted one day in a horrible nuclear holocaust? Will there be a major nuclear confrontation on this planet? Will the United States ever be conquered by the Soviet Union? . . . The Bible has a great deal to say about those questions and that subject."[2] Plenty of Americans were afraid of the end of the world via a nuclear war, but Falwell reassured his television audience that the End would actually come after the Millennial Reign of Christ, following which a nuclear explosion will melt the cosmos. Still, "We should build for our military defenses in this country. I support what the president's trying to do. I believe that we have human responsibility. But I'm talking to you from a biblical perspective."[3]

President Reagan, the darling of the newfound Religious Right and whom Falwell claimed was a close friend, had resumed a policy of nuclear build-up following years of détente between the United States and the Soviet Union. As candidate for president and later while holding office, Reagan made no secret of his belief in the impending battle of Armageddon. On November 5, 1979, almost a year to the day before he was elected president, he told Jim Bakker, then a televangelical celebrity (albeit one who would fall a few years later), that "if we let this be another Sodom and Gomorrah, that we might be the generation that sees Armageddon."[4]

Critics of prophecy belief tend to see it as fanciful and highly imaginative speculation that is so thin on Christian ethics that it features a bloodthirsty deity. In one sermon, Falwell spoke of a "grisly feast of God" that would occur halfway through the Tribulation, after the Almighty destroys five-sixths of the Russian army. Another grisly feast would occur in the aftermath of Armageddon, when hundreds of millions of bodies must be disposed of. The thrill to prophecy believers of what will happen to others during the Tribulation, the ability to talk calmly (or even eagerly) about the imminency of nuclear war and a cosmic genocide that will wipe out one-quarter of the population, is thrilling. Prophecy belief excites with a gripping tale that concerns other people, the horrors that will befall them (because they are not true Christians) but will not affect those who believe in prophecy.

Prophecy belief has always been politically charged, especially within dispensational thought. Those political connotations would become apparent during the Reagan presidency, when critics feared that he was making significant political decisions based on his belief in the impending battle of Armageddon. Kenneth Woodward, writing for *Newsweek* magazine in 1984, said, "Reagan's clerical critics suspect that the president really believes—as he has said—that the Soviet Union is an 'evil empire' and that the United States is therefore fighting God's own enemies. Further, they fear the president has adopted the hard-core fundamentalist view that the Biblical battle of Armageddon is at hand."[5] To Falwell, and presumably to his friend in the White House, society was on the cusp of the End Times, and current events really were building up to the battle of Armageddon. The way that Falwell spoke about prophecy, including Armageddon, was so closely intertwined with current events that for him, prophecy belief was a theological way of talking about the divine struggle between capitalism and communism, between conservativism and liberalism.

Dispensational Node
Armageddon

The church services in which Falwell spoke on prophecy, especially during the 1980s and into the 1990s, were highly performative affairs that drew the audience into the cosmic drama that was unfolding. "One nation under God. That is what our flag means. That is what it represents."[6] The pageantry that filled the auditorium of Thomas Road Baptist Church on July 3, 1983, bore more than a small resemblance to the "I Love America" rallies of the decade before. A military color guard marched down the aisles of the auditorium, bringing the American flag to the podium and presenting it to the congregation. "Proudly she waves, Old Glory," Robbie Hiner, a musician at the church, sang, "over the land of the free." Meanwhile, a montage of images from the national monuments in Washington, DC, played, and then Hiner led the audience in the Pledge of Allegiance. These services were all made for television, whether Falwell had purchased a prime-time spot or whether they would be featured on his standard *Old-Time Gospel Hour* programming. Services that featured topics such as nuclear war and Armageddon were carefully staged celebrations of the impending Rapture and the horrors that were to soon come.

Ironically to the movement Falwell built, Darby had placed little emphasis on the Tribulation and scarcely mentioned the looming battle of Armageddon. His organizing principle was separatism, both separatism from the established church and separatism between the church and Israel. God had distinct plans for both Israel and the church, and they could not be fulfilled simultaneously. Therefore, the church had to be raptured into heaven for God's purposes toward Israel to be fulfilled; the Tribulation would purge Israel of its sins, especially the sin of rejecting the Messiah, and prepare the nation for the coming of the Millennial Reign. This separatism resulted in an apocalyptic understanding of the future, but for Darby, separatism came first; the outcome of that separatism was the apocalyptic narrative that would ultimately become primary to Falwell. The 1909 edition of the *Scofield Reference Bible* contains no commentary on the battle of Armageddon. In fact, the passage in Revelation that speaks about Armageddon—Revelation 16:13–16—has the heading, "Parenthetical"; Armageddon was not the focus of Darby's or even Scofield's teachings.

Popular—as opposed to scholarly—dispensationalism became prominent in America amid the economic and social upheaval of the 1970s, and with this popular dispensationalism came a focus on the battle of Armageddon. This battle would occur at the end of the Tribulation, when the armies of the world—four hundred million soldiers, under the leadership of the antichrist—gather in Israel to wage war against God's chosen people. Before a drop of Jewish blood can be spilled, however, Christ will return and supernaturally destroy all who have taken up arms against Israel, with a special punishment reserved for the antichrist. The slaughter, which Falwell called a "grisly feast of God," will be so great that the blood will flow up to the horse's bridle for two hundred miles, and the people of Israel will spend months burying the dead. In the wake of Armageddon, Christ will set up his throne in Jerusalem and begin his Millennial Reign. "Armageddon," Falwell began in

December 1984, a year after Able Archer. "That word strikes fear into the hearts of people."[7]

Hal Lindsey's *The Late Great Planet Earth*, which was published in 1970 and sold upward of fifteen million copies during that decade, showed a curious American public—not merely dispensational fundamentalists who had long been savvy about the end of the world—how current events were leading up to the battle of Armageddon. Three years later, John Walvoord's *Armageddon, Oil, and the Middle East Crisis* likewise became a bestseller and explained America's current energy woes and economic collapse in terms of prophecy.[8] The dispensational narrative regarding Armageddon pushed back against the liberationist movements that were, in the eyes of conservatives, increasing social upheaval. While agitation for civil rights to be extended to women, queer individuals, and African Americans was upending the social and economic order, apocalyptic portions of the Bible contained sure and certain answers about the future of civilization. This upheaval was prophesied, the likes of Walvoord and Lindsey assured their readers, and there was no cause for alarm. God was in control, and he was supernaturally guiding events toward the Tribulation and ultimate battle of Armageddon. Christians had no need to fear, because they would soon meet the Lord in the air when he comes for his church in the Rapture.

Falwell took an entirely different approach. The Christians of America should not sit idly by while their nation shakes its fists at God and places itself under his wrath. No, they should be agents of conservative change, bringing the American Christian nation back into God's good graces so that it could receive divine blessing as it faced the End Times. All true Christians would soon depart in the Rapture, but until then, they had a duty to God and country to reject the nationwide adoption of the apostasy and take America out of the future reach of the antichrist. In other words, through conservative reform, American Christians could place their nation on the right side of prophecy. After all, Falwell himself stood to lose greatly if America continued sliding down the path of the apostasy, as his segregation academy had already come under scrutiny for racist admissions practices.

So instead of the fatalism of previous dispensational thinkers, he pushed for reform that would keep him in business and prevent more government hand-outs in the form of poverty-reduction programs. He could not change how prophecy would be fulfilled, including the coming battle of Armageddon; these things were biblically foretold and therefore immutable. What he could change was how America faced the End Times while the rest of the world, especially the Soviet Union, slid toward the wrath of God.

On July 3, 1983, Falwell based the sermon "The Two Flags in Today's World" on a biblical text that he consistently used to talk about the End Times, the Olivet Discourse of Matthew 24. "Nation will rise against nation, and kingdom against kingdom: and there shall be famines, and pestilences, and earthquakes in diverse places" (Matt 24:7 KJV). In the decades-long nuclear crisis of the Cold War, the prophecy of the Olivet Discourse was being fulfilled on the evening news. America was surely facing the End Times, as evidenced by the nuclear threat posed by the Soviet Union, even though in this sermon, he did not talk about those events directly. He did not go to great lengths to explain the "four horsemen of the apocalypse" or the "seven bowls of God's wrath," or even mention the coming battle of Armageddon. He only made a passing reference to the Rapture, saying, "I'm not expecting the undertaker but the Upper Taker."[9]

Yet the true meaning of the sermon in which he held up Soviet and American flags—nuclear war was on the horizon and Christians should be glad about the fulfillment of prophecy—could not have been lost on his audience. His audience knew that he was talking about the role of Russia in the End Times and that his talk of impending nuclear war—talk that must have both thrilled and terrified his listeners—was for everyone else, the unsaved, not for them. There was no need for him to directly connect current events to the unfolding of prophecy because his audience already understood what he was really talking about.

"The red, the white, and the blue," he began the sermon. "The United States flag represents a number of things." Those things included freedom of religion, freedom of speech, freedom of travel, freedom of work. Those freedoms, granted by God and capitalism, had to be preserved so that America could continue doing its great work of evangelizing the world. The way to preserve those freedoms was to stay the course of conservativism that Reagan had brought to America, especially the strengthening of the nuclear arsenal. Still, there was no need to fear nuclear war because, according to prophecy, the world would not be destroyed until after Armageddon.

Though Able Archer was still months away from July 3, 1983, Falwell's End Times sermons had long relied heavily on the nuclear threat. "The Soviet Union not only has more conventional military might, but almost twice the nuclear might as we do," he had warned the decade before in "America Back to God." Yet the message he brought forth in "The Two Flags in Today's World," though still hyper-conservative and nationalistic, was fundamentally different, for one critical reason: America was now winning. Citizens had elected a conservative president who was rolling back the economics of civil rights in favor of biblical capitalism. He was building up the nuclear arsenal, thereby ensuring God's blessing instead of his wrath. And like Falwell, President Reagan believed in the looming battle of Armageddon.

Apocalypticism and Dispensational Prophecy

One of the prevailing rules among conservative Bible scholars is to always uphold the divine origins of the Bible, meaning that whatever conclusions they come to, they should never suggest that the Bible says anything that is not true. The most conservative of these scholars consider themselves to be literalists, meaning that they interpret every passage in the Bible as having a literal rather than allegorical or mythological meaning. Those who do not cling to inerrancy might suggest that Noah's flood was a retelling of the flood myths seen in other ancient cultures, albeit with Yahweh at the center of the story, or that the story tells about a local flood of great significance. Literalists, on the other hand, insist that the flood really happened, that it really covered the entire earth, that all of humanity except Noah and his family perished, and that the only animals who survived were those that Noah brought on board the ark.

Literalism takes on increased significance when considering the genre of biblical literature considered to be *apocalyptic*. One example of this literature is found in Daniel, chapters 7 to 12. The passages contain vivid imagery of angels in heaven and on earth, a terrifying beast with a horn that speaks boastful words, spirits with dominion over different nations that war against each other, and the words, "Understand, son of man, that the vision concerns the time of the end" (Dan 8:17 NKJV). Daniel's vision begins with the particularly bizarre passage,

> I saw in my vision by night, and behold, the four winds of heaven were stirring up the Great Sea. And four great beasts came up from the sea, each different from the other. The first was like a lion and had eagle's wings. I watched till its wings were plucked off; and it was lifted up from the earth and made to stand on two feet like a man, and a man's heart was given to it. (Dan 7:2–4 NKJV)

Many observers have looked at passages such as this one as abstract ways of giving hope to people who were living under severe oppression, of interpreting events in a way that provides a cosmic and eternal victory despite temporary persecution, and of communicating coded messages that cannot be deciphered by the powers that be. Those who cling to biblical literalism, on the other hand, believe that there must be a literal fulfillment to passages such as the one above. If there were not four literal beasts that rose out of the sea when this passage was originally penned, then this event will occur in the future. In other words, literalists—Jerry Falwell included—tend to read apocalyptic passages in the Bible as prophecy about the future.

The book of Ezekiel contains imagery that rivals that of Daniel, with the opening of the vision saying,

> Then I looked, and behold, a whirlwind was coming out of the north, a great cloud with raging fire engulfing itself; and brightness was all around it and radiating out of its midst like the color of amber, out of the midst of the fire. Also from within it came the likeness of four living creatures. And this was their appearance: they had the likeness of a man. Each one had four faces, and each one had four wings. Their legs were straight, and the soles of their feet were like the soles of calves' feet. They sparkled like the color of burnished bronze. The hands of a man were under their wings on their four sides; and each of the four had faces and wings. (Ezek 1:4–8 NKJV)

Each of the creatures in Ezekiel's vision possesses a wheel, with another wheel inside. The rims of the wheels are full of eyes, and when the creatures ascend and descend from heaven, the wheels travel with them.

Scholars who do not see literalism as a necessity for biblical interpretation tend to view Ezekiel as part of the same genre to which Daniel belongs, Jewish apocalyptic literature. It has a specific context, during the period of ancient Israelite history known as the Babylonian exile, and especially the more apocalyptic passages of Ezekiel speak solely to that context. Literalists disagree with this approach and, as with Daniel, see Ezekiel as communicating literal history, whether that history already happened or future history, in the form of prophecy.

Of all the apocalyptic passages in the Bible, none compares to Revelation, the last book of the New Testament. Christians throughout history have seen many different ways of interpreting the imagery that seems to have no end to its otherworldliness and altogether strangeness.

> I looked when he opened the sixth seal, and behold, there was a great earthquake; and the sun became black as sackcloth of hair, and the moon became like blood. And the stars of heaven fell to the earth, as a fig tree drops its late figs when it is shaken by a mighty wind. Then the sky receded as a scroll when it is rolled up, and every mountain and island was moved out of its place. (Rev 6:12–14 NKJV)

Coupled with the bizarre depictions of the cosmos, such as of stars falling from heaven and the sky being rolled back like a scroll, are profound images of what is happening in heaven, especially in the throne room of God. Tens of thousands of angels fall down in worship and exalt the Lamb of God, understood by many to be the slain and resurrected Christ. These visions of heaven undoubtedly gave hope to Christians who, at the time of Revelation's writing, were experiencing severe persecution.

In the two millennia since the time of Christ, Christians facing uncertainty, chaos, and duress have looked to apocalyptic passages such as those above, sometimes leading to surges of interest in prophecy. One such time of renewed enthusiasm for prophecy occurred in Britain in the beginning of the nineteenth century, during the Napoleonic Wars (1803–1815). Prophecy conferences, which sought to understand the meaning of current events through the lens of Scripture, sprang up all across Britain and Ireland, and this milieu shaped the End Times calendar found in John Nelson Darby's system of dispensationalism. He drew from apocalyptic passages in books such as Daniel, Ezekiel, and Revelation and did something rather innovative. Prophecy teachers at the time were looking to certain events that were already occurring and showing how they were the fulfillments of certain apocalyptic passages of prophecy; this approach led many teachers to set dates for when further events of prophecy would unfold. Current events would invariably occur differently, and prophecy teachers would either re-work their prophecy interpretation or, disgraced, leave their profession.

Rather than suggesting that certain apocalyptic imagery applies to a specific event already occurring during the Napoleonic era, Darby said that prophecy is for the future, for the time of Tribulation that will occur after the Rapture. He was able to avoid the humiliation of other prophecy teachers by refusing to set dates on when these events would occur. Instead, he began developing what would become the End Times calendar of dispensationalism, the series of events between the Rapture and the Millennial Reign. This approach was known as futurism, meaning that all these events are still future and cannot be expected until after the Rapture. Futurism gave Darby's followers a way of literalizing the Bible's apocalyptic passages, of seeing them as part of human history, without the humiliation that faced those who set dates for when the next apocalyptic prophecy would be fulfilled. Dispensationalists came to see apocalyptic passages in the Bible as flooded with prophecy about what will happen as the earth enters its final days. No matter how bizarre the imagery, it depicts a literal event that, if it has not yet occurred in the past, will occur in the future.

Still, Darby's eschatology was highly influenced by the political events of his day, especially the Protestant-Catholic tensions that plagued Europe. With the apocalyptic imagery that he drew on in the books of Daniel and Revelation, he interpreted the "Roman Empire" of biblical apocalypticism as the Roman Catholic Church. To him, the Roman Empire had never truly gone away; it had merely changed form and would be fully revived in the End Times, with the pope gaining control of the world as the antichrist.

There were other political challenges, as well, that Darby's eschatology addressed. European politics of the nineteenth century, which were riddled with the theological challenges of Christendom, faced quandaries about what to do with Jews, the "people of God" who refused to worship Christ. To gain support for his campaign in the Middle East, in 1799, Napoleon had declared that Palestine is for the Jews and offered them the right to return to their ancestral homeland. Thus, Napoleon (perhaps inadvertently) resolved a perennial theological problem for European Christendom, of the conversion of the Jews so that they would join the church (and, for nineteenth-century Britain, be given full civil rights). Napoleon's "right of return" suggested that actually, rather than converting to Christianity, the Jews might return to Palestine while retaining their own religious and cultural identities. This new approach to European Jewry, that they might actually become their own nation rather than having to assimilate into European Christendom, had a profound impact on Darby's eschatology. He taught the return of the Jews to Palestine as part of the End Times, and over this nation Christ would—in literal fulfillment of the Bible's apocalyptic passages—reign over them, as an earthly king with an earthly kingdom.

Falwell's Signs of the Times

Falwell was nothing if not an innovator, especially with regard to prophecy. Since World War I, many American dispensationalists—while claiming to not set dates for prophecy fulfillment—have viewed current events through the lens of prophecy. Lindsey, who spoke at Thomas Road Baptist Church on several occasions, claimed in *The Late Great Planet Earth* that in the Bible, "one generation" meant about forty years. Since the state of Israel had gained official recognition in 1948, the Rapture must occur within one generation, or by 1988. Despite repeated claims to not be setting dates, Lindsey and Falwell both believed that the 1980s represented the Tribulation. At the very least, since the Rapture had to occur by the end of the decade, the way that the Cold War was unfolding meant that the Tribulation was near.

Falwell's innovation, above and beyond Lindsey's assertion that the Rapture had to happen by 1988, was the role that America would play as this End Times drama of the 1980s played out. Gone was the fatalism that had beset so many other prophecy teachers since Darby; American Christians could—and should, on a political level—change how their nation faced the End Times and the coming wrath of God. He prayed at the beginning of "The Two Flags," "But between now and [the Rapture], oh God, help us to occupy till you come. And our Father, help us not to be fatalists, but cause us to be spiritual and biblical activists, affecting the course of history." His followers could not change future history, as it had been divinely prophesied in the Bible. But America was not in the Bible, and they could, through nuclear build-up and biblical capitalism, change how it faced the dark days that surely lay ahead. America could be on the right side of prophecy.

During the 1970s, Falwell preached at least two major series on the events of the End Times. In 1973 and into 1974, he taught a Pastor's Bible Class series, entitled *The Book of Revelation*, which included thirty-eight one-hour lessons on how prophecy would unfold in the End Times. Later in the decade, in 1979 and 1980, he promoted an eight-part sermon series entitled *Dr. Jerry Falwell Teaches Bible Prophecy*, which included a study guide/workbook that participants could use to follow along with the sermon tapes. The workbook included the "signs of the times," events that were currently unfolding and indicated the Rapture was at hand. "Of course we are specifically told that neither man nor angel can know the exact time when Christ shall come again," Falwell said.[10] No one, not even the most ardent student of prophecy, could know the date when the Rapture would occur. Yet there were signs that the End was at hand, as Falwell repeatedly said that he believes he is of the terminal generation that will go up in the Rapture.

Falwell's "signs of the times" read as a list of contemporary events from the 1970s. They included "intense demonic activity," evidenced by vegetarianism, witchcraft, hard drugs, and astrology (paradoxically, Nancy Reagan was known to consult with an astrologer while in the White House), as well as the apostasy of liberal theology and the Social Gospel. Oddly for a man who extolled capitalism as the economic system endorsed by the Bible, Falwell warned that, prior to the Rapture, "soul-murdering materialism would also worm its way into the local church."[11] Overpopulation, an "intensification in knowledge"[12] that included America's public schools, and an absence of leadership were also, according to Falwell, biblically prophesied signs that indicated history is on the cusp of the Rapture.

Many of his signs of the times, such as the unification of the systems of the world, pointed to how current events were lining up, in accordance with prophecy, for the coming Tribulation. Falwell claimed of the events of the Tribulation that "the Antichrist will someday successfully unite the religious, political, and economic systems of the earth under his evil control. Although this goal will not be fully achieved until he assumes complete power, we can nevertheless see the approaching stormclouds."[13] Within the church, those storm clouds included Protestants "uniting with Roman Catholics"[14] and the formation of the United Methodist Church through a merger of the Methodist Church and Evangelical United Brethren Church. Most significantly, at least on the religious front, was the development and growth of the World Council of Churches; Falwell claimed that, in accordance with prophecy, "The World Council of Churches is uniting with various heathen religions."[15] He was pointing to interfaith efforts by the WCC to bring together Jews, Muslims, Buddhists, Hindus, and so forth, along with Christians of all denominations to advance the cause of peace. During the Tribulation, the antichrist would take over the WCC and declare himself to be God, forcing the entire world to worship him.

The counterpart to the WCC was the United Nations, whose formation in 1948 was also a sign that the End is near. Falwell believed that the UN was a precursor to a one-world government—the revived Roman Empire of Darby—through which the antichrist would become a global dictator and false messiah during the Tribulation. "The United Nations is nothing more than the political side of this Babylon, this confused coalition," he said in his 1973–1974 series on the End Times, "and the World Council of Churches is nothing more than the religious Babylon. They will marry each other very soon. When they do, and even now as you see these signs of the times, we can know that our redemption draweth nigh."[16] The UN and WCC would soon merge—"marry each other"—in such a way that the antichrist would be able to gain political and religious control of the world.

This control would be exemplified by the mark of the beast, the 666 that all people living during the Tribulation must have inscribed on their hand or forehead in order to engage in any commercial activity. In other words, the reign of the antichrist was the natural completion of communism. Rather than a capitalist, free market in which people of all faiths, especially Christians, can buy and sell goods, people living through the Tribulation will have to worship the antichrist to purchase the basics that they need. Those who refuse to worship him would die as martyrs, either of starvation from the inability to buy food or by the sword when they refuse to renounce their faith in Christ. Falwell called on America to disengage from the UN, a move that, according to his dispensational thinking, would make the country difficult for the antichrist to gain dominance over. At a minimum, America would be on the right side of prophecy, on God's side of the geopolitical struggle that would continue unfolding as the world sped toward Armageddon. For the time being at least, American Christians could retain their freedom, as they would not have to worship anybody other than Christ in order to buy and sell; they could continue worshiping as their consciences dictate. Additionally, without the UN and its looming shadow of antichrist communism, American capitalism could endure.

The surest sign that the End was near, that the Rapture would occur at any moment, was the regathering of world Jewry into the land of Palestine and the 1948 creation of the state of Israel. While Christian ethics has led many to express concern for the dispossessed Palestinians, Christian Zionism—which is openly hostile to Palestinians, including Palestinian Christians—was central to Falwell's conservative activism. The wrath of God during the Tribulation would prepare the land of Israel for the Millennial Reign of Christ, which would commence after the battle of Armageddon. Until that time, though, Christian America had a responsibility toward God to support Israel militarily against the Arabs who surrounded her; this imperative was so significant to

Falwell that he rejected entirely President Carter's Camp David Accords, which led to a truce between Israel and Egypt. He claimed of the treaty,

> In spite of the rosy and utterly unrealistic expectations by our government, this treaty will not be a lasting treaty. . . . We are certainly praying for the peace of Jerusalem . . . But you and I know that there's not going to be any real peace in the Middle East until one day, the Lord Jesus sits down upon the throne of David in Jerusalem and rules and reigns for 1000 years on this earth. We call this the Millennial Age, the Golden Age, the Age of our Lord and Savior, Jesus Christ.[17]

Support for Israel could not include efforts to reduce tensions between Israel and the surrounding Arab countries, as these tensions were biblical. Rather, support for Israel meant helping the country prepare for the Tribulation, when it would be ceaselessly invaded by other countries as part of its judgment by God.

The principal country that would invade Israel would be Russia. Recent developments in Russia were another one of Falwell's signs of the times, as the communist Soviets were the enemies of God. Ezekiel 38 speaks of an invading army from the north, the land of Magog, and Falwell was one of many dispensationalists to believe that this passage is a prophecy about an event that will occur during the Tribulation. Russia's growing influence on the world stage during the Cold War was evidence that events were aligning, accordingly with prophecy, toward this invasion.

In Falwell's paradox of End Times thinking, these "signs of the times" were both reversible and irreversible. They were irreversible in that the Bible had foretold the decline of society, especially in the days immediately preceding the Rapture. There was nothing that anyone could do to stem the tide of the End Times; as Falwell claimed in "America Back to God," "I think our society is damned." Yet he immediately followed that statement with, "But I do believe that we could have such a visitation from God. God could give us an extension of time and liberties and freedom for the ultimate purpose of carrying out the Great Commission." During the 1970s, the moral decay of society was *slightly and temporarily* reversible because he believed America had a special role to play in the End Times. Part of that role was supporting Israel against Arab and Soviet aggression, alongside promoting world evangelization; hence America, should it temporarily halt its social decline, could have an impact on cosmic history. Yet that history would unfold, with or without America, because it was biblically foretold.

In other words, the "signs of the times" that Falwell proclaimed in the 1970s became the core of his reformist agenda in the 1980s. Increased influence of the UN and WCC meant the antichrist would soon rise to power; America had to demand its own national sovereignty against the internationalism that the UN and WCC represented. Israel was facing persecution from the Arab states and Russia; rather than negotiating for a false peace, as President Carter had done, America had to arm Israel. Hard drugs being peddled to children meant that the Rapture was at hand; Falwell wanted to see the death penalty imposed on anyone who tried to sell drugs to children. Liberals were demanding that the government had to solve their problems, in such a way that would cause the antichrist to be seen as a savior; America had to end all government welfare programs and insist that people provide for themselves. In doing so, America could distance itself from the unfolding of prophecy, from the terrifying reign of the antichrist, from the wrath of God that would soon fall. The rest of the world was careening toward the Tribulation, but at least for Christian America, the signs of the times were reversible. God could bless America, even while the rest of the world was facing his wrath.

Righteousness Exalteth America

America's newfound conservativism under Reagan made the difference in how the country would face the End Times. In Falwell's view, the government was rolling back failed liberal policies in favor of Godly, unregulated capitalism and nuclear build-up. The Sunday after preaching "The Two Flags in Today's World," he laid the blame for America's demise in the 1950s, 1960s, and 1970s on the "Me Generation," the Baby Boomers upon whom parents lavished all the material products money could buy. For Falwell, the rise of the "Me Generation" was not a natural outcome of capitalism following the economic stimulus of World War II. No, the profit motive of capitalism combined with the exponential expansion of America's military had nothing to do with the rise of consumerism among the Baby Boomers. The problem was that well-intentioned parents who had lived through the Great Depression "gave things and things and things to their children, automobiles and comforts and luxuries."[18] But with this newfound material prosperity, "they failed to communicate and to pass on the values, the spiritual and moral values that make those things important. And those things became corruption in the hands of our children." As a result, he bemoaned, "our young people became captives of an anticapitalistic, anti-American, pro-socialist, pro-Marxist philosophy. And for two decades, the sixties and most of the seventies, this country almost went to hell."

Young people on college campuses, goaded by left-leaning professors, had burned the American flag in protest of the Vietnam War; they had no understanding of how to be God-fearing, capitalist-loving, patriotic Americans. Thus was fulfilled the prophecy of 2 Timothy 3:1–5, which says that in the End Times, "men shall be lovers of their own selves, covetous, boasters, proud, blasphemers, disobedient to parents, unthankful, unholy, without natural affection, trucebreakers, false accusers, incontinent, fierce, despisers of those that are good, traitors, heady, high-minded, lovers of pleasures more than lovers of God" (KJV). Here was irrefutable proof that prophecies about the build-up to the End Times were being fulfilled, and America was on the verge of collapse.

But then came Ronald Reagan, who began his presidency by dismantling social programs that had benefited the poor and marginalized of America in favor of big business, unregulated capitalism, and nuclear build-up. In the same sermon that he explained the social decline of the Me Generation, Falwell went on to extol the virtues of Reaganomics by asking, "Why is it Ronald Reagan's economy is coming back to health? Righteousness exalteth a nation, Proverbs 14:34." Yet the nation's prosperity went far beyond just the marks of wealth in a deregulated economy. "Why is it Mr. Reagan is getting his military budget through congress? Why is it that he is winning in his efforts to re-defense and restrengthen the military preparedness of this nation? Righteousness exalteth a nation." Though the decline of society was inevitable because it was biblically prophesied, America had proven that it could reverse course and be blessed by God during the End Times.

Ronald Reagan and Armageddon

Did Reagan share Falwell's view that current events were signs that the End is at hand? During the presidential debate between President Reagan and his challenger, Walter Mondale, on October 21, 1984, Marvin Kalb of NBC News said to the president, "You've been quoted as saying that you do believe, deep down, that we are heading for some kind of biblical Armageddon. Your Pentagon and your Secretary of Defense have plans for the United States to fight and prevail in a nuclear war."[19] Implied in Kalb's comment is the terror that some people really did feel about Reagan's nuclear build-up, that it was motivated by prophecy belief. Did the president see his role as leader of America during the Cold War as part of a cosmic struggle between good and evil? Enough people believed so for Kalb to ask him about Armageddon during a presidential debate.

Reagan shrugged off Kalb's comment by referring to "some philosophical discussions with people who are interested in the same things" and suggested that "a number of theologians for the last decade or more have believed that this was true, that the prophecies are coming together that portend [Armageddon]. But," he clarified, possibly to ease suspicion that his policies were based on prophecy belief, "no one knows whether Armageddon, those prophecies mean that Armageddon is a thousand years away or day after tomorrow."[20] He then segued into talking about how America would survive a nuclear war because of his new program, the Strategic Defense Initiative (SDI), nicknamed "Star Wars." SDI was a defense program that would essentially create a shield around America and shoot down any missiles that might come from the Soviet Union. Andrew Lang, a writer for the Christic Institute during the 1980s, claimed that "Dr. Falwell's support for President Reagan's 'Star Wars' program as 'our last and final hope' is predicated on the belief that the United States and the Soviet 'evil empire' are destined to collide."[21]

Surprisingly for many, the Reagan era, along with the decade of the 1980s, ended without the Rapture occurring. All of the events leading up to the fulfillment of prophecy had fallen into place, yet the End Times did not come. Then the Soviet Union collapsed, the Iron Curtain fell, and the Cold War ended, without Soviet Magog invading Israel. Yet prophecy belief is very malleable and able to absorb new political events, new eschatological enemies of God, and with them, new signs of the times. With Russia now in the background, prophecy belief during the administration of George H. W. Bush (president 1989–1993) came to center on a different power entirely: Iraq.

Babylon and Armageddon

On August 2, 1990, shortly after the Berlin Wall fell and while the Soviet Union was in its death throes, Saddam Hussein launched an invasion of the tiny Persian Gulf country of Kuwait. Iraq had recently come out of an eight-year war with Iran, during which Saddam had seemingly emulated the ancient Mesopotamian leader Nebuchadnezzar. Nebuchadnezzar had, as Saddam was attempting in his war with Iran, expanded his territory across the Middle East so that it spread from Persia to Palestine. And then in the midst of the Iran-Iraq War, Saddam began rebuilding Nebuchadnezzar's capital city of Babylon. "By rebuilding Nebuchadnezzar's city, Hussein has a natural opportunity to portray himself as Nebuchadnezzar's successor,"[22] wrote Charles Dyer, a dispensationalist scholar at Dallas Theological Seminary. "I could not help noticing the emphasis placed on Saddam Hussein and the comparisons between Hussein and Nebuchadnezzar." Perhaps in rebuilding Babylon, Hussein was attempting to cast himself as a new Nebuchadnezzar for the modern world. Whatever his motive, the rebuilding of Babylon and subsequent invasion of Kuwait stirred prophecy belief, moving it away from communism and the Soviet Union and toward the Middle East. "Babylon will be a great city again,"[23] Dyer declared, referring to prophecy. And before the world's eyes, Saddam, the self-styled Nebuchadnezzar, was rebuilding the ancient city.

In his efforts to reconstruct Babylon, Saddam had to channel massive financial resources to the building project, in addition to the enormous cost of the eight-year war with Iran. Iraq's oil reserves did not generate enough cash flow to pay for these projects, and to make things worse, overproduction in the late 1980s caused the price of oil to drop. Saddam began accusing the tiny country of Kuwait of siphoning off Iraqi oil from an oil field along the Iraq-Kuwait border. When the ruling house of Kuwait refused to give in to Saddam's demands, he sent his army to attack. Over 4,000 Kuwaitis died in the first fourteen hours of combat, after which Kuwait's resistance collapsed. Saddam was poised to gain control over a massive portion of the world's oil supply.

Fundamentalism in America, including dispensationalism, has long been deeply rooted in the belief that the Bible prescribes a particular approach to economics. The dispensationalist response to Saddam's invasion of Kuwait showed how these economics were now playing out in the oil fields of the Middle East, especially Babylon. "In August 1990 the armies of Iraq invaded Kuwait, a small but wealthy oil nation, which greatly increased the power of Iraq in controlling the oil of the Middle East,"[24] John Walvoord wrote in the 1991 edition of *Armageddon, Oil, and the Middle East Crisis*, updated from the 1974 version about another oil crisis and biblical prophecy. "If the invading armies had moved rapidly into Saudi Arabia, Hussein might have controlled 50% of the oil of the world."[25] God's purposes for the world in unfolding prophecy were being fulfilled through the economics of oil, in this case, by causing Iraq (Babylon) to dominate an increasing number of oil fields and attain unparalleled riches. Economics, specifically the economics of oil, were key to prophecy, as riches were to accumulate in the Middle East as part of the End Times. Walvoord said, analyzing the source of this wealth, "For many years, the explanation for this has been the presence of a major portion of the world's oil." He went on to ask, "Are the immense resources of oil in the Middle East part of the divine plan to make the Middle East the theatre of end-time events?"[26] The answer was yes; the current tensions caused by Saddam's invasion of Kuwait fit into the pattern of End Times prophecy.

As tensions were building, the atmosphere at Falwell's Thomas Road Baptist Church became tense and jubilant with expectation of prophecy fulfillment. "We've watched as the world has mobilized its forces," said gospel-singing legend Doug Oldham, as he opened a broadcast of Falwell's *Old-Time Gospel Hour*, "tanks, planes, ships, troops, all preparing for a face-off that could well lead to all-out war."[27] Yet despite the anxious tone of Oldham's voice, his message was not one of despair or doomsaying. "It fills men's hearts with fear," he went on, "unless they understand God's plan for his people." God's plan was to rapture his people into heaven before the world could spiral into the Tribulation and ultimately toward Armageddon; Falwell affirmed as much in his sermon, which was part of yet another series on prophecy, preached in response to Saddam's invasion of Kuwait.

Whether or not President George H. W. Bush believed that prophecy was being fulfilled in the Middle East,[28] America's, and the world's, supply of oil was at stake. On January 16, 1991, America entered the Persian Gulf War to liberate Kuwait and thereby ensure ongoing access to the oil fields of the Middle East.

The *Left Behind* Phenomenon

Still, the Rapture did not occur, and following the administration of President George H. W. Bush, America ended its twelve years of conservative presidents in favor of the apostasy. Bill Clinton, a liberal Democrat, became president in 1993. "Sodom and Gomorrah," Falwell said shortly after his election, referencing the biblical story that gave rise to the term "sodomy." "If you know how God dealt with Sodom and Gomorrah, it should concern you that we are entering such an era."[29] He had declared over a decade before that God had sent the AIDS epidemic to America as a punishment for toleration of gay lifestyles, and now president-elect Clinton wanted to appoint an AIDS czar immediately upon taking office, to coordinate the government's response to the epidemic. He even had openly queer people serving in his administration and wanted to end the ban on gay people serving in the military. In addition, he wanted to socialize healthcare—at the expense of America's nuclear arsenal—and expand abortion access across the country. With Clinton as president, the wrath of God was not far away. In fact, in his documentary *The Truth about AIDS* that Falwell produced immediately after Clinton's inauguration, he directly connected the AIDS epidemic to the destruction of Sodom and Gomorrah; AIDS was God's means of bringing apostate America to its knees.

"I believe God has given us the president we, the American people, deserve,"[30] Falwell declared on *Larry King Live* in 1998. "We are in serious trouble. I believe God is about to judge this nation." By legitimizing queer lifestyles and bringing the queer community into American public life, President Clinton was rejecting the nuclear family values that Falwell had been promoting since the 1970s. America was leaving unregulated capitalism and the nuclear family for the apostasy of liberalism—government-run welfare programs that included socialized medicine, the liberationism of civil-rights movements that had emerged from the Social Gospel, and a weakened military that now included gay people. The liberal apostates had, in keeping with prophecy, been organizing against God to push through their socialist agenda, and now they were in control of the American government. The queer agenda, the socialistic agenda, the feminist agenda that Clinton brought into the halls of power in Washington, DC, were part of a liberal, communist conspiracy—the same communist conspiracy that had included the civil rights movement during the 1950s and 1960s—to bring America under the wrath of God.

Yet for Falwell, the Clinton apostasy was so much more than promoting equal rights for the queer community and trying to provide a coordinated response to the AIDS crisis. In 1994, filmmaker Patrick Matrisciana produced the documentary *The Clinton Chronicles*, in which a former Clinton staffer in Arkansas, Larry Nichols, accused the governor-turned-president of crimes that included laundering drug money and political assassinations. During Nichols's time serving under Governor Clinton, he made hundreds of unauthorized phone calls from his office to the Nicaraguan Contra rebels of Central America, the same groups that the Reagan administration had illegally supported in the Iran-Contra Scandal. He was fired for the phone calls and came to believe that Clinton himself had long been engaged in gun-running, money-laundering, and cocaine shipments from Central America; he attempted to prove as much in the documentary and, by publicizing it, to convince the American public. *The Clinton Chronicles* gave rise to a new conspiracy theory, the "Clinton body count," claiming that untold opponents and whistleblowers had turned up dead or missing. Falwell promoted the video tirelessly, advertising it in his *National Liberty Journal* and even showing it to a national audience on his *Old-Time Gospel Hour*. The Clinton presidency could only be yet another Sign of the Times.

By the time of Clinton's election in 1992, Tim LaHaye and his co-writer, Jerry Jenkins, were working on a series called *Left Behind*, which dramatized the events of the Tribulation for a popular audience. The first book, *Left Behind: A Novel of the Earth's Last Days*, came out in 1995 and tells of the Rapture and its immediate fall-out. In an instant, millions of people around the world disappear into thin air, leaving behind their clothes and loved ones who did not know Christ (or, presumably, believe in Bible prophecy). Not far into the series, the antichrist, a charismatic man named Nicolae Carpathia, takes over the United Nations and moves its headquarters from New York to Babylon. A fierce persecution of Christians who come to faith during the Tribulation begins, and all who place their faith in Christ during this period of God's wrath can expect to die as martyrs.

Falwell had been preaching for decades about the vast numbers of people who would come to faith in Christ during the Tribulation and then die as martyrs; in LaHaye's books, virtually all the "Tribulation saints" convert to Christianity with the knowledge that they will die for their faith. Indeed, many of them do. Though most evangelical churches in America were not explicitly dispensationalist like Thomas Road Baptist (despite incursions of popular dispensational belief, such as the 666 and expectation of the Rapture), *Left Behind* was an unprecedented success. By the end of the decade, so many people had bought the books that they were hitting the *New York Times* bestseller list upon release. With an estimated eighty million copies sold (not including copies checked out from libraries and sold in used form), along with numerous spin-offs such as *Left Behind: The Kids* and *Left Behind* movies, people all across America had some level of contact with the story that the books told. Prophecy belief quickly consumed evangelical America, as evangelicals who had never seriously engaged with teachings about the Rapture prior to *Left Behind* suddenly began to believe that the Tribulation was at hand. Central to these evangelicals' newfound dispensational faith was the prospect of martyrdom. The *Left Behind* phenomenon, in which conservative Christians became, on an unprecedented scale, captivated with prophecy and the End Times, had begun.

And then on April 20, 1999, two students walked into Columbine High School carrying homemade bombs, two sawed-off shotguns, a carbine rifle, and a semi-automatic pistol. When the bombs they had planted in the cafeteria did not go off as planned, the boys began throwing homemade pipe bombs and shooting indiscriminately. One teacher and twelve students died before the shooters turned their guns on themselves, bringing the death toll of the massacre to fifteen.

Disinformation in the immediate aftermath of the Columbine massacre spread far and wide to people across America who were desperate for answers as to how this tragedy could have occurred. That disinformation fueled the *Left Behind* phenomenon in ways that no one could have anticipated. Two of the students killed, Cassie Bernall and Rachel Scott, were devout evangelical Christians. One of the disinformation stories that quickly spread was that the shooters had asked the girls—Rachel outside of the school as the shooters first began their rampage, Cassie in the library where most of the victims died—if they believe in God. Upon answering yes, the girls were shot and killed. (There was one girl in the library who did say yes, Valeen Schnurr, but she survived the massacre and was not sensationalized by the media.) Multiple investigations into the Columbine shooting revealed that Cassie and Rachel did not die as martyrs; the only witness to Rachel's murder could not attest to the martyr story, and Emily Wyant, the girl hiding under the library table with Cassie when she was shot, said numerous times that Cassie had not been asked anything. The gunman had banged on the table under which Cassie and Emily were hiding and said, "Peek-a-boo," before shooting her in the head. However, the results of those investigations did not sway Falwell and the tens of millions who had been reading LaHaye's *Left Behind* novels.

In fact, the Sunday after the massacre, Falwell's *Old-Time Gospel Hour* finished yet another weeks-long sermon series on the End Times. Through his preoccupation with the End Times, he had primed his followers to hear the message that he would bring in the weeks and months after the shooting: that the shooters had gone on their rampage to target Christians. He pointed to the evangelical faith of most of the students who had died, in addition to the supposed martyrdoms of Cassie and Rachel, to show that the massacre was really an effort to persecute Christians. What he did not say explicitly, though his followers certainly heard, was that the Bible had predicted that this persecution would come in the End Times.

In a mass email that he sent out on April 30, just ten days after the Columbine shooting, he pointed to the removal of "a granite tablet engraved with the Ten Commandments from a public locality"[31] in Manhattan, Kansas. He went on to claim that "the [American Civil Liberties Union] and Americans United [for Separation of Church and State] continue to tear at the only moral fabric that can penetrate and change the hearts of malicious teens like the two gunmen in Littleton, Colorado." In a later mass email that he distributed in the fall, he insisted that the families of the victims were facing religious persecution; elsewhere he said his ministry was distributing textbook covers with the Ten Commandments to teenage students who wanted to take a stand for their faith.[32] The point was clear: God had been kicked out of America's public schools, and the slide into immorality had only increased under Clinton. This failed experiment with liberalism had led to the massacre, and Christians had a duty to stand up for their faith in the face of this new persecution.

To Falwell, the Columbine shooting was about two things: Christian persecution and the moral decline of society, under the Clinton presidency, into liberalism and apostasy, a decline that caused teenage boys to become mass murderers. They were atheistic, amoral, haters of God—terms that he used to describe liberals; a liberal Supreme Court that had ruled to kick God out of public schools had caused them to kill. His followers, especially those who had been reading *Left Behind*, would have immediately connected those two elements to prophecies about the End Times. Liberals were trying to enact gun laws, but in his "Taking America Back" sermon that he preached in response to the massacre, he claimed that "passing gun-control laws is a waste of time."[33] The problem was spiritual and could be measured by the degree to which liberals were controlling America's culture, how much America had, since Clinton's election, slid back into the apostasy, thereby causing kids to kill kids. What the liberals did not know was that, with Christian persecution and even teenage martyrdom now a reality, in accordance with prophecy, Christians needed guns to protect themselves.

In fact, in the *National Liberty Journal* that Falwell had begun distributing in the 1990s, the July issue after the April massacre denounced the idea of gun control in terms reminiscent of communism. Similar to Soviet-era Russia, now-liberal America was "a Godless, immoral, and valueless society," even though Founding Father John Adams had said, "Our Constitution was made only for a moral and religious people." The real issue was that America's courts had taken God out of public schools and were attempting to force Christianity out of all public life. "The surprise is not that Littleton [the site of the Columbine massacre] occurred," the article read, "but that Littleton has not occurred more often."[34] The implication was that, unless America returned to God as it had under Reagan, unless America ended its liberalism that had begun anew under Clinton, unless America stopped trying to enact gun legislation and instead put God back in the public schools, more Littletons would mean that more Christians would die as martyrs.

But the entire End Times narrative about the Columbine massacre that Falwell and LaHaye helped build did not correspond with the facts that investigations revealed. Cassie and Rachel were not teenage martyrs, and their deaths had nothing to do with the Christian persecution that would come during the End Times. Yet in this climate of growing prophecy belief among America's fundamentalists and evangelicals, their right to worship freely as Christians was perceived to be at stake. This coming End Times persecution was, as with other aspects of prophecy, both inevitable and preventable. Christians could, and indeed should, continue pressing for policies that would preserve their religious freedom—policies that included bringing prayer and Bible-reading back into public schools, allowing Ten Commandments monoliths and manger scenes to be placed in public spaces, overturning Supreme Court rulings that prohibited teacher-led prayer and Bible-reading in public schools, and now more than ever, being able to carry guns that would protect Christians from their would-be persecutors. Yet despite efforts to legislate policies that would favor fundamentalist Christianity, the massacre was a sure sign the End Times persecution would come, that it was closer now than ever. Falwell may not have said as much directly, but in the sixth *Left Behind* book that was released four months after Columbine, a group of "Tribulation saints" attempts to assassinate the antichrist with a gun. The message was clear: Christians had to arm themselves against their End Times persecutors. Further, in the *Left Behind* video game that came out in 2006, players can opt to kill infidels who do not convert to Christianity to preserve their own lives.

In the face of the increasing End Times hysteria following the shooting, Falwell seemed to lose sight of the fact that Cassie and Rachel were seventeen-year-old girls who died at school. His narrative of Christian persecution and the End Times, of teenage martyrdom and students taking a stand for Christ with book covers, seemed to overshadow the tragedy of all the people who died that day. He did not acknowledge that the trauma of the massacre would mar the lives of the survivors and family members, that many would go on to develop drug addictions and even die of suicide, that the community of Littleton would be devastated for a generation. That the children and teacher who died were gone, would never go home to their families again, that "Columbine" would no longer be known as the name of a flower or even a high school but rather the archetype of modern mass shootings.

Global Terror and Armageddon

Still, the Rapture did not come. But in the summer of 2001, shortly after George W. Bush took the office of United States President, LaHaye founded the Tim LaHaye School of Prophecy at Falwell's Liberty University. There was to be no slowing down of prophecy belief; even without the Soviet menace locked in an arms race with the American Christian nation, Falwell and LaHaye promoting prophecy belief together would cause it to accelerate. As it accelerated, it would, like a snowball rolling down a hillside, attract more and more material—more snow, rocks, sticks; violence in public schools, socialistic government policies, the steady beat of the abortion drum, gay-rights activism, feminism, secular humanism, now alongside breakdown in the Middle East and religious pluralism in America.

Then one Tuesday morning, four commercial airplanes became missiles when a group of terrorists hijacked them shortly after takeoff. Two hit the Twin Towers of the World Trade Center in downtown Manhattan, one hit the Pentagon, and one was aimed for another national target in Washington, DC, but was diverted to a farm field in Pennsylvania. When America was attacked on 9/11, Falwell was already in the midst of yet another sermon series on prophecy and the Middle East. "The images replayed on our TV sets of the September 11 terrorist attacks on America will never be erased. The news footage of the World Trade Center buildings and the Pentagon reminded us of an apocalyptic scene lifted right out of the book of the Revelation,"[35] Falwell said two weeks later, in an *Old-Time Gospel Hour* broadcast that he dedicated to prophecy in light of 9/11. But his rhetoric around the attacks contained nothing new; it was merely the aggregate of this snowball that he had been pushing down the hill of society's decay since the 1950s.

"What we saw on Tuesday, as terrible as it was, could be miniscule if, in fact, God continues to lift the curtain and allow the enemies of America to give us probably what we deserve,"[36] Falwell said on Pat Robertson's *700 Club* two days after the attacks. "The ACLU has got to take a lot of the blame for this," he went on. "And I know I'll hear from them on this, but throwing God successfully, with the help of the federal court system, throwing God out of the public square, out of the schools . . ." Throwing God out of the public schools through the Supreme Court cases that began with *Brown v Board of Education* and went on to *Engel v Vitale* (1962, which prohibited state officials from composing a prayer for schoolchildren to recite) and *Abington v Schempp* (1963, which removed daily Bible readings and prayer) had already led to the Columbine massacre. And America had not responded to Columbine by putting God back into public schools but rather by attempting to institute gun-control laws that would make Christians sitting ducks for their would-be persecutors. Now, God was so angry with America that he had sent the terror attacks of 9/11 as both a punishment and a warning of what would come next, ostensibly in the Tribulation period, should America remain on this track of liberalism.

Falwell continued. "The abortionists have got to bear some burden for this because God will not be mocked. And when we destroy 40 million little innocent babies, we make God mad." He had been warning for decades that the national sin of abortion would bring the wrath of God upon America, would so weaken America that it would be unable to face the Tribulation. Now, the beginning of that judgment was here, and surely the Tribulation was not far behind. "I really believe that the pagans and the abortionists and the feminists and the gays and the lesbians who are actively trying to make that an alternative life-style, the ACLU, People for the American Way, all of them who try to secularize America." And then he left no question as to the real cause of the terror attacks: "I point the finger in their face and say, 'You helped this happen.'"

To be sure, more sophisticated dispensationalists have taught that the Bible contains various forms of the wrath of God, of which the Tribulation is only one. Yet Falwell possessed a very rudimentary understanding of dispensationalism, having chosen not to attend seminary and being cut off from the Baptist Bible Fellowship at the very beginning of his career. While he occasionally acknowledged different kinds of God's wrath—God's present judgment in direct response to sin, God's eternal judgment on unrepentant sinners by allowing them to spend eternity in hell—he was unable to make clear theological nuances and consistently preached of the wrath of God in terms of the Tribulation.

Perhaps even more significant than the terms he used in preaching was the environment that he created, an environment in which his audience knew that when he was talking about current events—nuclear build-up, war in the Middle East, the Clinton conspiracy, Columbine and martyrdom, 9/11—he was talking about prophecy and the Tribulation. Sometimes he gave sermon series about prophecy in response to events that seemed to directly resonate with how prophecy was being understood at that time. Sometimes his colleagues, who were more educated in dispensationalism but less media-savvy and charismatic than he was, produced books and tapes that showed exactly how current events were related to prophecy; he then promoted those products on his *Old-Time Gospel Hour*. And sometimes, the environment was just right for his audience to connect what he was saying about current events to the Tribulation, as when the tragedy at Columbine High School unfolded in the midst of the *Left-Behind* phenomenon.

For dispensationalists since Darby, understanding prophecy has been central to understanding the Bible. The God who reveals himself through prophecy is a God who wants to be known by his creation and a God whose word, the Bible, can be trusted down through the ages. Yet in the hands of Falwell, prophecy belief became shallow, little more than current events merged with conspiracy and paranoia; this low regard for prophecy—ironically, in spite of his obsession with it—allowed him to play *The Clinton Chronicles* on his *Old-Time Gospel Hour* for four full weeks, instead of preaching from the Bible. And when he did preach about prophecy, it was always in reference to what will happen to other people. The End Times would officially begin with the Rapture; after all Christians were gone, everything that would happen under the antichrist *would not concern a single born-again believer who was listening to him*. Still, he was able to grip his audience with a dramatic tale of what will happen to unbelievers, how they will suffer under the wrath of God. In Falwell's hands, prophecy belief became not only shallow but titillating, little more than theological pornography.

Yet this theological pornography has been having severe political ramifications for decades. Under a president who believed in Armageddon, prophecy belief supported putting billions of dollars toward nuclear build-up and a "Star Wars" defense program, while more and more people in America went hungry and slept on the streets. Under a president who became the subject of numerous conspiracy theories, including one of drug-running and a "body count" of whistleblowers and opponents, prophecy belief encouraged the further disenfranchisement of queer people alongside the spread of those conspiracy theories. And when hijacked airplanes struck the World Trade Center and Pentagon, prophecy belief would marry the War on Terror and convince millions of dispensational-influenced evangelicals that, as with the Cold War, this present crisis was the End Times. And over a decade after Falwell's death in 2007, the Clinton conspiracy that he promoted would shape a new, far-right political religion whose central figure was Hillary Clinton: QAnon.

CHAPTER 5

Global Warming as Fake News

"THERE IS A developing cultural divide occurring within the evangelical community over an unlikely subject: global warming."[1] So began a missive—dubbed a "Falwell Confidential"—that Falwell sent out to a vast network of over 160,000 pastors, laypeople, and public servants who had come together under the movement he had been building since the 1970s. He sent out many so-called "Falwell Confidentials" from the late 1990s until his death in 2007, but there was nothing confidential about them. The headings often read, "A weekly fax briefing for America's pastors and Christian leaders who may use this information without attribution." Not only was the information contained not "confidential" in even the loosest sense of the word, but it could be shared without giving credit to the author. Perhaps Falwell was trying to make the briefings' 160,000-plus recipients feel as though they were privy to his innermost thoughts and had exclusive access to his take on the most important issues of the day; he was making them feel as if they were his friends.

Whatever the case may be, during the last year of his life, he devoted a tremendous amount of energy to dispelling the "myth" of global warming. Three months before his death in May 2007, he sent out another "Falwell Confidential" to promote an upcoming service at his church, for February 25, 2007, in which he would thoroughly debunk the myth of global warming. He wrote of the upcoming service, "Pastor Falwell will expose from a Biblical perspective, the international global warming fraud. He will explain why global warming is not due to human contribution of

Carbon Dioxide."[2] Perhaps the surface of the planet is growing slightly warmer, he had conceded in other Falwell Confidentials, but this warming was purely a natural trend and could in no way be attributed to human activity, especially not the burning of fossil fuels.

The Confidential went on to say of the special sermon Falwell would preach, "He will reveal why Al Gore and others are promoting the 'earthism' movement and why this clandestine effort will eventually do great damage to America, unless it is unveiled, opposed, and stopped." Earthism, or worship of the earth, was a form of paganism and therefore a demonic religion that would support the rise of the antichrist. Al Gore, a "Southern Baptist in-name-only,"[3] had recently released the documentary *An Inconvenient Truth* to raise awareness of "the potential ruin of the planet." Evangelicals were becoming concerned about the impacts of human activity on the natural environment, and global warming was trending as a significant issue for the upcoming 2008 election cycle. Unless Falwell and the voters that he had been mobilizing acted decisively on the issue, American evangelicals in the Religious Right would move away from conservative politics in favor of ameliorating the effects of global warming.

"Well, unfortunately the scientists do not know what we are preaching on from the Revelation," Falwell said in a sermon on the antichrist. "They apparently have not read prophecy from the New Testament . . . They're talking about global warming, which I think is a myth."[4] Biblical prophecy had already declared how the earth would end. After the Rapture, the antichrist would arise and take control of the world. Christ would return after seven years of God's wrath to defeat the antichrist and establish his Millennial Kingdom. Global warming caused by humans burning fossil fuels was nowhere in the End Times calendar; this pseudo-science was deceiving Christians and causing them to fall into the apostasy of liberalism. These well-meaning Christians were now speaking out against the dangers that unregulated capitalism posed to the planet—especially with regard to fossil fuels—and were, in the process, threatening to cause America to fall under the antichrist. The myth of global warming was the enemy of capitalism—and Christianity.

Fundamentalism's relationship with the oil industry has long been a troubled one, not troubled in the sense of distressed, but troubled in how, through an alliance with the oil industry, fundamentalism came to reshape the Christocentric gospel of evangelicalism. While oilmen such as Lyman Stewart had used their petrodollars to finance fundamentalist institutions, Falwell would, throughout his career, advocate for the politics and economics of oil as piecemeal to his unique brand of dispensationalism. The world's—and especially America's—reliance on oil, which by 2007 was widely known to be driving climate change—was essential to protecting capitalism and Christianity. In Falwell's hands, denial of climate change and linking climate action to the liberal apostasy became a new version of the Cold War. In fact, in his special sermon on global warming, he referred to so-called "green scientists" as "red scientists," linking them to Cold War communism. Falwell helped make the denial of climate change and the doubling down on fossil fuels the new front in Christian America's war against socialism.

Dispensational Node

Christian Zionism

A perennial challenge for Christian theologians has long been the relationship between the people of God in the Old Testament (or Hebrew Bible), the Jews, and followers of Christ, Christians, collectively the church. In the New Testament, Acts 15 tells of the Jerusalem Council, which the early church held to determine whether or not the new Christian converts who were not Jewish had to also follow the Jewish law. The apostle Paul vehemently disagreed with the idea that new Christians had to assimilate into Judaism, saying, "But we believe that, through the grace of the Lord Jesus Christ, we [Jewish converts to the Way, sometimes regarded as the earliest Christians] shall be saved in the same manner as they [non-Jews, or Gentiles]" (Acts 15:11 NKJV). In the apostolic church as recorded in the book of Acts, new Christians did not have to convert to Judaism. In European Christendom, the challenge would take the opposite form, as Jews who refused to convert to Christianity were often denied the most basic rights and sometimes even killed.

Throughout Europe in the Middle Ages and beyond, a person's civil rights (or lack thereof) were consummate with one's faith. Catholics and Protestants could alternately face severe persecution; England's Queen Mary I, nicknamed Bloody Mary, had hundreds of Protestants burned at the stake, and her sister, Queen Elizabeth I, had Catholics hanged, drawn, and quartered. In a Britain that was overwhelmingly Protestant, a series of laws that came during the late eighteenth and early nineteenth century (as Darby was beginning his career) granted emancipation, or freedom from civil discrimination, to Catholics. Yet there was still the issue of emancipation for Jews. Should the Jews be emancipated, and what was their theological relationship with the other people of God, the church?

One solution to this theological quandary has been conversion, in which Jews have the opportunity to convert to Christianity, join the church, and assimilate into Christian culture. A component of the Jewish conversion approach is called supersessionism. Supersessionism teaches that the church has replaced Israel; the Jews were God's chosen people in the Old Testament, but because they rejected Jesus as the Messiah, the mantle of chosenness has passed from them and to the church. Now, all the promises and hopes that God gave to the Jews apply to the church. In a Europe that did not extend emancipation to Jews, supersessionism meant that Jews had to convert in order to receive God's grace; that grace came in the form of no longer being subject to blood libel and other persecutions that Christians subjected them to. The great reformer Martin Luther believed in conversion, and he prescribed a method for forcing Jews to join the church: "First to set fire to their synagogues or schools . . . Second, I advise that their houses also be razed and destroyed . . . Third, I advise that all their prayer books and Talmudic writings, in which such idolatry, lies, cursing, and blasphemy are taught, be taken from them."[5] His prescription for resolving the theological dilemma of the Jews' relationship to the church reads like a guidebook for the Holocaust. Sadly, there were some Christians who took his advice.

Conversion—sometimes as forced as that advocated by Luther, as in purges such as the Inquisition (several centuries before Luther)—has met limited success in the two millennia of the church's history. Some Jews converted, many of them to save themselves and their families from ongoing persecution and even death. Yet the theological and, in European Christendom, political challenge as to the relationship between the church and the Jews persisted, as many Jews chose to remain Jews.

Could the Jews of Europe attain emancipation without converting and assimilating into Christian culture? Darby's teachings suggested that they could. He rejected supersessionism, instead claiming that there are two chosen peoples of God, the Jews and the church, and both receive God's grace in different ways. The Jews remain under the covenants implemented during the Jewish dispensations, namely, the law given at Mount Sinai, and Christians are under the covenant of grace that comes through the sacrificial death of Christ. Jews did not need to convert into the church, though many dispensationalists have certainly evangelized Jews to that end. God's ultimate purpose for them lies elsewhere, in their restoration to the land of Palestine, over which Christ will reign for one thousand years. Not that Darby advocated for Jewish emancipation in Britain or even Jewish establishment in Palestine; he eschewed all political activity and urged his followers to do the same. Yet he believed the Bible prophesied the return of the Jews to Palestine, and over this regathered Israel, Christ would return and begin his Millennial Reign.[6]

Christian Zionism, the belief that the return of the Jewish people to the land of Palestine is the fulfillment of biblical prophecy, became a significant component of dispensationalism. Dispensationalists since 1948 have generally taught that this prophecy is still unfolding and will culminate soon in the Tribulation, which will center on Israel. "The final reason for the Tribulation will be to purge Israel," Falwell declared in his booklet, *Nuclear War and the Second Coming of Jesus*. "As gold is purified through the heat of the fire, so the nation of Israel will come through the Tribulation fit for the Master's use."[7] Here he echoed Darby's belief that the Tribulation would prepare Israel for the Millennial Reign, but with an important caveat. Darby did not believe that the Jews would be restored to Israel until the Tribulation was already taking place, but then in 1948, Israel became a country in its own right. This seemingly small difference has made a drastic impact on dispensational thought, especially with regard to how Israel has been interacting with its Arab neighbors.

With the rise of Falwell's marriage between American nationalism and dispensationalism, America's relationship with Israel became central to beliefs about how the continuing unfolding of prophecy would affect the American Christian nation. It had descended into the apostasy and wickedness, and God's judgment was surely not far off. Yet there were two reasons he often cited as reasons why God's wrath might have been delayed, at least temporarily: the role of America in world evangelization and America's support of Israel.[8] "We [as Americans] have always believed in the Abrahamic covenant, that God deals with nations in relation to how nations deal with the Jew," he declared in 1986. "And the Jew, the apple of God's eye, is very important to this country. We have given absolute freedom to the Jew in this country,[9] and the day we cease supporting Israel and supporting the Jewish people is the day God ceases supporting this country."[10] America's future, in the face of the imminent Tribulation, hinged primarily on support of Israel. Yet this support had economic overtones that reverberated alongside biblical capitalism and prophecies of Soviet Magog, because Falwell's Christian Zionism intersected with what may be the most central feature to biblical capitalism: the oil industry.

In 1892, Patillo Higgins, George Carroll, and George O'Brien formed the Gladys City Oil, Gas, and Manufacturing Company, hoping to strike oil in an area of Texas that, up until then, had been dominated by cattle ranches and lumber mills. Higgins had no formal theological training, yet he believed himself to be an expert in interpreting the Bible; similarly, he was a self-taught geologist who, despite no university education in the field, considered himself to be an expert in deciphering the signs of the earth's surface. After helping form the Gladys City Oil, Gas, and Manufacturing Company, he eventually partnered with Anthony Lucas; though Higgins himself would be cut out of the deal, the company he had helped form struck oil at Spindletop, Texas, on January 10, 1901. Higgins became known as the "prophet of Spindletop," owing to his unwavering faith in the Bible's ability to help him discern the presence of oil. The massive oil strike in

Beaumont, Texas, would help usher in a new era that would be dominated by oil.

The American West, along with the "plain-text" interpretation of the Bible that Higgins and many other evangelicals favored, would become transformed by oil and the new fundamentalist institutions that oil money helped finance. Capitalism would become sacrosanct, enshrined in Lyman Stewart's *The Fundamentals* (edited by Reuben Torrey and A. C. Dixon), the many publications from Biola, and eventually Bill Graham's magazine, *Christianity Today,* and that of his financier, J. Howard Pew, *Christian Economics*. Many of the schools that, at least at their inception, taught an Americanized version of dispensationalism—Biola, Fuller Seminary, Oral Roberts University—were funded with oil money. One place that would become particularly significant to the development of dispensational fundamentalism is Dallas, a center of the oil industry.

The firebrand, militant fundamentalist J. Frank Norris (1877–1952) would turn First Baptist of Fort Worth, Dallas's twin city next door, into the largest congregation in America. After beginning his pastorate there in 1909, he played a leading role in establishing Southwestern Baptist Theological Seminary. John Rice, who for a time partnered with Norris, founded in 1934 a biweekly fundamentalist publication called *Sword of the Lord*; Rice's ministry would eventually spawn a publishing company that published some of Falwell's material. Perhaps most significant to the marriage of the oil industry and dispensational fundamentalism in Dallas was the founding of Dallas Theological Seminary (DTS) in 1924 by Lewis Sperry Chafer. Chafer was a protégé of C. I. Scofield, whose *Scofield Reference Bible* greatly popularized dispensationalism throughout America; Chafer founded DTS with the intention of training pastors in dispensational thought so that they could bring it to pulpits across America. All these institutions together, what I refer to as the fundamentalist-oil empire, would, by the 1990s, shape Falwell's belief that global warming is a hoax.

By the time Chafer founded DTS in 1924, Rockefeller's Standard Oil Company was exploring in the Middle East and gaining concessions, legal rights from foreign governments, to drill for oil. In 1922, Standard Oil of New Jersey and Socony obtained 25 percent control of the Iraq Petroleum Company. Possibly the greatest success of Standard Oil, on an international scale, came in 1938, when a subsidiary of Standard Oil of California—what would become Saudi Aramco—struck oil in Saudi Arabia. World War II would dramatically increase America's need for oil, and as the war raged, President Franklin Roosevelt would begin negotiations with the Saudi monarch to buy the Saudi oil of Rockefeller's Aramco.

There was one significant problem with Roosevelt's arrangement, however, that of Jews fleeing Nazi-occupied Europe, many headed for Palestine. Though in need of the money that oil sales to America would bring, Saudi leaders—especially King Abdul Aziz ibn Saud—opposed the displacement of Palestinians that was increasing rapidly with the wave of Jewish immigration. In 1945, President Harry Truman said to the Saudi leaders concerned about the displacement of Palestinians, "I'm sorry, gentlemen, but I have to answer to hundreds of thousands who are anxious for the success of Zionism; I do not have hundreds of thousands of Arabs among my constituents."[11] Negotiations led to the Saudi monarch acknowledging that the United States would support Israel as part of the agreement to sell Saudi oil; Western interests became essential to Saudi's oil industry. In the post-war years, America's economy would boom as the country became increasingly dependent on cheap oil from the Middle East. Yet there would be tensions between America's support of Israel and

America's oil-supplying countries, especially those countries that supported the rights of Palestinians as they were being forced from their homes and becoming refugees.

What would emerge over the next few decades is a complex web of Western oil interests, Christian Zionism, Jewish Zionism (which is markedly different from Christian Zionism), and an ongoing event known as the Naqba. "Naqba" is the Arabic word for "catastrophe" and refers to the displacement of Palestinian civilians that began with the massive Jewish immigration from Europe in the early 1900s. That immigration increased dramatically with the rise of Hitler and the spread of Nazism throughout Europe and again when survivors of the Holocaust moved to Palestine, with the hope of rebuilding their lives. As more Jews moved in, more Palestinians were forced out, oftentimes at gunpoint. May 15, 1948, has two meanings in the contested strip of land in the Levant: to the Israelis, it is Independence Day, while to the Palestinians, it is Naqba Day. Following Israel's independence, Palestinian refugees poured into the surrounding countries of Jordan, Syria, and Lebanon, all of which were unable to take in and provide for such a large wave of desperate humanity. Many settled in refugee camps and remained there for decades, living and raising their children in squalor. Those who have remained in Palestine—particularly in the partitioned areas of the West Bank and Gaza—have faced ongoing violence, humiliation, and death at the hands of the Israeli Defense Forces, armed civilians, and a legal system that does not recognize Palestinian rights. This catastrophe is what Palestinians and their sympathizers commemorate each year on Naqba Day.

Yet to Falwell, the competing interests of Jewish Zionism and Palestinian rights, alongside the growing anger that Arab countries felt at a neighbor—Israel—that they saw as rogue and unwilling to engage in diplomacy, had nothing to do with the tensions in the Middle East. Everything could be explained in terms of prophecy, because the establishment of Israel in 1948 certainly meant that the present dispensation was nearing its end. "Today," Falwell declared a few weeks after Israel's 1967 war with its neighbors, "more so than in any age past, Israel is the greatest evidence of the fulfillment of Bible prophecy and the coming of the Lord Jesus for His church."[12] Surrounding this unwavering belief in biblical prophecy regarding Israel was the politics of oil, embedded in Falwell's insistence that the Cold War was a divine struggle between capitalism and communism. To make matters even more difficult, many of the countries with oil—Iraq, Iran, Saudi Arabia—were, at least at the time, sympathetic to the Palestinian cause.

The Re-Emergence of Babylon

Saudi Arabia, where Standard Oil began drilling successfully in the 1930s, was not the only country whose oil industry would become dominated by Western interests. In Persia (Iran), the Anglo-Persian Oil Company held such sway over the country's government and economy that in 1952, Mohamed Mossadegh became Iran's prime minister following a campaign to nationalize the country's oil industry. He canceled all of Britain's oil concessions, invoking the ire of Prime Minister Winston Churchill, who called on US President Dwight Eisenhower to help him regain unbridled access to Iran's oil. A global boycott failed to halt Iran's nationalization of its own oil industry, so in 1953, the foreign intelligence agencies of Britain and the United States enacted a coup that would end Mossadegh's brief tenure as prime minister. In 1965, the oil-producing countries of Saudi Arabia, Iran, Iraq, Kuwait, and Venezuela came together to form the Organization of Petroleum-Exporting Countries (OPEC). The goal was to attain national sovereignty over their own natural resources, particularly their oil, against the Western interests that were—particularly in the case of Iran—exploiting their countries.

These transformations of the global economic order—in which Western countries were becoming increasingly dependent on the Middle East and Iran for the oil that fueled their economies, and then through OPEC, the oil countries were pushing back—were not lost on students of prophecy at Dallas Theological Seminary. "A whole new alignment of international power was underway," John Walvoord, the president of DTS and future board member of Falwell's Liberty University, wrote in his 1974 book *Armageddon, Oil, and the Middle East Crisis*.[13] Walvoord also noted that, as America grew more and more dependent on oil from the Middle East, policies in America made drilling domestically increasingly difficult; oilers who wanted to access the oil deposits in the United States, such as those off the Gulf Coast and on the North Slope of Alaska, were bound by difficult legislation.

The ancient city of Babylon lay in Iraq, and the significance of Iraq's oil fields to the West correlated directly with new interpretations of prophecy. The Bible mentions Babylon more than any other city, except for the holy city of Jerusalem. Biblical prophecy is replete with references to Babylon, and dispensationalists, especially at DTS, held that these prophecies must have a literal fulfillment. "Although the fall of [ancient] Babylon marked the end of political rule of Babylonian rulers, much of the Babylonian culture, its pagan religions, and its ideology were continued in the kingdoms which followed," Walvoord wrote in his 1967 book *The Nations in Prophecy*. He went on to suggest, "Babylon, the symbol of religious confusion, was to appear again in the apostate church of Revelation 17, and its political power was to be revived in the final form of the Roman Empire as depicted in Revelation 18."[14] Babylon was to be the center of prophecy fulfillment during the

Tribulation, and the "whore of Babylon," described in Revelation 17 and 18, is none other than the liberal World Council of Churches—whose parent organization, the Federal Council of Churches, was underwritten by Rockefeller philanthropy and represented the liberalism of the Social Gospel. In other words, the wickedness of ancient Babylon had been playing out most recently in liberal theology—the apostasy that, according to Walvoord, the Bible referred to as a whore.

"Babylon is another term used for the one world religion [of the Tribulation],"[15] Hal Lindsey, a graduate of DTS, wrote in his 1970 bestseller *The Late Great Planet Earth*. This one-world religion would supposedly have its origins in liberal theology and the Social Gospel, financed by the same man—John D. Rockefeller—whose company pioneered American drilling in Iraq (Babylon) and the rest of the Middle East. Charles Dyer, a professor at DTS, went further in his 1991 book *The Rise of Babylon: Sign of the End Times*, linking Saddam Hussein with the legendary Babylonian ruler Nebuchadnezzar. In other words, to many American dispensationalists who believed that they were watching the fulfillment of prophecy, the conspiracy of liberalism that became associated with Rockefeller's international approach to oil—the World Council of Churches, Babylon, and a global socialist order—became the one-world religion of the End Times; this transformation was due to the growing wealth of the region that resulted from global, and increasingly American, dependence on Middle Eastern oil. This heritage of prophecy belief unfolding amid the troubles in the oil-rich Middle East would inform Falwell's gospel of unregulated capitalism.

Further, the wealth being amassed by oil-producing countries in the Middle East, countries that were (at least at the time) antagonistic toward Israel because of the Palestinian Naqba, could only mean one thing: Babylon was rising again, a rival to the holy city of Jerusalem. Middle Eastern oil was the means by which prophecy, centering on Israel, would continue to be fulfilled.

The 1973 Oil Embargo

What about the energy crisis? Three years ago, from out of the blue, we're out of oil. Strange, all of our lives we'd never hear of such a thing. Now we're hearing about food shortages in the future. Our air and water are polluted. This is all, I believe, the wrath of God upon a nation who has inside her borders a sleeping church.

Falwell said those words in 1976, the year of America's bicentennial, in his stump sermon of the decade, "America Back to God." The energy crisis he referred to was OPEC's international oil embargo that stretched from October of 1973 through March of 1974 and crippled America's economy. The embargo stemmed from a 1973 event that he saw as irrefutable proof that prophecy was being fulfilled in real time: the Yom Kippur War.

On October 6, 1973, the Jewish holiday of Yom Kippur, the countries of Egypt and Syria launched a surprise invasion of Israel, hoping to force the country to begin engaging in diplomatic relations with its neighbors and to end its oppression of Palestinians. This invasion was soon joined by Jordan and Iraq, which sent over troops, tanks, and aircraft; Saudi Arabia also supported the Arab invaders by sending some troops. Israel's military quickly began to deplete its supplies, and Prime Minister Golda Meir called on US President Richard Nixon for assistance. Nixon initially refused, as Egypt was an American ally. When the Soviet Union began supplying the Arab countries, Nixon changed his mind and had military supplies sent to Israel. What had begun as an Arab invasion into Israel quickly turned into a proxy war for the struggles between America and the Soviet Union. With American arms, Israel quickly defeated its invaders, but the war was enough for Cold War tensions to merge with prophecy belief about Soviet Magog and biblical capitalism.

The three-week war had an outsized effect on the movement Falwell was building. In his prophecy-tinted, capitalist mindset, communist Magog had just supported an invasion into God's chosen nation of Israel, exactly as dispensationalists believed the Bible foretold would occur in the End Times. Surely the final showdown between biblical capitalism and Soviet Magog was looming, but at this time, he was just beginning to marry dispensationalism with American nationalism. He had not yet toured the country to preach "America Back to God" in front of state capitols, had a military color guard march down the aisle of his church during worship, or dedicated an entire service to the US Constitution. His televangelical empire was still reeling from a scandal with the Securities and Exchange Commission (SEC) that had struck just a few months before, though, giving him the motivation to create his new understanding of the American Christian nation. The timing could not have been more perfect, because geopolitical events were surely lining up exactly as was needed for the Tribulation to unfold in accordance with his interpretation of prophecy. His hyper-nationalist movement would begin very soon.

Falwell was so inspired by the real-time fulfillment of prophecy that he began what would become his thirty-eight-part series on the book of Revelation. "The situation in Russia, China, and certainly the Middle East, is most critical," he declared. "As we see all the things happening in our country, as we see the total upheaval and the chaotic conditions, we must believe that the Lord is bringing all these things to a screeching halt." The reason, he went on to explain, is that "very soon, the trumpet will sound and God will take out his church, delivering us from the hour of temptation, and then will begin the seven years of tribulation."[16] At the end of the millennium, "Satan will be loosed out of his prison; he will go out to deceive the nations in the four corners of the earth, Gog and Magog."[17] Then the devil, along with all the enemies of God, will be cast into the lake of fire for eternal torment. The skies will be rolled up like a scroll, and the entire cosmos will melt in a nuclear explosion.

Saudi Arabia and Iraq, two of the countries involved in the invasion of Israel, were both founding members of OPEC. Up until 1973, OPEC had not been able to take much meaningful, decisive action with regard to the global oil industry, and the countries involved had been left with little control over oil outputs and prices. Yet America's arming of Israel, which the invading Arab countries saw as preventing diplomacy from occurring and enabling the continued oppression of Palestinians, gave OPEC its opportunity to remind America of who supplied its oil. On October 19, 1973, less than two weeks into the war, King Faisal of Saudi Arabia announced an embargo on OPEC oil to the United States. "We do not wish to place any restrictions on our oil exports to the United States," he had said on an interview with NBC News more than a month before the embargo began, "but as I mentioned, America's complete support of Zionism against the Arabs makes it extremely difficult for us to continue to supply the United States' petroleum needs and to even maintain our friendly relations."[18] When America armed Israel against the Arabs (and Soviet Magog), King Faisal stood by his word and helped implement the embargo.

Immediately, the American economy began to collapse. With automobiles, homes, and industries all dependent on an abundance of free-flowing oil, the sudden drop in supply caused the price of fuel to skyrocket. Because trucks that transported goods to stores required oil-derived products as fuel, the price of goods everywhere soared as inflation entered the double digits. Cars waited in lines at gas stations for hours, only for the gas to run out before they could be refueled. As the embargo entered the cold winter months, families could not afford to heat their homes, and those that could, found that fuel was in such short supply that heating was unreliable. With companies increasingly stressed financially, many American workers were laid off, and those that were not often did not receive their full paychecks. The economic breakdown surrounding the energy shortage of the 1970s would add a critical element to the movement that Falwell would soon begin building: social malaise and discontent with the supposed failures of liberalism. Economics, more than opposition to abortion and integration of Black bodies into historically white spaces, or even the prophecy that Falwell saw as intimately tied to the embargo, would draw people to his far-right nationalism.

The Dawn of Political Fundamentalism

Falwell's 1973–1974 series on prophecy lacked the creative finesse of his later teachings, as well as the nationalism that was just beginning to flavor his dispensationalism. Other than some references to the recent Yom Kippur War, any dispensationalist teacher of the era could have taught the series; it was standard prophecy fare. But that same year, 1973, his burgeoning empire would be rattled by a scandal that threatened to close his church, day school, newly found college, and media empire. Thomas Road Baptist had been selling bonds that promised 8 percent interest in order to finance the opening of Lynchburg Baptist College (what would become Liberty University) and launch a national radio and television ministry. But the bonds functioned as a giant pyramid scheme, and when they came due, they were essentially worthless. In July 1973, just three months before the Yom Kippur War and OPEC embargo, the Securities and Exchange Commission filed formal charges against Falwell's ministries for "fraud and deceit" in selling $6.5 million in bonds; the SEC also declared the church to be financially insolvent.

To Falwell, the government was attempting to legislate how his church could operate and was thereby depriving fundamentalist Christians of their religious liberty. This scheme looked perilously close to how the antichrist would demand religious worship as he ruled over the political sphere. In response, Falwell took his message about unregulated capitalism—which included allowing churches and church schools, including segregation academies, to operate how they see fit—to the road, but with a twist. "America Back to God," the message he toured the country with in the wake of the SEC scandal, married dispensationalism with something new, American nationalism. He did not explicitly talk about prophecy in "America Back to God," but as with plenty of other sermons about the End Times, he did not really need to. Listeners who were already "in the know" about current events, especially the Yom Kippur War, must have appreciated his message for what it really was.

"I do not think I'm an alarmist," he told his crowd, "when I tell you that the US is in its gravest and most serious trouble since she came into being 200 years ago."[19] America had gone the way of the Soviet Union by kicking God out of public schools through the *Abington School District v Schempp* decision that outlawed Bible-reading to schoolchildren. "Moral permissiveness pervades our schools today," he bemoaned, speaking from the dispensational belief that society is in a state of decline. "It is a matter of fact," he continued, "that not only sex education, but pornography and dirt are the order of the day." Then he went on to speak about a consequence of the Yom Kippur War, the six-month oil embargo. "What about the energy crisis?" he asked. "Three years ago, from out of the blue, we're out of oil. Strange, all of our lives we'd ever hear of such a thing." He then told his audience, with certainty, the true source of the energy crisis: "This is all, I believe, the wrath of God upon a nation who has inside her borders a sleeping church."

"If America allows herself to be blackmailed by the oil cartel [OPEC] and trade her allegiance to Israel for a petroleum 'mess of pottage,'" Falwell said in *Listen, America!*, "she will also trade her position of world leadership for a place in the history books alongside of Rome."[20] Perhaps in saying that America would find "a place in the history books alongside of Rome," he was not speaking of the ancient Roman Empire that fell in 476, but rather the revived Roman Empire to come, through which the antichrist would gain power over the world. America had so weakened itself by depending on Arab oil that it would be unable to withstand the events that were sure to continue unfolding. The country was under God's wrath, as he had declared in "America Back to God," and the evidence was the energy shortage brought about by the 1973–1974 OPEC embargo. His solution was for America to end its dependence on Arab oil so that it could exclusively support Israel without worrying about whether it would offend OPEC.

President Jimmy Carter (president 1977–1981) had attempted to accomplish exactly that goal shortly before Falwell published *Listen, America!* in 1980. Carter's energy plan included calling on Americans to conserve as much as possible while developing alternative sources that would dismantle the country's dependence on oil—not only Arab oil but fossil fuels altogether. Additionally, the Camp David Accords, in which he mediated between the leaders of Israel and Egypt, addressed the tensions between the two countries that had flared in the Yom Kippur War, leading to the OPEC embargo.

Yet Carter's plan, no matter how well-intentioned it may have been, was not consistent with how prophecy was unfolding.

And further, his program for green energy supposedly, as Falwell suggested, placed the energy supply under government control, just one step away from Soviet-style communism. "In spite of the rosy and utterly unrealistic expectations by our government, this treaty will not be a lasting treaty," Falwell said of the Camp David Accords, certain that prophecy superseded diplomacy. "We are certainly praying for the peace of Jerusalem . . . But you and I know that there's not going to be any real peace in the Middle East until one day, the Lord Jesus sits down upon the throne of David in Jerusalem and rules and reigns for 1000 years on this earth."[21] Falwell needed a conservative like himself, someone who understood that the oil industry had always been piecemeal to both American capitalism and fundamentalism. Someone who understood that the events in the Middle East could not be stabilized—as Carter had attempted with the Camp David Accords—but were rather leading to Armageddon. He found that man in Ronald Reagan.

The relationship between Falwell's movement and the oil industry was not merely a matter of coincidence regarding the timing of the OPEC embargo and his scrutiny by the SEC. In May of 1979, Dudley Hughes, a leader in America's oil industry, wrote a letter to Howard Phillips, leader of the Conservative Caucus, and began by saying,

> At the Dulles Marriott meeting on May 21st, we discussed the possibility of getting oil groups involved in the conservative coalition, particularly in view of the poor public image which the business has.
>
> At the urging of several people at the meeting, I am attempting to arrange a meeting between several top conservative leaders and leaders in the oil industry.[22]

One of the conservative leaders contacted for this purpose was Paul Weyrich, with whom Falwell formed the Moral Majority very shortly after the meeting described as scheduled for May 21, 1979, with the Moral Majority's arrival occurring on June 6, 1979.[23] In other words, the flagship organization of the Religious Right may have been a direct response to an appeal by the oil industry.

To accomplish the task of disengaging from Arab oil, America had to open more of its own land for drilling, and President Reagan had just the person for the task: James Watt. Watt professed his premillennialist beliefs when he said, as recorded in a *Washington Post* article from April 1983,

> All Christians and all Jews believe that the Messiah will come. Now, because we don't know when He's coming, we have a responsibility—and the Bible's very clear, it does not tell us when He's coming—to show compassion, to feed the hungry and care for the widows and orphans, and the land and everything. Until He comes."[24]

Here, the biblical mandate to "care for the widows and orphans" is tied into "care for . . . the land" as part of waiting for the Messiah (in the Rapture and/or the Millennial Reign), and Watt had a very controversial view of what caring for the land meant. During the early 1980s, Watt's belief in the impending Rapture led him, as President Reagan's Secretary of the Interior, to turn public lands— including national parks—over to private developers, often in the form of leases to drill for oil and mine for coal. He believed that in promoting private business—particularly oil and coal—over the environment, he was doing the Lord's work.

"And Jim Watt, I don't know if any of you know Secretary Jim Watt or not, but he's the secretary of the interior on the cabinet of President Reagan, a man of real moral integrity," Falwell said in a 1982 sermon. "He's a great Christian. He gives his testimony of faith in Christ wherever he goes. He's a man of moral commitment, and oh, has the media been after him, I mean from the day he walked in." Falwell went on to acknowledge the relationship between Watt's premillennialist beliefs and the values received through the fundamentalist-oil empire. "You know what he's trying to do? He is trying to follow the cue of his president in bringing America to a place where we are no longer dependent upon the OPEC nations for our energy. He's trying to bring us to the place where we don't have to bow down to Saudi Arabia, bow down to the ayatollah, bow down to the Arab nations in order to run our automobiles and heat our houses."

He went on to recognize that this position did not reflect environmental stewardship, yet there was no need to steward the environment if Christ should rapture his church at any moment. "And . . . all the environmentalists are after his jugular vein. God bless the environmentalists. Everybody's got to do something. But may I say to you that we have a secretary of the interior who really is earnestly trying to bring the country to self-dependence, dependence on its own resources."[25] That self-dependence would not come through the development of renewable energy, the allegedly socialistic enterprise that President Carter had promoted, but rather through increased drilling in America. When increased drilling was not enough, the eyes of prophecy watchers returned to Babylon.

America's Oil Wars

"No blood for oil," read the signs of protestors gathered at Lynchburg's Monument Terrace, not far from Falwell's Liberty University. Three weeks after the United States joined the Persian Gulf War in January 1991, to ward off the Iraqi military that had invaded Kuwait to gain access to its oil fields, tensions in Falwell's hometown were at a fever pitch. While many residents of

Lynchburg opposed the war, there was near-unanimous support at Liberty University and Thomas Road Baptist Church. In addition to airing more sermons on prophecy, Falwell responded to the war by reviving his "I Love America" campaign from 1976, in which he toured churches and public venues preaching "America Back to God." This tour was less extensive, possibly because by 1991, he had so many other commitments at his church, day school, and university; possibly because after successfully building up a resurgent conservativism inspired by his take on dispensationalism, and after more than a decade of a conservative White House, there was less work to do this time around. And shortly after he began the tour, the war ended, with Iraq retreating from Kuwait.

The short-lived war helped ensure that oil politics and the economic system they inspired would remain at the center of fundamentalist politics. Shortly after President George H. W. Bush reneged on his promise of not implementing any new taxes, in 1992, Howard Phillips, who had helped Falwell build up the Religious Right, created the Taxpayers Party. In the Taxpayers Party's founding documents, Phillips stated,

> We call attention to the continuing need of the United States for a sufficient supply of energy to sustain the nation's standard of living and its agricultural, business, and industrial activities. Private property rights should be respected and government should avoid interference with the development of potential energy sources, including hydroelectric power, solar energy, wind generators, and nuclear energy. We also encourage the use of coal, shale, and oil sands for the production of power and the conversion of coal, shale, and agricultural products to synthetic fuels.[26]

Protests against a war fought over oil, coupled with growing calls from scientists about the dangers of burning fossil fuels, had led to increased pressure to begin a transition to renewable energy.

In response, those in Falwell's movement—including Howard Phillips and his Taxpayers Party—dug in over the need to continue dependence on oil.

"The scientists say the atmosphere has warmed by one degree in the past hundred years. I don't think they could possibly know that," Falwell said in a 1997 sermon on prophecy.[27] Showing that he was acquainted with the statistical models that scientists had developed about the threat of climate change should the burning of fossil fuels continue, he went on. "And they're saying it could be three to six degrees in the next hundred years, which would melt the glaciers and raise the oceans 21 feet and all that hogwash." He went on to compare the myth of global warming with the myth of the hole in the ozone layer—a hole that stabilized in the 1990s and began to shrink in the early 2000s, in response to policies that banned the use of chemicals that were detrimental to the environment.

The message Falwell conveyed to his listeners was clear: fossil fuels are beneficial because they promote the biblical capitalism that will keep America on the right side of prophecy. Alternative energy sources, such as solar and wind, are not only unnecessary but detrimental, as they promote government control of the energy sector, bringing America perilously close to communism. A communist-type government would take over the world in the End Times, as he hinted in the 1997 sermon on the antichrist and denial of climate change. Until that time, however, American Christians could remain capitalist and free by supporting policies and even wars that ensured access to oil. At the same time, reliance on OPEC countries placed America in a difficult predicament, because Arab oil compromised unconditional support of Israel. The popular dispensationalist focus on Babylon would recede a bit in the 1990s but emerge in greater force than ever before when President George W. Bush launched an invasion of Iraq.

Perhaps American control of Babylon's oil could ensure an ongoing energy supply, one that did not include the alleged socialism (and even communism) of renewable energy, while not compromising unconditional support of Israel.

"The good news is that today's higher CO_2 levels are producing more abundant plant life and greater agricultural yields," read an advertisement in a far-right, conspiracy-laden newspaper that Falwell published through the 1990s, *National Liberty Journal*. "You can't see it or smell it, but CO_2 is all around us. Humans exhale it. Plants thrive on it. And natural geological processes produce most of the CO_2 in our atmosphere. The use of fossil fuels also contributes to atmospheric CO_2. Without CO_2, life on earth would cease."[28] The advertisement was by the Greening Earth Society, an organization that is now defunct but had been formed by the Western Fuels Association as a vehicle for denying climate change.

In Falwell's hands, the denial of climate change had become critical to dispensational thought, as the impending apocalypse that environmentalists were warning of stood in stark contrast with the Tribulation of biblical prophecy. Further, with the oil industry essential to preserving America's biblical capitalism, the acknowledgment of climate change would—in Falwell's view—necessarily instigate a move toward socialism, especially via the development of alternative energy. Yet perhaps if America controlled the oil fields in the Middle East, at least the oil fields of Babylon, support of Israel could continue without the diplomatic and theological hurdles around Arab oil. The Tribulation would still come, but perhaps if America held Iraq, it would be better positioned to assist Israel as both countries—Israel in particular—faced the wrath of God. Perhaps if America held the wealth of Babylon for itself, keeping oil from a modern-day Nebuchadnezzar who was amassing the riches of the world for himself, the Tribulation might actually be delayed. Falwell never said as much, at least not explicitly, but he constantly warped dispensationalism to fit new demands placed on his version of American nationalism.

When President George W. Bush sent American troops to Iraq in the wake of the September 11 attacks, in a move that many saw as a mirror to his father's entrance into the Persian Gulf War in 1991, Falwell energized his movement to lend support to the invasion. In fact, he preached yet another series on prophecy in the build-up to the invasion, though the series contained no new information. It was more reheated prophecy leftovers from the Persian Gulf War, about the antichrist and the wrath of God in the Tribulation, but in other circulations he gave a more nuanced view of Bush's war on terror.

"Today, America continues to face the horrible realities of our fallen world," Falwell wrote in a January 2004 Falwell Confidential entitled "Is God Ever Pro-War?"[29] Citing "suicide bombings and terrorist actions" that people saw daily on the evening news, he asserted, "It is apparent that our God-authored freedoms must be defended." He had spent over three decades detailing what he meant by those freedoms: unregulated capitalism and the privileging of fundamentalist Christianity in the public sphere. Though he did not say as much explicitly, since World War 2 those freedoms had been guaranteed by unlimited access to the oil reserves of the Middle East—a critical component of Bush's war on terror and invasion of Iraq. Yes, God was on the side of Christian America in the war; Falwell claimed, "President Bush declared war in Iraq to defend innocent people. This is a worthy pursuit. In fact, Proverbs 21:15 tells us: 'It is joy to the just to do judgment: but destruction shall be to the workers of iniquity.'"

He went on to chastise Christians who opposed the war on theological grounds. After all, the sixth of the Ten Commandments does not say, "Though shalt not kill." It says, rather, "Thou shalt not murder," and going to war for a righteous cause surely did not count as murder in the eyes of God. "In fact," Falwell went on, placing himself as judge of the wicked against whom America was warring, "many times God commanded capital punishment for those who break the law." Killing the terrorists was surely God's will. Protecting the capitalist, Christian freedoms of America, against the encroachments of terrorist Babylon and its attempts to gain the riches of the world—oil—for itself was God's will. "We continue to live in violent times," he went on, showing the pragmatism of his view. "The Bible tells us war will be a reality until Christ returns. And when the time is right, Jesus will indeed come again, ending all wars."

In attempting to give a theologically sound exposition on why Christians should support America's righteous war in Iraq, Falwell revealed his altogether poor grasp of dispensational thought. Dispensationalism divides history into distinct periods of time—dispensations—in which God dispenses grace in different ways. To Adam and Eve in the garden of Eden, he dispensed grace by walking with them in the cool of the day while requiring that they obey him, by not eating the forbidden fruit. In the dispensation of Mosaic Law, God dispensed grace to the Hebrews by forgiving their sins through sacrificial offerings that they made, in accordance with the law. He also led them, as his chosen people, into victory as they faced battles. And in a dispensational framework, the verses in the Hebrew Bible that talk about war belong to that specific dispensation, not to today's Church Age, the Dispensation of Grace. Falwell made a critical dispensational error by applying verses and principles from a previous dispensation to the Church Age.

Yet there was an even greater error, one that spanned his entire public career from the time he turned to promoting American nationalism in the 1970s. Dispensationalism is avowedly anti-supersessionist, meaning that verses that apply to Israel do not, cannot ever, apply to the church. Most Christians historically have been supersessionist, at least to an extent, meaning they believe that many of the promises that God gave to Israel in the Hebrew Bible now apply to the church. For example, 2 Chronicles 7:14 says, "If my people, who are called by my name, humble themselves, and pray and seek my face, and turn from their wicked ways, then I will hear from heaven, and I will forgive their sin and will heal their land" (NASB). Many non-dispensationalist Christians have looked to verses such as this one as promises for themselves and their present era, yet dispensationalism teaches against this use of the Hebrew Bible. Second Chronicles 7:14 is a promise for Israel, and only for Israel; it can never apply to the church. The church never assumed the covenants and promises given to Israel, and the church must be raptured into heaven so that God's prophetic program can return to Israel in the End Times.

Yet Falwell frequently applied verses about Israel from the Hebrew Bible, including 2 Chronicles 7:14, to Christians, and especially to his imagined American Christian nation. "I want you to open your Bibles to Joel chapter 2," he said in July 1983, in a sermon that was part of the same series as his Fourth of July sermon "The Two Flags in Today's World," "because I'm going to take four passages out of Joel 2 to describe what has happened in America, what is happening to America, and what I believe is going to happen in America." He went on to recognize dispensationalism's rejection of supersessionism when he said, "Now, I'm fully aware of the dispensational significance of Joel 2. I fully realize that the United States is not Israel." Then he made a remark that set him at odds with the dispensational thought that he had received, but had little training in: "However, biblical principles are without revocation. Biblical principles are the same for everybody. God is not respecter of persons."[30] Yet within dispensational thought, biblical principles are not for everybody, particularly when they apply to Israel; the covenants that God has made with Israel are exclusive to Israel.

Falwell was a dispensationalist, but by the time he expressed his views on the Iraq War, he had spent decades re-inventing dispensationalism so that it supported his own ideas about capitalism, the American Christian nation, the Cold War, and the unfolding of prophecy. This re-invented dispensationalism allowed him to speak about America as if it was the Israel of the Hebrew Bible, chosen by God and supported in battles against its enemies. America would surely triumph, as had Israel of old, against its enemy of Babylon, because God was on her side. As he said in his missive "Is God Ever Pro-War?," "God actually strengthened individuals for war, including Moses, Joshua, and many of the Old Testament judges who demonstrated great faith in battle." Whether or not he was using an accurate reading of the Hebrew Bible, he was failing as a dispensationalist by using verses about ancient Israel to provide context for a war by twenty-first century America. A well-educated dispensationalist might have looked at his use of these verses from the Hebrew Bible and immediately rejected his argument, as these verses about ancient Israel only apply to Israel, not to the church and certainly not to America.

Despite Falwell's inability to read the Bible from a dispensational perspective, he proved himself supple in reading current events in terms of prophecy. The Iraq War was yet another example of how the world's geopolitics were aligning consistently with how he was interpreting prophecy at the present moment. The world did not need to fear climate change; not only was it based on faulty science, but it did not take into account the prophecy that was unfolding in real time, on people's television screens. Christian America could, indeed should, remain dependent on oil, even if doing so meant invading a sovereign country; the alternative was a socialism that would put the nation on the wrong side of prophecy as God's wrath was sure to descend on the world. Supporting America's righteous war in Iraq was yet another way to ensure that, when the Rapture occurred and the Tribulation descended on the world, the country would not become one nation under God's wrath.

CONCLUSION

QAnon

"ERA, A SATANIC Attack Upon The Family And The Bible," read the title to a 1970s pamphlet that Falwell's ministries distributed. The ERA, or Equal Rights Amendment, was a constitutional amendment that stated, "Equality of rights under the law shall not be denied or abridged by the United States or by any State on account of sex." Feminists in the 1920s had championed the effort to pass legislation guaranteeing equal rights for both men and women, and in 1971, the House of Representatives passed the ERA; this passage was followed by the Senate's in 1972. The amendment then went to state legislatures for ratification; with bipartisan support, it seemed sure to pass before the 1979 deadline.

Then Phyllis Schlafly, a lawyer and conservative activist, began a massive organizing campaign among women in the growing conservative movement to defeat the ERA. Dubbed an "antifeminist" for how she opposed the gains of Women's Liberation, Schlafly had previously campaigned for the far-right presidential candidate Barry Goldwater, who opposed passage of the Civil Rights Act; like Falwell, Schlafly also criticized arms-control agreements with the Soviet Union, in favor of nuclear proliferation. In her STOP (Stop Taking Our Privileges) ERA campaign, she insisted that women enjoyed special privileges, such as dependence on their husbands under Social Security and an exemption from the military draft. Not only would these privileges be threatened if the ERA passed, but women would no longer be able to use public restrooms that were separate from men's. Her "pink protests," in which anti-feminist women held rallies outside of state capitols and other public buildings, helped stage the defeat of the ERA.

"This is an amendment which strikes at the foundation of our entire social structure," read the pamphlet that Falwell distributed. "If passed, this amendment will accomplish exactly the opposite of its outward claims. By mandating an absolute equality under the law, it will actually take away many of the special rights women now enjoy." According to Falwell, stopping the passage of the ERA was not merely a political or moral issue; it was a scriptural one, as well. His argument against it was embedded in the rhetoric of "family values"—capitalism, male dominance over women, and a wife's duty to stay at home and care for the children. There was nothing overtly "satanic" in the information he provided in the pamphlet, nothing about demons, the occult, astrology, or witchcraft. Yet to Falwell, because the ERA—along with women's liberation, gay rights, and civil rights—was an attack on his interpretation of the Bible, the only place it could have originated was in the pits of hell. These movements were, after all, products of the liberal apostasy that signaled the End Times and would bring about the reign of the antichrist over the world.

Throughout his career, Falwell did not talk much about Satan, Satan worship, demons, the occult, or anything of the like. He would mention them in passing when talking about the End Times, yet his lack of formal training in dispensationalism precluded him from being able to develop a coherent Satanology or demonology. His approach to "Satanism," as evidenced in the ERA pamphlet, was based on his binary worldview that consistently divided society into "us" and "them." "We," he and his followers, were unconditionally good and incapable of corruption. This "we" came to include the American Christian nation, chosen by God for a divine task that, at least under Reagan, it absolutely was accomplishing. "They" were always the liberals, people tearing at the fabric of America by insisting on more equitable distribution of resources, rather than punishing crime more severely; by demanding equal rights for people regardless of race, gender, or sexual orientation, rather than allowing unregulated capitalism to automatically correct the injustices—real or imagined—that people complained of. "They" were Russia—Soviet Magog—along with other communist countries, and in the 1990s, "they" were especially Bill and Hillary Clinton, who advanced the rights of the LGBTQ+ community. "They" were incapable of doing good, while "we" were attempting to restore moral sanity to America.

"They" were the people pushing the ERA, and "they" hated the idea of the family, but perhaps even more significantly, "they" were criminals. "They" were always the pedophiles, the thieves, the gang members, the murderers, the arsonists, the drug addicts, the drug dealers. People who committed those crimes could not possibly be members of fundamentalist churches and certainly not conservative activists. In building his movement, Falwell did more than make conservative politics mainstream among fundamentalists and evangelicals. He polarized the nation into "us" and "them." "We" had to be afraid of "them," because "they" were always the bad guys. "They" were the people "we" did not want our children around, that "we" did not want our children to become, because "they" were evil. To use the language of his pamphlet about the ERA, "they" were satanic.

And then throughout the 1980s and into the 1990s, numerous defendants in criminal trials, defendants eventually found innocent because there was absolutely no evidence when the evidence should have been overwhelming, found out how damaging being one of "them" was. Through those decades, Falwell's fundamentalist and conservative insurgency helped shape what has since been dubbed a "Satanic Panic," a mass hysteria that would ultimately play out at the US Capitol on January 6, 2021.

The 1960s was a decade of rapid change in America, and the 1970s was a decade of fear. In the South, resistance to the civil rights movement, followed by the conservative backlash to the economic collapse of the OPEC embargo, became Falwell's fundamentalist insurgence. Hippie culture and free love on the West Coast descended into the shock and horror of the Manson murders. Meanwhile, the liberated feminists of the 1960s became working mothers needing daycare for their children in the 1970s. Just as Californians feared for their safety as the Manson Family tore through the state, there was a perpetual fear among working parents who had to leave their children in the hands of strangers at daycares and preschools.

In 1968, a horror move came out that would bring the occult and Medieval ideas about devil worship to movie theaters and television screens across America. Based on the book that came out the previous year, *Rosemary's Baby* portrayed the fictional account of a woman who conceives after being forced into a satanic ritual and gives birth to the devil's own son. In 1973, William Blatty's book about a young girl's possession by a demon became the box-office hit *The Exorcist*. And in 1976 came a movie in which a couple unknowingly raise a child who is, in fact, the prophesied antichrist—*The Omen*. Though these movies featured Catholic characters, they all contained iconography that many dispensationalists would have recognized as belonging to the occult, as well as relating to the Tribulation: demons and demonic possession, the number 666, devil worship, witchcraft, and rumors of dead infants who may have been sacrificed to Satan.

Meanwhile, heavy-metal groups such as Black Sabbath—which used occult-like symbols that included pentagrams and the ram's head—were gaining notoriety, especially among teenagers. Illicit drug use was climbing, as LSD came to symbolize the counterculture of the 1960s and MDMA, or ecstasy, gained popularity throughout the 1970s. Further exacerbating the increasing hysteria surrounding occultic influences, Anton LaVey had founded the Church of Satan in 1966 and, in 1969, made his religion of Satanism available to a mass audience when he published *The Satanic Bible*. As the fear and paranoia of the era grew, parents across the country became terrified that their teenage children were sneaking off to hippie communes, where they were taking mind-altering drugs and invoking the presence of Satan.

The fears of parents across America were realized when reports came out about the McMartin Preschool in Manhattan Beach, California. Accusations emerged that one of the male preschool teachers had repeatedly sodomized a two-year-old boy. Soon, the accusations came to include this worker flying through the air, of the little boy and his classmates traveling in hot-air balloons, watching witches perform magic, and leaving the preschool in underground tunnels. As police contacted parents about the accusations and urged them to talk with their children about possible abuse, the allegations against the preschool teachers became increasingly bizarre. The children claimed that their teachers had flushed them down toilets into secret chambers, locked them in closets with spiders, put them into swimming pools with sharks and alligators, forced them to watch orgies at airports, and made parrots peck at their genitals. The smoking gun was a rhyme that some of the children would sing on the playground: "What you say is what you are / You're a naked movie star." Surely this children's rhyme was evidence that the preschoolers were being used in pornography, a "game" that they childishly called "naked movie star."

"We believe the children." The words became almost a mantra across America and into Canada as similar stories emerged at one preschool after another. The cases seemed to all share a common thread of Satanism, and "satanic ritual abuse" became the catchphrase for describing what these children were suffering. Taking children into satanic temples, forcing them to watch babies being sacrificed to the devil and to drink the babies' blood, taking them across the border to be raped by soldiers in Mexico, shooting them in the arms with rubber bullets, these horrors were all forms of satanic ritual abuse that preschool teachers across America were supposedly inflicting on young children while their parents were gone. The allegations of abuse were almost always believed without question, leading to numerous arrests and court cases. The McMartin Preschool case went to trial, held from 1987 until 1990, and ultimately cost $15 million over the seven years of investigation and courtroom proceedings; it was the longest-running and most expensive criminal case in American history up until that time.

Across the country, Child Protective Services offices and police departments opened special units for investigations of satanic ritual abuse. Conferences were held that taught officials and investigators how to interview children suspected of being victims of satanic ritual abuse and of how to spot the signs that this nightmare was occurring in one's own community. Surprisingly (or perhaps not surprisingly), as the same people attended the same conferences and received the same information, the allegations of satanic ritual abuse that children made came to look extremely similar. Perhaps the similarity would have served as evidence of abuse, were the stories centered on symbols long associated with the occult, such as pentagrams and black candles, or even the

Satanism espoused by LaVey. But the most bizarre claims, such as the ones about parrots pecking at children's genitals, were the ones most repeated, and the children who made these accusations had no physical evidence on their bodies. After a while, the whole affair of preschool teachers being accused by young children of satanic ritual abuse started to look like the 1693 Salem Witch Trials; the altogether strangeness of the accusations was matched only by the lack of evidence. Still, one case after another went to trial as dozens of preschool teachers and even parents were arrested.

The McMartin Preschool trial resulted in no criminal convictions because there was absolutely no evidence that the accused teachers had committed the crimes, nor that the crimes had even happened at all. Furthermore, what came to light is that the people who had interviewed the children had used coercive techniques to demand accusations of abuse, even when the children repeatedly insisted that nothing had happened to them. Yet not all the preschool teachers accused of satanic ritual abuse were as fortunate as those at McMartin Preschool. There were numerous cases in which allegations led to criminal convictions; some children spent years in foster care because their parents—who had been accused by other members of their communities—went to prison for abuse that never even occurred. Despite the absurdity of the cases, major talk-show hosts, including Geraldo Rivera and Oprah Winfrey, fanned the flames of mass hysteria by airing episodes that focused specifically on the specter of Satanism and satanic ritual abuse.

While the Satanic Panic was certainly an effort to protect children, it actually diverted attention away from the real causes of sexual abuse and child neglect. The 1989 congressional report on the 1980 Child Welfare Act, referenced in chapter 3, demonstrated a clear link between growing poverty, inability to access social services, drug use, and child neglect. The Satanic Panic, which was occurring from the passage of the 1980 Child Welfare Act until well beyond the 1989 report on it, caused people to look at daycare workers as guilty of heinous crimes against children, when poverty was actually the main culprit. Further, Falwell's fixation on the nuclear family completely disregarded the fact that the overwhelming majority of childhood sexual abuse comes not from satanic cults lurking in the darkness, but rather from family members. Many of the children who really needed help, those who were suffering neglect because of their parents' poverty or abuse by a family member, were left to fend for themselves because the country was obsessed with the fictitious threat of satanic ritual abuse.

In other words, after Reagan gutted children's services, which were part of what Falwell saw as the liberal apostasy, child protection was no longer about helping children in difficult circumstances attain what they needed to thrive. Rather, child protection had turned into witch trials that prosecuted preschool teachers for outrageous crimes that never even happened. This new approach to child protection was consistent with Falwell's nuclear family values: women should stay home with their children rather than hold jobs and have to place their children in daycare. The result of not adhering to his nuclear family values was the trafficking and gross assault of toddlers and preschoolers by Satan worshipers. As such, the Satanic Panic was almost a natural effect of Falwell's dispensational politics hitting the mainstream.

Falwell certainly did not create the Satanic Panic, and he does not seem to have had a significant *direct* role in the hysteria that gripped much of America. He was not bringing charges of satanic ritual abuse against local preschools, testifying in court about the prevalence of Satanism and the ever-present realness of the demonic realm, or sending private investigators to explore the woods around Lynchburg for evidence of satanic activity (or if he did, no record seems to exist in public archives). Yet this forgotten piece of American history is crucial to understanding Falwell because it was an inescapable outgrowth of the movement that he was creating. What he was doing was more significant to the Satanic Panic, and the even greater conspiracy theory that would emerge from it, than what he was not doing: he was dividing America into the good guys and the bad guys, the righteous and Godly conservatives versus the hell-bent, demonic liberals.

"It is an amazing insight that we do not, as Ephesians 6 warns us, we do not battle against flesh and blood,"[1] he said in a sermon on spiritual warfare. "Our struggle is not with the temporal, or the visible, or that which we can touch and see and communicate with," said the pastor who had organized fundamentalist and evangelical Christians against political—seemingly temporal—causes. "But against the forces, the principalities, the powers of darkness, Satan himself." The Ephesians 6 passage he referenced says that followers of Christ war against spirits, not people; however, Falwell's demonology was centered on people, on the liberals waging a satanic war against America. Perhaps the reason why his war against liberalism was not against people was because the liberals themselves were inspired by the demonic forces of hell; he was warring against those forces that animated liberals and their political agenda. Even if Falwell himself held to a more nuanced demonology, at least some of those listening to him regularly would have been inclined to believe that the God-hating liberals were, in fact, the demons.

By the early 1990s, the Satanic Panic was beginning to loosen its grip on America. FBI Agent Ken Lanning established meaningful standards for how cases of satanic ritual abuse should be prosecuted when he released *The Investigator's Guide to Allegations of "Ritual" Abuse* in 1992. In 1993, journalist Debbie Nathan and criminal-defense lawyer Michael Snedeker published *Satan's*

Silence: Ritual Abuse and the Making of a Modern American Witch Hunt, based on their first-hand research into not only the hysteria but also real cases in which people had been sent to prison for crimes that had not even occurred.

The belief in an underground network of Satanists operating daycare centers was debunked, and judges and juries began requiring hard evidence that went beyond the coerced testimony extracted from very young children. Yet the conspiracy theory, that there is an underground network of satanic pedophiles, persisted and developed fresh nuances as Bill and Hillary Clinton moved into the White House. A few years before directing *The Clinton Chronicles*, Pat Matrisciana directed a fifteen-part documentary series called *Pagan Invasion*. The first installment of the series was entitled "Halloween: Trick or Treat?" and it rehashes the Satanic Panic themes of witchcraft and the occult. Another installment, entitled "Preview of the Antichrist," features the dispensationalist author Hal Lindsey, whose book *The Late Great Planet Earth* popularized dispensational belief about the End Times throughout the 1970s. The dispensational overtones of "Preview of the Antichrist" show that Matrisciana's conspiracy-minded films were firmly embedded in a popular approach to dispensationalism—an approach that looked a lot like Falwell's. Indeed, Falwell was a major supporter of Matrisciana's work, especially of *The Clinton Chronicles*.

In *The Clinton Chronicles*, the smoking gun of the conspiracy theory known as the Clinton body count was the death of Vince Foster. Foster had worked as a partner at the same law firm as Hillary Clinton in Arkansas, and he followed the Clintons to Washington to serve as White House Counsel. Foster had a history of depression, which grew worse while serving in the White House. Six months after Bill Clinton's January 20, 1993, inauguration, Foster was found dead of a self-inflicted gunshot wound. *The Clinton Chronicles* spread conspiracy theories around the death of Foster, claiming that a murder—likely orchestrated by the Clintons themselves—was covered up by investigators who ruled his death a suicide. The "murder" of Vince Foster was, to Falwell who avidly promoted *The Clinton Chronicles*, public evidence that the Clintons were silencing people who got too close to their secret, double lives.

Central to the conspiracies of *The Clinton Chronicles* was a failed real-estate deal from 1978 that the Clintons were involved in. Whitewater, as the affair came to be known, was based on the allegations that the Clintons had engaged in criminal financial dealings. Following the failure of the Whitewater real-estate deal, the Clintons' business partner, James McDougal, formed a bank, Madison Guaranty, which collapsed as a result of another failed real-estate deal; that collapse cost the government $73 million because of FDIC insurance that the government provided. Because the Clintons had done business with McDougal in the Whitewater deal, they came under investigation for criminal acts; however, there was insufficient evidence against them for any of the allegations, and they were cleared. Yet the lead investigator of Whitewater, Kenneth Starr,[2] continued the case, alleging that as governor of Arkansas, Bill had unduly pressured businessman David Hale to make an illegal $300,000 loan to McDougal's wife, Susan. The allegation against the former governor had no credibility, however, though the McDougals spent time in prison for separate financial crimes that they committed. Yet to those who believed the conspiracy theories promoted by *The Clinton Chronicles*, Whitewater was a massive cover-up for the many illegal acts that the Clintons had engaged in, including drug-running from Central America and pedophilia, back in their home state of Arkansas.

There is no way to estimate how many people viewed *The Clinton Chronicles*, as people could copy the VHS tapes to distribute them, and Falwell aired the documentary on his *Old-Time Gospel Hour*. Still, the conspiracy theories it described, about the Clintons master-minding a drug-running ring between Arkansas and Central America and the murders of people who got too close to the truth, seemed to find its home on the margins of American public life. Mainstream America did not care too much for the conspiracy theories of *The Clinton Chronicles*; when major media outlets, such as the *New York Times* and *Los Angeles Times*, did feature the film, the purpose was largely to uncover why participants had agreed to promote wild claims with little more than thin speculation. Another scandal—this one real, not based on fictitious evidence and conspiratorial thinking—would soon envelop the country and cast a shadow over the Clinton presidency: his inability to keep his pants on, exemplified by a sexual affair in the Oval Office with a White House intern. Stories of sexual assault and numerous affairs going back decades ultimately led to a new investigation, and the president would be impeached for lying under oath.

While much of America, including the media, was salivating over the salacious details of President Clinton's sexual escapades, Falwell was promoting a conspiracy theory that was far darker. The documentaries that Matrisciana produced during the early 1990s show that there was a sort of "mega-conspiracy" brewing in certain corners of Falwell's Religious Right. This mega-conspiracy included Satan worship, witchcraft, pedophilia, the occult, Bill and Hillary Clinton's drug-running scandal in Arkansas, the Clinton body count, the covered-up murder of Vince Foster, a rejection of internationalism (especially that represented by the United Nations), hatred of "socialism," and an intense dread of a one-world dictator. This mega-conspiracy coalesced around secular humanism, otherwise known as liberalism, what Francis Schaeffer, Tim LaHaye, and Falwell had preached against in the 1960s, 1970s, and 1980s, as the enemy of Christianity. Secular humanism had consisted of the civil rights movement, women's liberation, and gay rights—the liberationism against which Falwell had built his movement. Now with the conspiracy of a Satan-worshiping cabal of pedophiles that had Hillary Clinton as their ringleader, secular humanism—at least the secular humanism that served as the bogeyman of the Religious Right—could assume a more concrete, human (pun intended) form: the gay-loving, drug-running, abortion friendly, socialist, murderous Bill and Hillary Clinton.

The investigator who pursued the president's year-and-a-half affair with a then-twenty-two-year-old White House intern (her name has been sullied enough through the scandal, and she has since turned to activism against the kind of bullying that she herself endured, so out of respect I will not use her name here) was none other than Kenneth Starr, the man who doggedly pursued criminal charges in the Whitewater scandal after the Clintons had been cleared. What lurid details would Starr find, not with regard to Clinton's sex life but the other criminal conspiracies found in *The Clinton Chronicles*? As the investigation began in January 1998, Falwell said in his weekly Falwell Fax, "I deeply suspect that another Clinton sexual conquest is far from what's on Starr's mind. Why else would the three-judge Whitewater panel and Clinton apologist Janet Reno allow him to enter this investigation? I expect much deeper issues are being investigated."[3]

If those "deeper issues" referred to the Clintons' history of drug-running in Arkansas, then they were never prosecuted. The president was charged with perjury, obstruction of justice, and abuse of power; the House of Representatives impeached him, though the Senate acquitted him and allowed him to complete his second term. Following this ordeal, Hillary went on to win a seat in the US Senate before becoming President Obama's Secretary of State, keeping her in the upper echelons of Washington's elite. Her secret double life had not yet been uncovered and prosecuted, but it surely would be. In the conspiratorial thinking that led to the production of *The Clinton Chronicles*, the criminal evidence would eventually be found and presented to law enforcement officers, who would then prosecute Bill and Hillary Clinton to the fullest extent of the law.

Jerry Falwell died of a heart attack on May 15, 2007, and by then, the movement he had begun three decades earlier was ready to move on without him. A far-right populist and Pentecostal Christian from Alaska, Sarah Palin, ran alongside John McCain in the 2008 presidential election and stirred up public anger in her anti-establishment rhetoric. When the GOP campaign lost to the first African American president in history, Palin became a leading figure in the far-right movement known as the Tea Party. While the Tea Party was certainly not synonymous with the Religious Right and included plenty of disaffected non-Christians, it showed that Falwell's movement was evolving. Mirroring his "biblical capitalism" in which the economic sphere is completely deregulated, the Tea Party advocated for a national economy that had no government oversight. Tea Partiers who were elected to congress pushed back against virtually every single one of President Obama's financial programs, which would expand healthcare access and lessen America's reliance on the fossil fuels that have been driving climate change.

Yet Tea Partiers went beyond Falwell and his use of dispensationalism in reshaping American conservative politics, in no small part by being less reliant on the Bible. While Falwell had preached on the End Times and Armageddon, and by the late 1970s on America's supposed role in these events, Tea Partiers preached about their interpretation of the US Constitution. In this evolving movement, the Constitution was replacing the Bible as the Religious Right was becoming more and more divorced from its fundamentalist origins. The message was clear: this movement is no longer a Christian one; it is about who occupies the halls of power in Washington rather than anything contained in the Bible.

As the Tea Party grew—and, by about 2015, became mainstream within the Republican Party—many of the evangelicals and fundamentalists of the Religious Right were becoming more politicized and more polarized in their thinking. The movement that Falwell began, by pushing the conspiracy theories of influencers such as Robert Welch and fighting against desegregation, was, by the time Donald Trump announced his candidacy for President of the United States in 2015, a site of radicalization. With Hillary Clinton, the bogeyman (or rather bogeywoman) of Falwell's conspiracy theories from the 1990s, as Trump's Democratic challenger, there was bound to be trouble.

The Clinton conspiracy theories of the 1990s would merge with the Satanic Panic of the 1980s in a strange new religious movement that would begin about a year after the 2016 election of Donald Trump. Q, an anonymous poster who began dropping cryptic messages on the ill-reputed website 4Chan and later on 8Chan, suggested that Hillary was part of a secret cabal of Satan-worshipping pedophiles. Members of this cabal supposedly hold high-ranking offices in American politics, and a government official with top-secret clearance—"Q," for his high security clearance—is working undercover to weed them out. With the true identity of Q remaining anonymous, the movement around Q became known as QAnon. QAnon followers overwhelmingly came to believe that the mysterious figure known as "Q" is none other than Trump himself. The conspiracy theory grew to include what is known as "frazzledrip," a claim that there is a video of Hillary and her aide, Huma Abedin, mutilating a young girl, supposedly fileting her face off. In a throwback to the Satanic Panic, in the alleged video (which has never been uncovered), Hillary and her aide drink the girl's blood as part of a Satanic ritual.

Another aspect of the QAnon conspiracy includes "the storm," which claims that a day is coming when Trump will publicly arrest the thousands of political leaders involved in this Satanic cabal. The "storm" became a prophecy of sorts, one not foretold in the Bible but rather handed down, supposedly, from Trump posting as Q. Prophecy became a significant part of QAnon culture, with believers certain that the day was coming when Hillary's crimes would be publicly exposed, and she imprisoned. Falwell had done more than probably anybody else (except for possibly Tim LaHaye and Hal Lindsey) to popularize prophecy belief within American politics, especially through his association between nuclear build-up and Armageddon during the 1980s and his response to turmoil in the Middle East in the 1990s and early 2000s. By then, prophecy belief had become an indispensable component of evangelical politics, and as this political tradition evolved through the Tea Party and QAnon, the Religious Right became primed for the political prophecies of Q.

The political prophecies about Hillary and the storm were perhaps distant relatives of the End Times prophecies that Falwell had promoted in geopolitical terms. These prophecies were from an authority—for Falwell, from the Bible, for QAnon believers, from Q—and would be fulfilled in the world of politics, either through the geopolitics of the Cold War or through the politicking that goes on in Washington. The faith of believers, a faith that became less and less biblical as it became more and more political, was shaped around these prophecies.

Despite being mostly underground rather than in the public eye for the first couple of years, QAnon grew at an exponential rate. Concerned "patriots," as they tended to consider themselves, regularly shared videos on YouTube and networked with other "patriots" to interpret the messages from Q that came to be known as "Q drops." And then in December of 2019, a news story came out of China, saying that a new form of pneumonia was killing patients and that officials were locking down entire cities to contain the spread of this illness. The culprit was a novel virus known as Covid-19, and by the middle of March 2020, most of the world would be on lock-down. With movie theaters, restaurants, and playgrounds closed, many Americans spent their extra time on the internet, where they found a movement of people committed to ending pedophilia and child trafficking. "Patriotism" became a code word for becoming part of this growing movement, and in the conspiratorial mindset of QAnon, the pandemic was nothing more than a cover-up for those who wanted to continue trafficking children so they could sacrifice them to the devil.

The internet, more than possibly any other factor, allowed this new political religion to spread at such a dizzying rate that, by 2021, 15 percent of Americans believed that the government is controlled by a ring of satanic pedophiles. Polls released by the Public Religion Research Institute in May 2021 showed that among white evangelical Protestants, who have become all but synonymous with Falwell's movement, only 21 percent fully reject QAnon, while 22 percent embrace the conspiracy theory entirely. There is another explanation, in addition to the internet, that would cause so many people to believe the conspiracy theory with absolutely no evidence: the Satanic Panic of the 1980s never went away; it merely evolved. Long before the first Q drop, more Americans than we realize already believed that Satan-worshipping pedophiles were ritually abusing and murdering children, again, despite zero evidence to support the claim (or to support the numerous court cases and prison sentences that emerged out of the Satanic Panic). Falwell helped develop this conspiracy theory so that it included the Clintons; though Falwell's Clinton conspiracies never hit the mainstream in the 1990s, they never disappeared. Instead, they continued growing and evolving on the margins of the far right, so that they eventually helped give rise to QAnon. People were ready to believe QAnon because they already believed the central conspiracy theory years, if not decades, before Trump's election: that Hillary Clinton is a leader in a global ring of Satan-worshipping pedophiles.

In the months leading up to the 2020 election between Donald Trump and Joe Biden, QAnon surged in popularity, owing largely to supporters' focus on child trafficking and pedophilia. #SaveOurChildren—a slogan that had been used in the 1970s to defeat legislation aimed at providing equal rights to queer individuals—dominated social media, including from people who had never even heard of QAnon or the cabal of Satanists who were sacrificing children in ritual abuse. Over one hundred Facebook groups that were dedicated to raising awareness of child trafficking were dominated by the content of the QAnon conspiracy theory, creating an even greater relationship between QAnon and the fight against child trafficking; concerned citizens looking up child trafficking online would inevitably be met with QAnon content. Yet as with the Satanic Panic, the misguided focus of these child-protection efforts has driven attention away from the predominant culprit of child neglect and abuse, including trafficking: child poverty. As with Falwell and Reagan, QAnon followers have been overwhelmingly opposed to anti-poverty government programs, *thereby inadvertently placing children at greater risk of trafficking.*

And then the unthinkable happened when Biden defeated Trump in the 2020 election. Prophecies had predicted that Trump would remain in office to continue dismantling the Satan-worshiping, child-trafficking cabal, yet he lost. As with Falwell's prophecies about the End Times, QAnon political prophecy is very malleable and able to adjust; in this case, QAnon followers subscribed to Trump's claim that Biden had stolen the election. Surely this election theft must have been the doings of the very cabal that Trump had been working to destroy; his loss soon became seen as evidence of the cabal. And there was a greater prophecy that followers could put their faith in: the storm. Not only would Trump publicly arrest the thousands of child traffickers involved in the cabal, but the nation's rightful leaders—including Trump himself—would be restored to power.

For this reason and others, QAnon devotees of Trump traveled to Washington, DC, on January 6, 2021, to protest outside of the Capitol as the US Congress was to formally declare Joe Biden the next president. "We fight like hell," Trump told his supporters, before telling them to march down Pennsylvania Avenue. Many believers initially saw this event as the prophesied storm, and the efforts of the protestors would restore America's true and righteous leaders to power. Trump went on, "And if you don't fight like hell, you're not going to have a country anymore." They did fight like hell, breaking glass doors and windows as they stormed the Capitol building and entered the congressional chambers. Falwell was not present in the mayhem, having died fourteen years previously, but in the crowd were untold numbers of evangelicals and fundamentalists whose conservative activism is due in no small part to his influence. Indeed, QAnon might have never hit the mainstream had he not spent decades goading and shaping the conspiracy theory that underpinned it.

Looking back from the Capitol Riot of January 6, 2021, and having studied hundreds of documents and sermons, I can say this about Jerry Falwell: by the end of the 1970s, he was no longer seen as a theological authority, if he had ever been seen as one at all. During the decade of the 1970s, he garnered some traction for himself by preaching sensationalized sermons on the End Times, and though his favorite sermon topic seemed to remain Armageddon, his preaching became more and more politicized as the years went on. Demonization of liberals, and especially of efforts to ensure civil rights for queer individuals, came to dominate sermons that were otherwise on topics such as the birth of Christ and the resurrection. This politicized preaching remained embedded in popular dispensationalism, and this approach to the Bible became increasingly warped and twisted as Falwell consistently breathed new life into old prophecies that he wrapped, over and over again, in the American flag and veneers of patriotism.

Despite his lack of theological recognition, for constituents of the Religious Right, he was an authority on American economics, the threat of liberalism, current events, climate change, and international affairs. His interpretation of all these goings-on was based on extrapolations of dispensational beliefs in the coming End Times, the rise of a one-world government and one-world church that the antichrist would take over to become a one-world dictator. Many believed him and his insistence that prophecy was being fulfilled and God's wrath poured out in events such as the rise of the AIDS epidemic, Saddam's invasion of Kuwait, the Columbine massacre, September 11, and America's invasion of Iraq. These followers may not have understood his theological calculations, but they trusted him when he insisted that climate change was invented by the liberals as a new means of advancing communism.

In effect, Falwell created a new political religion, one born of a distortion of fundamentalist theology married with far-right conspiracy theories, racism, fears of Christian martyrdom, and unconditional embrace of a completely deregulated economic sphere. This political religion has been called "Christian nationalism," yet it has little to nothing in common with historic Christianity or New Testament mandates, such as to love neighbor as self and to even love enemies. Indeed, in this political religion, trying to play nice with the other side and even engage the long-standing American political tradition of compromise is seen as selling oneself out to the enemy. And the enemy is none other than the blood-lusting, child-trafficking, demonic agents of Satan—liberals, especially Hillary Clinton, whose ideological forebears embraced the Social Gospel as a means of following Jesus's message of caring for the poor.

I do not use the term "Christian nationalism" because this political religion is anti-Christian, indeed, anti-Christ. The rioters of January 6 may have invoked the name of Christ in prayer, but by that time, Christianity's central figure had become a mere mascot; his message of humility and grace was entirely disregarded by people insistent on using him to push conspiracy theories and enact a coup of American democracy. The events of January 6 reveal a movement that has divorced itself completely from the Bible while retaining Falwell's conspiratorial thinking.

One question I have found myself asking repeatedly is whether Falwell and his dispensationalism matter anymore, if the movement has moved so far beyond him that his thought has become irrelevant. I do not believe that it has. His hyper-nationalist, anti-UN, anti-one-world-government paranoia; his embrace of unregulated capitalism and insistence on dismantling all social-aid programs; his fears of Christian martyrdom and of non-Christians having a place in America's public sphere; his hatred of the queer community; his rejection of civil rights for African Americans with the smokescreen of the anti-abortion movement; his unwavering belief in the imminent fulfillment of prophecy even when global events change direction; these things and more have all shaped the belief that America is indeed one nation under God's wrath. And that belief persists to this day.

AUTHOR'S NOTE

An Evangelical Jeremiad

THE FIRST LITERARY form to develop in America was a type of sermon called the American jeremiad. Named for the Hebrew prophet Jeremiah, the jeremiad recognizes the greatness to which the American nation is called. Yet the people have failed to live up to that greatness and must repent of their sinfulness, so that they can achieve their God-intended destiny. Abraham Lincoln's "Gettysburg Address" and Martin Luther King Jr.'s "I Have a Dream" speech were both classic American jeremiads. "Fourscore and seven years ago our fathers brought forth on this continent, a new nation, conceived in liberty, and dedicated to the proposition that all men are created equal," begins the Gettysburg Address. The American people started their grand experiment of representative government with the belief that equality should be given to all, yet as King famously noted in his "I Have a Dream" speech, "Instead of honoring this sacred obligation, America has given the Negro people a bad check, a check which has come back marked 'insufficient funds.'" Yet he went on to declare, "We have come to cash this check—a check that will give us upon demand the riches of freedom and security of justice." America could change its ways and live up to its high calling that says all men—and yes, all women—are created equal. I wish to conclude this intensive study of Jerry Falwell with an American jeremiad for evangelicals.

God has called us to something great. We can set the standard for what America can be, a haven of liberty and justice for all, a site of freedom for the dispossessed, and a symbol to the world of opportunity. Regardless of the faith backgrounds of the people around us, we can be a city on a hill that lights the way for all. But we have failed to live up to this high calling, as we have capitulated to the seductions of power and the deceptions of greed. We have confused capitalism with the gospel and forgotten that our message must always be good news for the poor. We have been worshiping America, as if the nation is able to save us, forgetting that our salvation is in Christ. We have failed to see how our political and national idolatries have created suffering and oppression in our communities and around the world. We have allowed ourselves to forget that "they," whoever "they" may be, are image-bearers of God and deserving of the same dignity that we would show Christ himself. Christ who showed compassion to the poor, Christ who left heaven and was crucified, not a political messiah who sought power here on earth. Christ who is risen and knows that true greatness is in heaven, not in Washington.

We can do better, but we must repent of our sins. We must confess that we have not, as Micah 6:8 says, loved mercy, acted justly, and walked humbly with our God. We have not, in accordance with Amos 5:24, let justice roll down like waters, and righteousness like an ever-flowing stream. We can repent of our sins against God and against our fellow humans; then we can seek the way of compassion for those that our unregulated capitalism has left behind. We can help develop renewable energy projects that will uplift the poor by putting resources back into local communities. We can support public schools and restore the services that foster children and families in need require, so that they can stay together. We can stop championing wars fought over oil and instead champion the poor, because they are bearers of the image of God. And we can make society more equitable for those who may not look like us, pray like us, think like us, or believe like us.

And in the process, we can draw people to a light that can warm their hearts and turn their faces toward God.

NOTES

INTRODUCTION

1. Patricia Pingry, *Jerry Falwell: Man of Vision* (Milwaukee, WI: Ideals Publishing Corporation, 1980), 6.
2. Teachings on human depravity may be associated with Calvinism, but one need not be Calvinist to believe in human depravity. Many Baptists are not Calvinists, but Baptist doctrine has historically taught human depravity.
3. Jerry Falwell, "Our Citizenship as Americans," preached on March 7, 1976. Acquisition number OTGH 179.

CHAPTER 1

1. Jerry Falwell, *Listen, America!* First Edition (New York: Doubleday, 1980), 62.
2. Jerry Falwell, "America Back to God," undated (1976?).
3. Falwell, "America Back to God."
4. Jerry Falwell, "I Love America!" expanded version of "America Back to God" produced in *America Can Be Saved* (Murfreesboro, TN: Sword of the Lord Publishers, 1979), 21.
5. Falwell, "I Love America!" 35.
6. Falwell, *Listen, America!* 70.
7. Falwell, *Listen, America!* 12.
8. Jerry Falwell, "Judge Not That You Be Not Judged," undated. Acquisition number OTGH 476.
9. Jerry Falwell, "What Miracles and Wonders God Has Wrought," preached on November 18, 1984. Acquisition number OTGH 631.
10. John Nelson Darby, "What the World Is and How a Christian Can Live in It" (London: G. Morrish).

11. American Protestantism already had a strong premillennial (though not dispensationalist) thread that included some Puritan thinkers and, during the 1840s, the Millerite sect that became Seventh-Day Adventism. By the early 1850s, some British adopters of Darby's teachings were preaching dispensationalism in America, though Darby himself did not come until 1863.

12. At the time of Darby, many Protestants saw the Bible as containing different dispensations. His contribution to theology was not to divide biblical history into dispensations but rather the doctrine of the Rapture. While one can certainly see the Bible as divided into dispensations and not be a *dispensationalist* in the Darbyite meaning of the term, this book refers to dispensationalism as the Darbyite system.

13. Darby himself did not see the Paradisical State (also referred to as Innocency) as a true dispensation, but many dispensationalists who have built on his foundation have considered it as such.

14. Darby was embroiled in the Protestant-Catholic tensions in Europe that regularly erupted into violence. Darbyite dispensationalism was built on these tensions, though they are much less relevant in America.

15. To Darby, the revived Roman Empire was the Roman Catholic Church, though later dispensationalists in America have held that ten nations that were once the original Roman Empire will come back together as a political bloc.

16. From *The Letters of J.N.D.*, retrieved from Ernest Sandeen, *The Roots of Fundamentalism: British and American Millenarianism, 1800–1930* (Chicago: University of Chicago Press, 1970), 32.

17. John Nelson Darby, "Reflections on the Ruined Condition of the Church; and on the Efforts Made by Churchmen and Dissenters to Restore It to Its Primitive Order" (London: G. Morrish, 1841).

18. John Nelson Darby, "What the World Is and How a Christian Can Live in It" (London: G. Morrish).

19. Darby, "What the World Is and How a Christian Can Live in It."

20. Falwell, "America Back to God."

21. C. I. Scofield, *What Do the Prophets Say?* (Greenville, SC: The Gospel Hour, 1918), Foreword, 9.

22. Jerry Falwell, "Twelve Things to Come." This sermon is undated, but based on his reference to the Vietnam War as currently happening, was preached before 1973.

23. Falwell, "Twelve Things to Come."

24. Falwell, "Twelve Things to Come."

25. B. M. Pietsch, *Dispensational Modernism* (New York: Oxford University Press, 2015), 4.

26. Charles Ryrie, a prominent twentieth-century teacher of dispensationalism based out of Dallas Theological Seminary, addressed what he referred to as the "charge of recency" in his 1965 book *Dispensationalism Today* (revised in 2007 as *Dispensationalism*). He asserts that, while Darby formulated dispensationalism into a comprehensive system of biblical exegesis, the principles and outlines of dispensationalism existed in the early centuries of Christianity. (See Charles Ryrie, *Dispensationalism* (Chicago: Moody Publishers, 2007), especially Chapter 4.)

27. Darren Dochuk, *Anointed with Oil: How Christianity and Crude Made Modern America* (New York: Basic Books, 2019), 8.

28. There is a strong Christian humanist tradition, deeply rooted in the *Imago Dei*. The innovative approach of Falwell and his associates, including Tim LaHaye, routinely disregarded historical Christian teachings.

29. Falwell, *Listen, America!* 56.

30. Pietsch, "Lyman Stewart and Early Fundamentalism," 621.

31. Pietsch, "Lyman Stewart and Early Fundamentalism," 621.

32. Falwell, "Our Citizenship as Americans."

33. Falwell, "Our Citizenship as Americans."

34. Falwell, "Our Citizenship as Americans."

35. Jerry Falwell, *The Book of the Revelation, as Taught by Dr. Jerry Falwell in Pastor's Bible Class, Thomas Road Baptist Church, Lynchburg, Virginia* (Lynchburg: Thomas Road Baptist Church, 1974), 183.

36. From *The Letters of J.N.D.*, retrieved from Sandeen, *The Roots of Fundamentalism*, 33.

37. "King's Business, January 1910" (1910). *King's Business All*, 3.

38. "King's Business, January 1910" (1910). *King's Business All*, 16.

39. Falwell, "America Back to God."

40. Charles Erdman, "The Church and Socialism," in *The Fundamentals* Vol. 4, ed. R. A. Torrey and A. C. Dixon (Grand Rapids: Baker Book House, 1980), 101. Reprinted from the original *The Fundamentals* published by The Bible Institute of Los Angeles.

41. Falwell, *Listen, America!* 11.

42. J. Edgar Pew, "The Oil Industry, Its Importance, and Some of Its Problems," in *AAPG Bulleting* 1923, Vol. 7, No. 3.

43. Curtis Lee Laws may have spoken too soon when he grouped adherents of the Princeton Theology with dispensationalists as all being "fundamentalists." Both groups rejected the liberal theology that they felt was

undermining the Bible as a sacred book, but Princeton-Theology evangelicals were generally less averse to the Social Gospel than dispensationalists. Four decades after the Fundamentalist-Modernist Controversy, Jerry Falwell would reveal the deep commitments to business, and especially to the business of oil, that dispensationalists still had, and how these commitments were shaping ideas such as prophecy interpretation, racial segregation, and abortion. Many evangelicals who had closer ties to the Princeton Theology would be harder to convince on his movement than dispensationalists who had long believed that liberalism and the Social Gospel were signs of the End Times. For this reason, I do not consider Princeton-Theology evangelicalism to be part of fundamentalism, though ultimately an overwhelming majority of both evangelicals and fundamentalists would join the movement that Falwell created.

44. Paul Boyer, *When Time Shall Be No More* (Cambridge, MA: Belknap Press, 1994), 156.

CHAPTER 2

1. Southern Baptist Convention, "Resolution on Abortion." June 1, 1971.
2. Southern Baptist Convention, "Resolution on Abortion." June 1, 1976.
3. Falwell, *Falwell: An Autobiography*, 357–358, 360.
4. John Nelson Darby, "Considerations on the Nature & Unity of the Church of Christ" (Plymouth: J. B. Rowe, Whimple Street, 1828).
5. John Nelson Darby, "Remarks on Puseyism," 1854.
6. Brown, *The National Churches of England, Ireland, and Scotland*, 248.
7. W. G. Turner, *John Nelson Darby: A Biography* (London: CA Hammond, 1926), 18.
8. Falwell, "Ministers and Marchers," March 21, 1965.
9. Andrew J. Douglas and Jared A. Loggins, *Prophet of Discontent: Martin Luther King Jr. and the Critique of Racial Capitalism* (Athens: University of Georgia Press, 2021), 2.
10. Falwell, *The Book of Revelation*, 249.
11. Robert Welch, *The Blue Book of the John Birch Society* (Pickle Partners Publishing, 2016 (reprint)), 30.
12. Howard Thurman, *Jesus and the Disinherited* (Boston: Beacon Press, 1994), 39.
13. To show that his support of BJU did not come from a racist stance, his colleague at Liberty University, Ed Hindson, said that "in defending Bob Jones we would need to be very clear that we are not defending their position."
14. Jerry Falwell, "America Back to God," (revised) 1980.

15. Randall Balmer, *Thy Kingdom Come* (New York: Basic Books, 2006), 13–14.
16. Jerry Falwell, "Fact Sheet Regarding South Africa and My Recent Visit There," based on trip made on August 14, 1985.
17. Falwell, "Fact Sheet Regarding South Africa."
18. C-SPAN, "South Africa," hosted by Susan Swain. August 29, 1985.
19. C-SPAN, "South Africa."
20. C-SPAN, "South Africa."
21. Martin Mawyer, "Who Cares about South Africa?" in *Moral Majority Report*, October 1985.
22. Ed Hindson, "Apartheid—The Custom That Must Change," in *The Fundamentalist Journal*, August 1985.
23. Falwell, "Fact Sheet Regarding South Africa."
24. Tim LaHaye, *Rapture under Attack* (Sisters, OR: Multnomah, 1998), 137.
25. LaHaye, *Rapture Under Attack*, 138.
26. Tim LaHaye, *The Battle for the Mind* (Old Tappan, NJ: Fleming Revell Company, 1980), 10.
27. Tim LaHaye, *The Unhappy Gays* (Wheaton: Tyndale House, 1978), 20.
28. Daniel K. Williams, *Defenders of the Unborn: The Pro-Life Movement before Roe v Wade* (Oxford: Oxford University Press, 2016), 77.
29. LaHaye, *The Battle for the Mind*, 29.
30. Jerry Falwell, "One Nation under God on the Rebound, Part 1."

CHAPTER 3

1. Jerry Falwell, "Here Is Where Moral Majority Stands on the Vital Issues Affecting America Today," circular published approximately 1979.
2. Falwell, *Listen, America!* 157.
3. Falwell, *Listen, America!* 161.
4. Falwell, *Listen, America!* 161.
5. Jerry Falwell, *Listen, America!* 106.
6. The Manpower Development and Training Act of 1962, signed by President John F. Kennedy, had sought to create economic opportunity for poor whites and disenfranchised African Americans through job-training programs. President Johnson had recently signed the Civil Rights Act of 1964, which outlawed discrimination based on race, color, religion, sex, and national origin; the Act also prohibited racial segregation in public places, including schools, and required that voting requirements be applied equally across races. His Economic Opportunity Act of 1964 created job programs for the rural and urban poor to help

address the gap between the wealthiest Americans and the destitute. He signed the Voting Rights Act of 1965 at about the same time that his administration published the Moynihan Report, in August of that year.

7. Daniel Patrick Moynihan, *The Negro Family: The Case for National Action* (Washington, DC: Office of Policy Planning and Research, United States Department of Labor, 1965).

8. John Nelson Darby, "Notes on the Epistle to the Romans," 1868.

9. Jerry Falwell, "Nuclear War and the Second Coming of Christ," 1983.

10. National Conference of Catholic Bishops, *The Challenge of Peace: God's Promise and Our Response* (Washington, DC: United States Catholic Conference, 1983).

11. United Church of Christ, "Pronouncement on Affirming the United Church of Christ as a Just Peace Church," 1985.

12. Jerry Falwell, "A Call to Christian Service," preached on August 22, 1982. OTGH 514.

13. Jerry Falwell, "Nuclear War and the Second Coming of Jesus Christ" (Lynchburg: Old-Time Gospel Hour, 1983).

14. Falwell, "Nuclear War and the Second Coming of Christ."

15. Falwell, *Listen, America!* 106.

16. Falwell, *Listen, America!* 104.

17. Jerry Falwell, "Why the Moral Majority?" (Washington, DC: Moral Majority Inc., 1979), 1.

18. Seth Dowling, *Family Values and the Rise of the Christian Right* (Philadelphia: University of Pennsylvania Press, 2015), 4.

19. This idea has significant overlap with John Rousas Rushdoony's Christian Reconstruction.

20. Falwell, *Listen, America!* 112–113.

21. Falwell, *Listen, America!* 112.

22. HR 7955 Family Protection Act, introduced in the US House on August 19, 1980.

23. Jerry Falwell, "America Back to God," preached on February 3, 1980. OTGH 386.

24. Jerry Falwell, "Is America a Christian Nation?" preached on April 20, 1986.

25. Jerry Falwell, "America, You're Too Young to Die," Prime-Time Special, 1980? OTGH 401.

26. Falwell, *Listen, America!* 160.

27. Jerry Falwell, "Wake Up America," preached on April 27, 1980 (estimated). OTGH 398.

28. Falwell, *Listen, America!* 84.

29. *America's Pro-Family Conference: The Alternative to the White House Conference on Families.*

30. "What It Means to Be Pro-Family," in *America's Pro-Family Conference: The Alternative to the White House Conference on Families*, 2.

31. Jerry Falwell, "Nuclear War and the Second Coming of Christ," preached in 1983.

32. 101st US House of Representatives, "No Place to Call Home: Discarded Children in America. A Report Together with Additional and Dissenting Views of the Select Committee on Children, Youth, and Families." November 1989, 2.

33. "No Place to Call Home," 46.

34. "No Place to Call Home," 52.

35. Texas Freedom Network, "The Texas Faith-Based Initiative at Five Years: Warning Signs as President Bush Expands Texas-style Program at National Level," 1.

CHAPTER 4

1. Jerry Falwell, "The Two Flags in Today's World," preached on July 3, 1983. OTGH 559. (Note that the archives have misdated this sermon.)

2. Jerry Falwell, "Nuclear War and the Second Coming of Christ," 1983.

3. Falwell, "Nuclear War and the Second Coming of Christ."

4. Jim Bakker interview with Ronald Reagan. Taken from the DVD "Jim's Historic Interview with Ronald Reagan," *The Jim Bakker Show*, 1979.

5. Kenneth Woodward, "Arguing Armageddon" in *Newsweek*, November 5, 1984, 91.

6. Falwell, "The Two Flags."

7. Jerry Falwell, "The Battle of Armageddon," preached on December 2, 1984. OTGH 633.

8. Walvoord was serving as president of Dallas Theological Seminary at the time he wrote *Armageddon, Oil, and the Middle East Crisis*, and the vast majority of his work can be considered as belonging to a scholarly approach to dispensationalism. This book stands in contrast, though, as it was a bestseller that brought dispensationalism out of fundamentalist circles and into mainstream culture. Rather than teaching dispensational doctrine, as many of his other works do, *Armageddon, Oil, and the Middle East Crisis* engaged with current events in a manner suited for a popular, nondispensational audience.

9. Falwell, "The Two Flags."

10. Jerry Falwell, *Dr. Jerry Falwell Teaches Bible Prophecy* Study Guide, 1.

11. Falwell, *Dr. Jerry Falwell Teaches Bible Prophecy* Study Guide, 2.

12. Falwell, *Dr. Jerry Falwell Teaches Bible Prophecy* Study Guide, 3

13. Falwell, *Dr. Jerry Falwell Teaches Bible Prophecy* Study Guide, 6.

14. Falwell, *Dr. Jerry Falwell Teaches Bible Prophecy* Study Guide, 6.

15. Falwell, *Dr. Jerry Falwell Teaches Bible Prophecy* Study Guide, 6.

16. Falwell, *The Book of the Revelation*, 45.

17. Jerry Falwell, "1980 Update on Bible Prophecy, Part 1," from cassette series *Dr. Jerry Falwell Teaches Bible Prophecy* (Lynchburg, VA: *Old-Time Gospel Hour*, 1979).

18. Jerry Falwell, "America, in Grave Danger," preached on July 10, 1983. OTGH 0560.

19. October 21, 1984, Debate Transcript. The Commission on Presidential Debates.

20. Reagan's comment about not knowing whether Armageddon was imminent or one thousand years away indicates a belief that was less radical than that of Falwell and other dispensationalist pastors. According to Joseph Cuomo, whose article about Reagan and Armageddon for the *New York Times* likely inspired Kalb's question, the real problem was how close Reagan let himself get to Falwell. Falwell confused faith in the Bible with knowledge and certainty about how Armageddon was related to current events, and his knowledge of Armageddon may have unduly influenced the president.

21. Andrew Lang, "The Politics of Armageddon: Reagan Links Bible Prophecy with Nuclear War," in *Convergence* (Fall 1985), 3.

22. Charles Dyer, *The Rise of Babylon: Sign of the End Times* (Wheaton, IL: Tyndale House, 1991), 41.

23. Dyer, *The Rise of Babylon*, 19.

24. John Walvoord, *Armageddon, Oil, and the Middle East Crisis (Revised)* (Grand Rapids, MI: Zondervan Publishing House, 1991), 47.

25. Walvoord, *Armageddon, Oil, and the Middle East Crisis (Revised)*, 48.

26. Walvoord, *Armageddon, Oil, and the Middle East Crisis (Revised)*, 48.

27. Falwell sermon. POT 0945, from November 18, 1990.

28. A biography of John Walvoord on the website Walvoord.com claims that President George H. W. Bush requested a copy of *Armageddon, Oil, and the Middle East Crisis*, as the book "made a powerful impression" on the White House. (https://walvoord.com/about-dr-john-walvoord, accessed on February 2, 2023). The author was not able to independently verify this claim.

29. Jerry Falwell, "The Clinton Agenda for the Unborn and Gays," preached on November 8, 1992. POT 1056.

30. Jerry Falwell, "The Falwell Fax Online," September 4, 1998.

31. Jerry Falwell, "Falwell Confidential," April 30, 1999.

32. Falwell, along with like-minded fundamentalists and evangelicals, had been pointing to Supreme Court decisions of the 1950s and 1960s relating to public schools, including *Brown v Board of Education*, *Abington v Schempp*, and *Engel v Vitale*, long before the Columbine massacre to explain the moral decline of society. He had also been promoting his Ten Commandment textbook covers for at least a year to encourage Christian teenagers to defy the Supreme Court. This trend took on renewed significance in the wake of Columbine.

33. Jerry Falwell, "Taking America Back," preached on May 2, 1999.

34. Matthew Staver, "Take Back America!" in *National Liberty Journal*, July 1999.

35. Jerry Falwell, "The Book of Revelation, Part 1," preached on September 23, 2001. OTGH 1467.

36. *The 700 Club*, September 13, 2001.

CHAPTER 5

1. Jerry Falwell, "Falwell Confidential: Evangelicals and Global Warming." November 17, 2006.

2. Jerry Falwell, "Falwell Confidential: Sunday Special, the Myth of Global Warming." February 21, 2007.

3. Falwell, "Evangelicals and Global Warming."

4. Jerry Falwell, "Is the Antichrist Alive Today?" POT 1272. Preached in about 1997, date uncertain.

5. Martin Luther, *The Jews and Their Lies*, 1543.

6. In the past century, a growing number of Christians have joined dispensationalists in rejecting supersessionism, primarily because it has gone hand-in-hand with anti-Semitism. Dispensational rejection of supersessionism is unique because of its approach to Israel, especially within the context of the End Times. Other Christians who have dismissed supersessionism for being anti-Semitic are not necessarily Christian Zionists, but dispensationalists, especially since 1948, have categorically been Christian Zionists.

7. Jerry Falwell, *Nuclear War and the Second Coming of Jesus* (Lynchburg: Old Time Gospel Hour, 1983), 14.

8. Walvoord claimed before Falwell, in his 1967 book *The Nations in Prophecy*, that God has withheld a judgment that America deserves because of America's support of Israel and role in evangelizing the role.

Falwell likely borrowed this view from Walvoord and other scholarly dispensationalists.

9. No, we haven't.

10. Falwell, "Is America a Christian Nation?"

11. Dochuk, *Anointed with Oil*, 274.

12. Jerry Falwell, "What Is Happening in the Middle East?" (Lynchburg: Old-Time Gospel Hour, 1967), 1.

13. John Walvoord, *Armageddon, Oil, and the Middle East Crisis* (Grand Rapids, MI: Zondervan, 1974), 44.

14. John Walvoord, *The Nations in Prophecy* (Grand Rapids, MI: Academie Books, 1967), 68–69.

15. Hal Lindsey, *The Late Great Planet Earth* (Grand Rapids, MI: Zondervan, 1970), 115.

16. Jerry Falwell, *The Book of Revelation*, preached in 1973–1974, 74.

17. Jerry Falwell, *The Book of Revelation*, preached in 1973–1974, 287.

18. From "Can the Arabs Really Blackmail Us?" by Robert E. Hunter, *New York Times* September 23, 1973, 283.

19. Falwell, "America Back to God."

20. Falwell, *Listen, America!* 98.

21. Jerry Falwell, "1980 Update on Bible Prophecy, Part 1," from cassette series Dr. Jerry Falwell Teaches Bible Prophecy (Lynchburg, VA: Old-Time Gospel Hour, 1979).

22. "1979-06-04 Oil Business Poor Public Relations," found in the online database for the Moral Majority in the Jerry Falwell Library.

23. Jerry Falwell, "The Moral Majority, Inc.: Fighting for a Moral America in This Decade of Destiny," pamphlet in the Moral Majority archives at Liberty University.

24. Conaway, "James Watt, in the Right with the Lord."

25. Jerry Falwell, "Talking Right and Living Right," preached on August 29, 1982. Acquisition number OTGH 515.

26. From "Energy," in the US Taxpayers Party Platform for 1992.

27. Falwell, "Is the Antichrist Alive Today?"

28. Advertisement by Greening Earth Society on page 8 of *Jerry Falwell's National Liberty Journal*, July 1999.

29. Jerry Falwell, "Falwell Confidential, Is God Ever Pro-War?" January 29, 2004.

30. Jerry Falwell, "Our National Healing," preached on July 24, 1983 (approximate; based on the sermon's context, the transcript was misdated to 1987). Acquisition number OTGH 562.

CONCLUSION

1. Jerry Falwell, "Spiritual Warfare," preached on August 9, 1998. POT 1306.
2. Starr had also been in charge of the investigation into Vince Foster's death.
3. Jerry Falwell, "Falwell Fax," January 23, 1998.

BIBLIOGRAPHY

King's Business, January 1910.

101st US House of Representatives. "No Place to Call Home: Discarded Children in America. A Report Together with Additional and Dissenting Views of the Select Committee on Children, Youth, and Families." Washington, DC, 1980.

Balmer, Randall. *Thy Kingdom Come, An Evangelical's Lament: How the Religious Right Distorts the Faith and Threatens America*. New York: Basic Books, 2006.

Bass, Clarence. *Backgrounds to Dispensationalism*, 2nd ed. Grand Rapids, MI: Baker Book House, 1977.

Blome, Wendy Whiting. "Reasonable Efforts, Unreasonable Effects: A Retrospective Analysis of the 'Reasonable Efforts' Clause in the Adoption Assistance and Child Welfare Act of 1980." *The Journal of Sociology and Social Welfare*, 1996.

Boyer, Paul. *When Time Shall Be No More*. Cambridge, MA: The Belknap Press of Harvard University, 1994.

Brown, Stewart Jay. *The National Churches of England, Ireland, and Scotland, 1801–1846*. Oxford: Oxford University Press, 2001.

Centers for Disease Control and Prevention. "Morbidity and Mortality Weekly Report." 50, no. 21 (June 2001).

Champagne, Anthony. "The Segregation Academy and the Law." *The Journal of Negro Education* 42, no. 1 (1973): 58–66.

Convention, Southern Baptist. "Resolution on Abortion." June 1, 1971.

Cook, Vanessa. "Martin Luther King, Jr., and the Long Social Gospel Movement." *Religion and American Culture* (University of California Press) 26, no. 1 (January 2016): 74–100.

Darby, John Nelson. "Notes on the Epistle to the Romans." 1868.

———. "Reflections on the Ruined Condition of the Church; and on the Efforts Made by Churchmen and Dissenters to Restore It to Its Primitive Order." London: G. Morrish, 1841.

———. "Remarks on Puseyism." 1854.

———. *Studies on the Book of Daniel: A Course of Lectures.* London: John B. Bateman, 1864.

———. "What the World is and How a Christian Can Live in It." Lancing, Sussex: Kingston Bible Trust, n.d.

Dochuk, Darren. *Anointed with Oil: How Christianity and Crude Made Modern America.* New York: Basic Books, 2019.

Dochuk, Darren. "Blessed by Oil, Cursed with Crude: God and Black Gold in the American Southwest." *The Journal of American History* 99, no. 1 (2012): 51–61.

Dorn, Jacob. "The Social Gospel and Socialism: A Comparison of the Thought of Francis Greenwood Peabody, Washington Gladden, and Walter Rauschenbusch." *Church History* (Cambridge University Press) 62, no. 1 (March 1993): 82–100.

Dorrien, Gary. *The Making of American Liberal Theology: Imagining Progressive Religion, 1805–1900.* London: Westminster John Knox Press, 2001.

Douglas, Andrew, and Jared Loggins. *Prophet of Discontent: Martin Luther King Jr. and the Critique of Racial Capitalism.* Athens, GA: University of Georgia Press, 2021.

Dowland, Seth. ""Family Values" and the Formation of a Christian Right Agenda." *Church History* 78, no. 3 (2009): 606–631.

———. *Family Values and the Rise of the Christian Right.* Philadelphia: University of Pennsylvania Press, 2015.

Dowling, Seth. *Family Values and the Rise of the Christian Right.* Philadelphia: University of Pennsylvania Press, 2015.

Falwell, Jerry. "A Call to Christian Service." Lynchburg, VA: Old-Time Gospel Hour, August 22, 1982.

———. "America Back to God." 1976(?). https://tinyurl.com/jryth54m.

———. "America Back to God." *OTGH 386.* Lynchburg: The Old-Time Gospel Hour, February 3, 1980.

———. "America Can Be Saved." n.d.

———. *America Can Be Saved.* Murfreesboro, TN: Sword of the Lord Publishers, 1979.

Falwell, Jerry. *Dr. Jerry Falwell Teaches Bible Prophecy.* Old-Time Gospel Hour Productions. Lynchburg, 1979.

———. *Dr. Jerry Falwell Teaches Bible Prophecy Study Guide.* Lynchburg: Old-Time Gospel Hour Productions, 1979.

———. "Fact Sheet Regarding South Africa and My Recent Visit There." Lynchburg, August 15, 1985.

———. "Falwell Confidential." Lynchburg, VA, April 30, 1999.

———. "Is America a Christian Nation." *OTGH 705.* Lynchburg: The Old-Time Gospel Hour, April 20, 1986.

———. "Judge Not, That You Be Not Judged." Lynchburg: Old-Time Gospel Hour, n.d.

———. *Listen America! First Edition.* New York: Doubleday, 1980.

———. "Ministers and Marchers." Lynchburg, March 21, 1965.

———. "Nuclear War and the Second Coming of Christ." The Old-Time Gospel Hour, 1983.

———. *Nuclear War and the Second Coming of Jesus.* Lynchburg: The Old-Time Gospel Hour, 1983.

———. "Our Citizenship as Americans." *OTGH 179.* Lynchburg: The Old-Time Gospel Hour, March 7, 1976.

———. "Taking America Back." Lynchburg, VA: The Old-Time Gospel Hour, May 2, 1999.

———. "The Falwell Fax Online." September 4, 1998.

———. *The Truth about AIDS.* Performed by Jerry Falwell. 1993.

———. "The Two Flags in Today's World." *OTGH 559.* Lynchburg: The Old-Time Gospel Hour, July 3, 1983.

———. "Twelve Things to Come." Lynchburg: The Old-Time Gospel Hour, n.d.

———. "Twelve Things to Come." undated.

———. "What Miracles and Wonders God Has Wrought." Lynchburg: Old-Time Gospel Hour, November 18, 1984.

———. "What's Happening in the Middle East?" Lynchburg: Old-Time Gospel Hour, July 1967.

———. "Why the Moral Majority." Washington, DC: Moral Majority, Inc., August 1979.

Foster, Carly Hayden. "The Welfare Queen: Race, Gender, Class, and Public Opinion." *Race, Gender, and Class* 15, no. 3/4 (2008): 162–179.

Gallagher, John, and Chris Bull. *Perfect Enemies: The Religious Right, the Gay Movement, and the Politics of the 1990s.* New York: Crown Publishing, 1996.

Geary, Daniel. *Beyond Civil Rights: The Moynihan Report and Its Legacy.* Philadelphia: University of Pennsylvania Press, 2015.

Haberman, Aaron. "Into the Wilderness: Ronald Reagan, Bob Jones University, and the Political Education of the Christian Right." *The Historian* 67, no. 2 (2005): 234–253.

Handy, Robert T. *The Social Gospel in America*. New York: Oxford University Press, 1966.

Luther, Martin. *The Jews and Their Lies*. 1543.

Mawyer, Martin. "Who Cares about South Africa?" *Moral Majority Report*, October 1985.

Moynihan, Daniel Patrick. *The Negro Family: The Case for National Action*. Washington, DC: United States Department of Labor, 1965.

National Conference of Catholic Bishops. *The Challenge of Peace: God's Promise and Our Response*. Washington, DC: United States Catholic Conference, 1983.

Nelson, Brent, and James Guth. "European Union or Kingdom of the Antichrist? Protestant Apocalyptic Narratives and European Unity." *National Identities* 19, no. 2 (2017).

Phillips, Paul. *A Kingdom on Earth: Anglo-American Social Christianity, 1880–1940*. University Park: Pennsylvania State University Press, 1996.

Pietsch, B.M. *Dispensational Modernism*. Oxford: Oxford University Press, 2015.

———. "Lyman Stewart and Early Fundamentalism." *Church History* 82, no. 3 (2013): 617–646.

Pingry, Patricia. *Jerry Falwell: Man of Vision*. Milwaukee, WI: Ideals Publishing Corporation, 1980.

Rock, Stephen R. "From Just War to Nuclear Pacificism: The Evolution of US Christian Thinking about War in the Nuclear Age, 1946–1989." *Social Science* 7, no. 6 (May 2018).

Ryrie, Charles. *Basic Theology*. Chicago: Moody Publishers, 1986.

———. *Dispensationalism*. Chicago: Moody Publishers, 2007.

Sandeen, Ernest. *The Roots of Fundamentalism: British and American Millenarianism, 1800–1930*. Chicago: University of Chicago Press, 1970.

Schoenwald, Jonathan. *A Time for Choosing: The Rise of Modern American Conservativism*. Oxford: Oxford University Press, 2002.

Scofield, C.I. *What Do the Prophets Say?* Greenvile, SC: The Gospel Hour, Inc., 1918.

Shapiro, Joseph, Teresa Wiltz, and Jessica Piper. "National Public Radio." *States Send Kids to Foster Care and Their Parents the Bill—Often One too Big to Pay*. December 27, 2021.

Smith, Robert. *More Desired Than Our Own Salvation: The Roots of Christian Zionism*. Oxford: Oxford University Press, 2013.

Texas Freedom Network. "The Texas Faith-Based Initiatve at Five Years: Warning Signs as President Bush Expands Texas-style Program at

National Level." n.d. *POT 0945*. Performed by The Old-Time Gospel Hour. 1990.

Turner, W. G. *John Nelson Darby: A Biography*. London: CA Hammond, 1926.

United Church of Christ. *Pronouncement on Affirming the United Church of Christ as a Just Peace Church*. UCC, 1985.

Welch, Robert. *The Blue Book of the John Birch Society*. Pickle Partners Publishing, 2016.

Williams, Daniel. *Defenders of the Unborn: The Pro-Life Movement Before Roe v Wade*. Oxford: Oxford University Press, 2016.

Williams, Daniel. "Jerry Falwell's Sunbelt Politics." *The Journal of Policy History* (Cambridge University Press) 22, no. 2 (2010).

Williams, Daniel. "The Partisan Trajectory of the American Pro-Life Movement: How a Liberal Catholic Campaign Became a Conservative Evangelical Cause." *Religions*, 2015: 451–475.

Woodward, Kenneth. "Arguing Armageddon." *Newsweek*, November 5, 1984: 91.

INDEX